DATE			
OCT 14 89			
1 7 199			

SHAKESPEARE BY HILLIARD

To
W. B.
C. V. W.
M. M. P. H.

Hilliard: *Unknown Man Clasping a Hand issuing from a Cloud.*
above, *V & A*; below, *Howard*

SHAKESPEARE

BY
HILLIARD

LESLIE HOTSON

UNIVERSITY OF CALIFORNIA PRESS
Berkeley and Los Angeles 1977

University of California Press
Berkeley & Los Angeles, California

ISBN: 0-520-03313-2
Library of Congress Catalog Card Number: 76-24584

© Leslie Hotson 1977

Printed in Great Britain

Contents

Illustrations

I

The Case of the Clasping Charm

CONSIDER for a moment the opening of a hunt in real life for a Wanted Man. Does he not—at first, anyhow—bring to mind the Invisible Man? For while the police are spreading their net, pressing forward the search for him, certainly there, somewhere, is the Man. There, but not seen. In the upshot, if luck is with the law, sooner or later some sharp eye spots him. Sees the Unseen. And caught, he at last takes shape, becomes visible to all.

Yet police annals also present that awkward customer, the Wanted Man who never materializes. In his case, as for decades in Martin Bormann's, though everything is known—his name and every alias, physical appearance, peculiarities, habits, associates—his photograph sown broadcast, and countless eyes looking for him, there is no arrest. But why? How to account for it?

Perhaps this rare Wanted Man is like Poe's familiar Purloined Letter. Strange as it seems, he may actually be sitting there throughout the search, in plain open sight. Yet somehow passed over by every eye. And because not recognized, still unseen. In brief, so long as he is not *effectually seen for what he is*, the Wanted Man remains secure, Invisible.

Strikingly similar is the problem now drawing us on to the pursuit. More than that, this absorbing and formidable manhunt of ours offers a special attraction. For it lies not in the field of Crime, but the Arts. And who does not know that Art and Science often employ identical detective methods? Certainly when we stand checked, at a loss whether in strategy or in tactics, we shall find the expert criminal investigators joining those sleuths of Art, the *Kunstforscher*, to point us to the true line.

Our Invisible Man is more than four hundred years old: an

Elizabethan both familiar and unknown. That is to say, his face is familiar, and his identity is unknown. A blond Englishman, handsome, sensitive, thoughtful. When he sat for his picture 'in little' in 1588, the Wonderful Year of the Spanish Armada's defeat, he was an alert, hazel-eyed young man, with fair curling hair, moustache, and slight beard. And it was Nicholas Hilliard, the master portrait-painter of Elizabeth's England, who limned his likeness. The work ranks as one of the best-known masterpieces of Hilliard's brush—his peerless 'fine pencil'.

It exists in two authentic examples. One of the two—'damaged on left cheek of sitter'—is now in the Victoria and Albert Museum. We shall refer to it as the *V&A*. The other, more carefully painted, excellently preserved, and by modern experts described as 'famous' and 'magnificent', may be called the *Howard*, for until recent years it was long at Castle Howard, Yorkshire. Ever since before 1700 the *Howard*'s frame has been mistakenly labelled 'Earl of Essex'.

Of the two, the *V&A* is the one more widely known, having been exhibited at the Museum for a generation, and also reproduced in excellent colour for Carl Winter's *Elizabethan Miniatures* (King Penguin 1943, 1949, 1955), in half-tone enlarged for Sir John Pope-Hennessy's *A Lecture on Nicholas Hilliard* 1949, and again in colour for Dr. Roy Strong's *Nicholas Hilliard* 1975. The privately owned *Howard* has come into prominence more recently, figuring notably at British and Dutch exhibitions of late years, and appearing in half-tone in Dr. Erna Auerbach's full-length study, *Nicholas Hilliard* 1961.

How is this portrait described? We turn to the late Carl Winter's excellent book, and read of the *V&A*—

MAN CLASPING A HAND FROM A CLOUD
Inscribed: Attici amoris ergo. Año · Dñi · 1588.
. . . The identity of the subject and the meaning of the motto are unknown.

To this admirably candid 'MAN unrecognized, motto unread' our author might have added, 'We also don't know *whose* hand from a cloud the MAN is clasping.' For we should not overlook the fact that *two* persons were represented here. Of the second, only his hand was shown: *himselfe behind Was left unseene, save to the eye of mind: A hand . . . Stood for the whole to be imaginëd.*

Now since in fact we have here Two Invisible Men, and one of them considerably more Invisible than the other, the detective's double task—to recognize both the Clasper and the Owner of the Hand—is quite simply imposed. And at first sight it looks like attempting the utterly impossible. For what means of identification are offered? The hand-holding gesture looks as though it should convey something. But what? Eric Westbrook observes of it,

> To an Elizabethan this symbol was probably quite comprehensible; but we have lost the clue, and all that has come down to us is the ludicrous yet disturbing image of a pre-occupied gentleman strap-hanging in a mad Underground railway. *The Studio*, 142 July 1951, 2

That is to say, when the real object presented (*viz.* the Hand) means nothing to our critical minds, to give it 'relevance' we turn Don Quixotes, and instantly transform it into some air-drawn shape (*e.g.*, Underground-strap) standing in our own mind's eye, like the dagger in Macbeth's.

Such an approach would not impress the C.I.D. Shunning the mad method of that seductive Don, let us cling to reason. We face the controlling fact that this picture, which seems to confront us, in reality is *far away and long ago*. We are separated from it by nearly four centuries of change. If we imagine that at such a distance the unaided modern eye can be trusted to discern its intention, to *read* the picture, we are self-deceived. For that modern eye is 'rapt in ignorant admiration'. We gaze with our modern eyes at Elizabethan objects, and completely mistake their meaning. Just as we do with their words. When these *look* so familiar, who would suppose them foreigners? For example, when an Elizabethan refers to an 'income' and a 'document', we ask how can he possibly mean an *entrance-fee* and a *piece of instruction*? But he does. And when he mentions 'horse meat' and the 'mortuary', he is talking of *oats and hay* and the *parson's gratuity, due to him from the estate of a deceased parishioner of his.* Would you suspect that by describing a man as 'high-minded' he is putting the fellow down as *haughty or arrogant*? Or that by 'obnoxious' and 'crazy' he merely means *liable or subject* and *ailing or infirm*? Or yet when an author complains 'I could not recognize this my work' he is saying 'I could not *proof-read* it'? No foreign tongue could trick us like this.

To the Elizabethans the position was elementary: *Things far off seen seem not the same they are*; or again, *Things seen far off are lessen'd in the eye, When their true shape is seen being hard by*. Before we can possibly give our eyes a chance—that is, get this portrait under intelligent scrutiny in true perspective—we must somehow *move our minds nearer to it*. For as Goethe says, *we see only what we know*. A close parallel to the modern Underground strap-hanger view of our miniature was drawn long ago by the following report of Boswell's:

> When I observed to him [Dr. Johnson] that Painting was so far inferiour to Poetry, that the story or even emblem which it communicates must be previously known, and mentioned as a natural and laughable instance of this, that a little Miss on seeing a picture of Justice with the scales, had exclaimed to me, 'See, there's a woman selling sweetmeats;' he said, 'Painting, Sir, can illustrate, but cannot inform.'
>
> *Boswell's Johnson*, ed. G. B. Hill, 1887, 4.321

There it is. So long as we do not know *what our miniature illustrates*, our strap-hanger remains as natural as that woman selling sweetmeats. The psychologist Merle Lawrence has proved by experiment a rather self-evident conclusion: namely that 'what you see when you look at something depends not so much on *what is there* as on the assumptions you make when you look'. With our CLASPING A HAND, certainly, it will be only when we have enabled our modern minds *to assume approximately what the lookers of 1588 assumed* that we may hope to see *what is there*.

'On a huge hill, Craggëd, and steep, Truth stands.' It would be foolish to underrate the difficulties ahead. And only the experts know how great they are. Sir John Pope-Hennessy doubtless had this very portrait in mind when he wrote, 'The

Elizabethan miniature presents an iconographical problem of the first magnitude.'

No evidence, so far as I can learn, has ever been offered for the identity of our blond MAN CLASPING A HAND. To suggest the brown-haired Earl of Essex is of course laughable. But must that identity, known in 1588, remain for ever unrecovered? Or could there be somewhere a key, which like Sabrina can unlock the clasping charm?

In the nervous moments before the start we need every sanguine thought anyone can offer us; and we catch at the thrilling possibility held out by the expert Duffield Osborne:

> In portraiture we have a multitude of portraits of characters humbler than rulers or great men, with always the hope that an identification . . . may reveal the lineaments of some man in whom history has created a deathless interest. *Engraved Gems*, 1912, 4

We draw encouragement too from Eric Westbrook's conclusion about our CLASPING A HAND: 'To an Elizabethan this symbol was probably quite comprehensible.' For who can deny or rule out the possibility that what this symbol meant in 1588 may be recovered? What is more, we may confidently extend this 'quite comprehensible' to apply to *every detail* painted in the picture. To John Calvin, Queen Elizabeth's contemporary, this fact was self-evident: 'Only those things be painted and graven whereof our eyes are capable'*—that is, 'which our modern sixteenth-century eyes are able to comprehend'.

This Elizabethan miniature was painted, as Elizabethan poems were written, to be understood. It therefore does not present a *mystery* hermetically sealed, but (as Sir John Pope-Hennessy warned) a *problem*. A problem to be solved by *hermeneutics*, the art or science of interpretation. Strange-looking to the uninitiated eye centuries later, naturally, like Shakespeare's *Warwick was a bug that fear'd us all*. But hermeneutics has solved problems harder than that.

There are many wrong ways of tackling a problem of this kind. One of the wrongest and most common is Lestrade's

* *Institutes*, tr. T. Norton 1561, 1.26, qu. *OED*. Spelling modernized.

way—Don Quixote's method at one remove. In '*the hopeful arrogance Sprung from ignoring of our ignorance*' of the data, we rush in with a rash hypothesis. And so obsessed is our mind with it, that when we confront a difficult piece of the evidence we promptly distort this into something familiar, something which we assume supports our darling conjecture. The clever RACHE scrawled in letters of blood at the murder-scene becomes 'Rachel', and off we go. Completely off.

Equally fatal is it to secure good sources of information only to misapply them. Here the truth lies under our eyes for the taking; yet—purblind and blunder-prone—all we can make of it is the howler: well illustrated by the student who had to interpret the French phrase *La rose, émue, répondit*. A good dictionary, a little close work, and up he came with the happy solution—'The pink emu laid another egg.'

We are convinced that with CLASPING A HAND we have already made what Sir George Thomson calls 'the first discovery: that there are things worth discovering'. But in the pursuit, if we are not to find ourselves either chasing Rachel or laying another egg, we dare not deviate from the well-tested directions set down by Experience. Despite recent revolutions in science, these rules—the basic precepts of Sherlock Holmes—remain unchanged and in force. The frontispiece to *Fabian of the Yard* (1950) shows the expert Superintendent with a magnifier, scrutinizing a mark or break made on a wall near a door. And under it the legend, *The most meticulous examination of every piece of evidence may often reveal the missing clue*.

2

In Less Compass, More Cunning

Every work of art contains within itself all that is necessary for its comprehension. So Edgar Allan Poe, assuring us that every piece of evidence we need lies before us, already painted in this little picture. Yet if therefore a most meticulous examination is indicated—holding the precious possibility of a clue—how are we equipped to conduct it? *He that will seek for a pearl must first learn to know it when he sees it.* A famous Chief of the C.I.D. sums up our predicament: 'Pure reasoning is all very well, but the blood and bones of all practical detective work is information.'*

What we need for this iconographical problem of the first magnitude is *more light to find your meaning out*: illumination from the age which produced the picture. The fabulous Holmes, with his 'You see, I have a lot of special knowledge which I apply to the problem', is of no help at all. We must carry on with Superintendent Fabian's more modest watchword, 'We have a lot to learn.'

Elementary caution warns us to begin with background. To look first, that is, at the history of paintings in miniature. Quietly, and apart from the large-scale works of the Italian Renaissance, the native North European tradition of painting 'in little' continued firm and unbroken. It had come down through Holbein, as the name *limner* shows, from the *lumineur* (illuminator) of the medieval manuscript. The illuminator emulated not the grand monuments of art, but Nature; for Nature's force was seen as *maxima in minimis*—'Nature, greatest in the least.' The age of Shakespeare held it an axiom:

A description of Nature.
Al-working mother, Foundresse of this All . . .
Was it because thou takest most delight
To print the greatest worth in smallest things?

* Frederick P. Wensley, *Forty Years of Scotland Yard*, 1931, 18.

So both in Art and Nature tis most cleere,
That greatest worths in smallest things appeare.

Thomas Moffett, *The Silke wormes*, 1599, G4, F1ᵛ

Nature sets Her rarest Gems in smallest Cabinets.

W. Loe, verses to Slater's *New Yeares Gift*, ... 1636

Shakespeare's contemporary the poet Giambattista Marino presents the god Mercury instructing Adonis on the point:

> In all her fair works Nature shows admirable art: one cannot deny it. But just like the painter, who discloses far more genius and study in a small figure than in a great, now and again in the smallest things she exerts greatest diligence, greatest care. This 'more' therefore rises above the wonted height of all her other miracles.
>
> *Adone*, 1623, 7.39

It may have been from Marino that William Drummond added the following to his *A Cypresse Grove* (*Flowres of Sion*, 2nd ed., 1630):

> ... Nature (who like a wise Painter showeth in a small Pourtrait more ingine than in a great) ...

And this conviction remained current in the eighteenth century. Count Francesco Algarotti (*Saggio sopra la Pittura*, 1762) writes, 'It is on the smallest that Nature's energy is bent; and in the smallest lies the excellence of art.'

As John Canaday observes, in considering the *Hours* of Catherine of Cleves, painted about 1400,

> It requires severe readjustment for most people today to realize that a painting that could be covered by the palm of a child's hand may hold infinite delights, that it must be allowed to reveal itself as if layer by layer, and that its expressive force, rather than being inhibited by tiny dimensions, may in a very special way be expanded by them.*

* Review of *The Hours of Catherine of Cleves*, 1966, Introduction and Commentaries by John Plummer. *New York Times Book Review*, 30 October 1966, p. 7.

Only major readjustment and full realization will qualify us to understand our miniature. And to the question vital to our present problem—Is miniature painting essentially *significant*? —Mr. Canaday quotes the considered reply of the specialist John Plummer:

> Medieval thought, pre-occupied as it was with parallels, analogies, and symbols, found the broadest meanings in small things.

Thus in every minute feature their work mirrored their conviction, *By the little is known the much*. The modern scientist shares this belief with the medieval. Lawyers of old had a maxim, *In obscurities we always follow what is smallest*.*

The poets, such as Marino and Drummond, were not alone in holding that the painter 'discloses far more genius and study in a small figure than in a great'. We have evidence that under Elizabeth, James, and Charles, limners in England were still purposefully striving for the excellence of the *multum in parvo*. And the proof comes, like so much other illumination of the period, from a playwright. Every reader of those plays recalls the miniature as a feature of them both favourite and frequent; and some may remember their common term for 'small portrait or likeness'—*model*. Thus Middleton:

> WIDDOWE.   [*Drawing out her husbands Picture*.
> Deare Copie of my husband, oh let me kisse thee.
> How like him is this Model! this briefe Picture
> Quickens my teares.   *The Puritaine* I.I

And Massinger:

> BAPTISTA. Take then this little modell of *Sophia*
> With more then humane skill limde to the life . . .
> *The Picture* I.I

Now to the evidence. It is given by Henry Glapthorne in 1640, some nine years after the death of his uncle Will Hatcliffe, Shakespeare's fair Friend—who as a youth *ca.* 1588 was portrayed presenting True Loving Friendship in Hilliard's

* *Semper in obscuris quod minimum est sequimur*. Cited by Rabelais, *Pantagruel* 3.39.

masterly full-length miniature. Glapthorne is dedicating his published play *The Hollander* to Sir Thomas Fisher; and he writes,

> ... as cunning painters expresse more significant Art in modell, then in extended figures, I have made election of this little of-spring of my braine to show you the largest skill of my many indearments to you.   [*ground, reason*

Glapthorne's opening phrase is neither an opinion nor a fancy. It merely brings forward a fact familiar to all: 'As everyone knows, pictures painted "in little" express not *less*, but *more* significance than large ones do.' As the Elizabethan Brian Melbancke had put it, 'A good Painter shadoweth a great counterfeit in a small roome.' (*Philotimus*, 1583, K2ᵛ.)

In less compass, more cunning. Facing us, therefore, inescapable, stands the warning: If we latter-day lookers do not find *more* significance in the features of an Elizabethan miniature than we do in a large portrait of the time, we are simply not finding what was painted in it to be found. We are not seeing *what is there*.

We look again at CLASPING A HAND. If *more significance* is there, we ask, where is it? Beyond three Latin words of inscription and a date, what means of communication does the work contain? We see the cloud. We see gestures of hands and fingers. We see articles of dress and ornament, with colours, forms, and figures. But nothing more.

Yet our information holds that all these features said something. Put together, they formed a particular concentration of unified meaning intelligible to Englishmen in 1588. For us, therefore, 'acting on information received' means a determined effort to dig up that buried message. And the adventure of such digging in itself presents singular points of interest. *Time, which antiquates antiquities, and hath an art to make dust of all things, hath yet spared these minor monuments.* Our problem is posed. It is to persuade that old wrecker Time to tell us what this reprieved minor monument of ours means.

As a preliminary, we look over the field for a possible sign. And we notice that our CLASPING A HAND belongs to a very limited class of miniatures: those carrying not a bare date with the sitter's age, but *an inscription or lemma*. Of such inscriptions we at once find two types. First there is the sitter's motto, chosen to convey a clear personal meaning or intent, such as that on Isaac Oliver's miniature of Queen Anne, *Seruo per regnare*. And second, *a difficult 'word' or lemma darkly allusive*, such as Lucan's *Dat pœnas laudata fides* on Hilliard's full-length miniature of Will Hatcliffe *ca.* 1588, or the baffling *Attici amoris ergo* on his CLASPING A HAND dated 1588.

The difficult 'word' (as we learned in studying *Dat pœnas laudata fides* for *Mr. W. H.*) belongs to the *impresa* or heroical Device: forming the 'soul' or 'spirit' of its figure or 'body'. Known as 'the noble mind's hieroglyphic', the *impresa* or Device presented *a high personal thought or intent to be guessed from the combined picture-and-word*.

Queen Elizabeth's own delight in Devices is betrayed both by her large collection of them at Whitehall and in the lines describing the entertainment specially prepared for her by the Fairy Queen:

> *Within hir bower she biddes her to a feast,*
> *Which with enchaunted pictures trim she dightes,*
> *And on them woordes of highe intention writes.**

And they go on to extol Elizabeth's rare skill in Device-solving:

> Now since, by that more than mortall power of your more than humane wisdome, the enchanted tables [pictures] are read ...   *The Phoenix Nest*, 1593, ed. Rollins 1931, 24

The Device was so much the rage of educated Europe in its time that it has come down to us in hundreds of examples. And modern scholars are finding that (like the more common and easily understood moral Emblems) their solution can throw unexpected light not only on the poems and pictures, but on the life of their period as well.

A familiar description of the Device is given by the learned antiquary and herald William Camden:

> An Impress (as the Italians call it) is a device in picture

* Anon., qu. Bond ed. *Lyly* 1.456; but see E. K. Chambers, *Elizabethan Stage* 3.404, 407.

with his motto, or word, borne by noble and learned personages, to notify some particular conceit of their own, as Emblems (that we may omit other differences) do propound some general instruction to all. . . .

There is required in an Impress (that we may reduce them to a few heads) a correspondency of the picture, which is as the body, and the motto, which as the soul giveth it life. That is, the body must be of fair representation, and the word in some different language, witty [*i.e.*, full of meaning], short, and answerable thereunto; neither too obscure, nor too plain, and most commended when it is an hemistich, or parcel of a verse.

Remains, 1605 ed. 1870, 366–367. Spelling modernized

But Camden here omits one essential difference from the Emblem too important to be overlooked. And that is the special rule strictly governing the Device: namely, that *neither picture nor motto may be intelligible separately or by itself.* This central requirement—set down by Scipione Bargagli as 'the two must be so strictly united together that being considered apart they cannot explicate themselves distinctly the one without the other'—is recited in the very year of our CLASPING A HAND, 1588, by the English poet Abraham Fraunce in his book on the Device, as follows:

The joining of motto with figure

Here one must beware lest the words declare the figure, or lest by themselves alone they make full and perfect sense, as we have already often said; but, if they be removed, and separated from the figure, that they leave behind an imperfect indescribable something, a *je ne sais quoi*, such as you cannot understand.

Abrahami Fransi, Insignium Armorum, Emblematum, Hieroglyphicorum, et Symbolorum quæ ab Italis Imprese nominantur, explicatio. . . . Londini . . . 1588. N4[v]

Little wonder, therefore, when the meaning of *Attici amoris ergo* remains unknown, that we do not grasp the significance of the figure in CLASPING A HAND.

Yet this strict rule, when we chew upon it, brings not discouragement, but aid. Aid of the first importance. For that requirement gives us, we now realize, an infallible means of checking the correctness of conjecture. Because of it, we know that any guess at the meaning of the picture which does not *complete* as well as explain the sense of the 'word' is wrong. And the same is true *vice versa* of the 'word'. Nothing but its true meaning will *complete* and explain the picture. So that if we are wrong we shall know it at once. And if we are right, there will be no question about it.

To lift our latter-day minds to the height on which the devotees of the Device placed it is beyond hope. But to attend to their appraisal will at least warn us against taking a superficial view. For they held that in its powers of communication it surpassed all other arts. Thus Père Pierre Le Moyne calls the Device

> a Poem; but a Poem which does not sing, which is composed but of a mute Figure, and of a Word which speaks for it to the eye. The marvel is that this Poem without Music does in a moment, with this Figure and this Word, what other Poesy could not do but with a long time and great preparations of harmonies, fictions, and contrivances.
>
> *De l'Art des Devises*, 1666, qu. Mario Praz, *Studies in Seventeenth Century Imagery*, 1964, 60

And Henri Estienne puts the portrait-Device *full of high intent* above Painting,

> since this onely representeth the body and exquisite features of the face, when as a Devise exposeth the rare conceipts, and gallant resolutions of its Author, far more perspicuously, and with more certainty, then Physiognomy can.
>
> *L'Art de faire les Devises*, 1645, tr. T. Blount 1646, 14

Picta poesis—a painted poem, yes; but not a free unattached flight of fancy. For Scipione Bargagli, the Aristotle of the *impresa*, lays it down that

> In the main subject of the devices there can be no room

... for mere fictions; since we must deal with real things, and we have to explain and prove them.

Qu. and tr. Praz, *op. cit.*, 69

Poetical, then, surely; but poetry based firmly on actual fact. Yet also according to the rules, the Device must on sight *strike the mind with wonder*. Therefore, as Ercole Tasso points out, to rouse the requisite wonder this 'truth however can be enhanced by some hyperbolical adjunct'. And Emanuele Tesauro elaborates: 'in which the picture, . . . overstepping the ordinary laws of Nature, holds the mind somewhat suspended or astonished'. (Praz, 69, 64.)

Certainly the astonishing act of clasping a hand from a cloud makes a notably hyperbolical and wonder-stirring adjunct to the poetical *impresa*-portrait of a recognizable man.

Informed by these authorities of the time, our view of CLASPING A HAND draws steadily both nearer and clearer. Listing the items of information together, we can now see

(a) that this miniature somehow expresses an eloquent poetical intent or thought of the sitter's;
(b) that the poet's theme is based on actual fact, known to the London of 1588;
(c) that this actual fact is symbolized for us by a wonderful or marvellous hyperbole: the MAN's supernatural action in clasping a hand extended from the sky; and
(d) that picture and 'word' are, as they stand, each *imperfect* in meaning. Only the true interpretation will enable each *to complete and explain* the other.

Multum in parvo with a vengeance. A load of significance packed into a couple of inches. This dense concentration makes it obvious folly to imagine any slightest feature of it an irrelevant *parergon*, 'by-work', or a 'needless grace'. There is no possible room for adventitious embellishment. As Francesco Albani—who excelled at painting 'in little'—put it, 'a fine Invention, with most beautiful conceits well set out; and all the figures work to the intent: nothing useless.' (Qu. C. C. Malvasia, *Felsina Pittrice*, 1678, 2.255.)

With this warning, we shall not repeat the ignorant type of

modern blunder which took the conspicuous cat in the oil-painting 'Southampton prisoner in the Tower' for a *parergon*: 'his favourite cat'. So far from being a needless grace, that cat —common symbol of Impatience of Imprisonment and Desire for Liberty—in reality embodies the whole *argument* or message of the portrait. Nothing more is required to tell an Elizabethan not only that the sitter is a prisoner, but also that he 'wants *out*'. (See my *Mr. W. H.*, 1964, 207–208.)

And just as that cat does not display a notion of the artist's, but *the intent of Lord Southampton the sitter*, so every detail in our Device CLASPING A HAND sets forth not something of Hilliard's imagining, but *the high personal thought of this MAN A.D. 1588*. As Abraham Fraunce emphasizes, 'in making a Device, I speak mine own intent, not that of others. I do not instruct others. Others I do not consider.' (*Op. cit.*, N3.)

Here we are given an imperative pointer. To lose sight of it is to invite defeat. We shall in fact be well advised to approach the features of this *impresa* precisely as De Quincey approached the works of Shakespeare—

> which are to be studied with entire submission of our own faculties, and in the perfect faith that in them there can be ... nothing useless or inert—but that, the farther we press in our discoveries, the more we shall see proofs of design and self-supporting arrangement where the careless eye had seen nothing but accident.

From Abd-el-Kader Salza's classic study of the literature of the Device* and Professor Praz's illuminating chapter† on its interpretation, we learn a fascinating deal about this curious fad of educated Europe's so amazingly widespread and long-lived. We realize that the exacting laws and standards which governed it naturally made Device-devising a high speciality. Many were the gentlemen who longed to be in style with a Device which would win approving attention. But relatively few could command either the literary skill or the wit needed

* *La Letteratura delle 'Imprese' e la fortuna di esse nel 500*, appended to his *Luca Contile*, 1903.
† 'The Philosophy of the Courtier', *op. cit.*, 54–82.

to excogitate the interlocking elements of so elegant a personal puzzle. Most of them must have confided their more or less fumbling 'noble thought' to a recognized expert. And he (for love or money) worked it up into a delicate poetic conundrum in figure-and-word. Then it was executed (for money) by a draughtsman; and the proud owner brought it out for display, 'to be understood by some but not by all'.

Such Device-specialists, now long forgotten, in their own day were accorded high consideration, doubtless higher than that enjoyed by many a good minor poet. Italy's prince of the *impresa* was Marcantonio Epicuro, as Scipione Ammirato testifies, offering in proof several samples of Epicuro's devising. 'Two most beautiful Devices, certainly.' 'Enough to say that they are by Epicuro.'

And in Sir William Skipwith (died 1610) England had her own distinguished practitioner, eulogized by William Burton, and commended by Thomas Fuller in these terms:

> He was deservedly knighted, being a person of much valour, judgment, and wisdome, dexterous at the making [of] fit and acute Epigrams, Poesies, Mottoes, and Devices, but chiefly at Impreses, neither so apparent that every rustick might understand them, nor so obscure that they needed an Œdipus to interpret them.

We shall find this expert Sir William Skipwith turning up in our own *impresa*-story. He will figure significantly in the sequel.

A court of the quality of Queen Elizabeth's could boast others among its eminent cavaliers. Sir Philip Sidney produced a large number of Devices for the *Arcadia*. And skilful too was the Earl of Essex, in the discerning judgment of Sir Henry Wotton, long resident in Italy, chief home of the *impresa*. From his early intimate knowledge as the Earl's secretary, Wotton concludes,

> for his writings, they are beyond example, especially in his Letters and things of delight at Court ... as may yet be seen in his Impresses and Inventions of entertainment.
>
> *Reliquiæ Wottonianæ*, 173

Yet naturally more expert still were the leading poets. Nashe's and Marston's works both furnish interesting *imprese*. The many Devices which Ben Jonson contrived for his numerous masques—his 'Court Hieroglyphics'—and the handful for his *Cynthia's Revels* have survived. But from his epigram *To Sir Annual Tilter* and the dunning one *To Fine Grand* we learn that he also made a lucrative side-line of devising others, now lost, for courtiers of more wealth than wit.

And Shakespeare? He must have proved his excellence in the art. Nothing less could have moved Francis Manners the new Earl of Rutland to entrust to him (not to Jonson) the important devising of his *impresa* for his Court *début* in the 'jousts of incomparable magnificence' on King's Day 1612/3, where he 'made a very rich appearance' reported second only to the Earl of Dorset's 'gallant show'. And further, we note that since Henry Peacham significantly repeats in 1612 his complaint of 1606—

> I am sory that our . . . great personages must seeke farre and neere for some . . . Italian to . . . inuent their deuises, our Englishmen being held for *Vaunients* [Good-for-noughts].

—Lord Rutland's choice shows 'our Shakespeare' distinguished as *a rare expert*.

That Device for Lord Rutland is an authentic lost work of Shakespeare's. And it is certainly not impossible, even at our late day of the world, that another—and more important one—might come to light.

To bring before us in action the rage for symbolism and Device-guessing rampant in the London of about 1588 I find nothing to equal a brief letter of Stephen Powle's to Walter Cope. Powle in 1587 is recently back in town after a year of 'intelligencing' in Germany for Lord Burghley. With a courtier's eye to his standing with his lord's influential gentleman-usher Master Walter Cope, Powle sends him (doubtless as a New Year's gift) a cunning piece of German carving in ivory —here pressed into the service of symbolism—instead of *a naturally expected impresa*.

Good Mr. Cope, Instead of an Italian Impresa to acquaint your eyes with my mind, I send you a German's handiwork; and this letter to manifest my secret meaning therein. Let the whiteness thereof signify my sincerity; the roundness in length, the perfection of my good will long to continue; and the degrees and stairs therein, the desire I have to mount higher in your acquaintance and favour.

Your very loving and assured friend to command,

S. P.*

It is plain that we are not to imagine CLASPING A HAND something exceptional. On the contrary. It is merely a sample of the fashionable means of acquainting cultivated London eyes with the sitter's mind.

Yet take away all man's works of significant art, and Duke Senior will still find tongues in trees, books in brooks, sermons in stones. The inventing and unriddling of Devices was but one typical diversion of the quick Elizabethan mind: a mind not only richly stored, but also symbol-haunted.

We have seen that *Dat pœnas laudata fides* (about 1588) and our *Attici amoris ergo* (CLASPING A HAND) of 1588 are, each one, a portrait and a Device. Examples of such *impresa*-portraits, while not common, are well known. We have a familiar one in the *impresa*-portrait of Philip II and his son Ferdinand, bearing the lemma *Maiora Tibi*, in the Prado.†️ Another—of Mary Stuart—is described by Drummond of Hawthornden: 'a Crucifix, before which with all her Royall Ornaments she is humbled on her knees most lively, with the word *undique*.'‡️ And in the next chapter we shall be recognizing a third—a famous portrait of Queen Elizabeth I.

As for the special way in which this peculiar 'loaded' type of portrait is to be viewed, the thoughtful Giovanni Ferro points it out to us:

Properly speaking, these bodies and images [drawn in Devices] cannot be strictly termed 'portraits'; since a man

* Bodl. MS. Tanner 78, f. 105^v. Powle's copy; spelling modernized.
† Erwin Panofsky, *Meaning in the Visual Arts*, 1955, 148n.
‡ Qu., *Ben Jonson* ed. Herford and Simpson, 1.208.

when put as the body in a Device would not be taken as an image pure and simple representing So-and-so, but would be regarded as representing *So-and-so performing some act.* [Consequently, in these *impresa*-portraits it is not the *likeness* of the figure which is important, but] *some action of it upon which the Device is founded.*

Teatro d'Imprese, 1623, 1.83. Italics added

Recognition of the central action of the figure: will this prove to be the key to our puzzle?

Yet the question *May the human figure be used at all in a proper Device?* had been much debated by its law-givers. Paolo Giovio's rule excluded it. But the poet Samuel Daniel prefaced his translation in 1585 of Giovio's treatise with this qualification:

> *Jovius* also addeth for a precept in the rules of *Imprese,* that in them there ought to be no human form; which precept is most true, if it be in the ordinary and simple form of a man . . .; but yet when the human form *shall be in a strange & unaccustomed manner,* it beareth a great grace.*

This significant qualification had been Ruscelli's point. Although admitting the human figure, Ruscelli held that in order to produce the requisite 'rare and unusual'

> in the Device it is not becoming that one should represent men and women ordinarily dressed as they usually are, but that those human figures one represents should somehow wear garments of a strange fashion, and somewhat different from those in which we see them every day.†

* *A worthy tract of Paulus Iovius . . . of . . . Imprese,* 1585, A7ᵛ. Spelling modernized, and italics added.

† From *Imprese illustri,* 1566, tr. Praz, 71. Ercole Tasso later gave his own opinion: 'But if this man be considered in respect of happenings which befell him, or of some memorable achievement, or action undergone . . . in such case, the said human Figure yet remains a most worthy "body" of this Device.' *Della realtà, & perfettione delle Imprese,* 1612, ed. 1614, 389.

Abraham Fraunce sums it up in these words:

The human figure.

This is a great question; many arguments are brought forward on each side. Giovio stays in doubt: he excludes it in his rules, and gives it in his examples. Ruscelli approves it, but [only if] *altered, unusual*. Contile also retains it, but [only if it be] *poetical*. *Op. cit.*, O4

And we find that what Contile meant by *poetical* was figures such as 'Mars, Apollo, Venus, Mercury, Neptune, Pallas, Jove, and Saturn'. (Qu. Ercole Tasso, *op. cit.*, 189.)

On putting these pointers together, we now have before us the very sort of definite contemporary eye-opener we have been lacking. For if our CLASPING A HAND conforms to the rules, we begin to see more clearly where the necessary clues must be presented.

First comes the cardinal sign of the MAN's poetical intent: the *supernatural action* symbolizing a fact known in 1588, upon which the Device is founded. Next, we are to expect to find the MAN presenting himself here *not* as his familiar ordinary self, but *in some unusual or 'poetical' character*: *e.g.*, one of the Homeric *gods*. Finally, by two means we are to guess who that character is. First, by *the MAN's supernatural action*. And second, both by his looks and by *marked or unusual features of his articles of costume*.

You will agree that our puzzle, even with all this clarification, is not so transparent that every rustic might solve it. 'The meaning of the *impresa* should not be so plain that every common fellow at first sight would know it by seeing it naked, and without the veil of the allegory.' (Bartolomeo Taegio, *Il Liceo*, 1571, qu. Robert J. Clements, *Picta Poesis*, 1960, 114.)

But we have been assured that no Œdipus is required. And if that is the case, who could tamely leave to someone else the keen satisfaction of reading the riddle? Curiosity is unleashed. With these clear hints now in hand, are we not fresh enough to hunt farther along these tracks pointed out for us by old Nimrods skilled in the chase?

3

The Clue of the Royal Hand

IN competition with our ancestors, skilled in this kind of hieroglyphic, we feel painfully like Dr. Watson, trying his prentice hand. Of what use is it to be told, 'You know my methods, Watson'? Our only hope is to begin with two resolves: (*a*) not to overlook *anything whatever*, and (*b*) to scrutinize every feature not merely for 'some significance', but for *an apt meaning demonstrably recognizable by an Elizabethan.*

The need for such most meticulous examination of every piece of evidence *in the light of its own time* vividly appears in a familiar example: the excellent large 'Siena' portrait (*ca.* 1580–1585) of Queen Elizabeth with a sieve in her hand. Camden tells us that 'Queen Elizabeth, upon occasions, used as many heroical devices as would require a volume; but most commonly a Sieve without a Mot'—that is, a 'word' or lemma. But her *intent* in displaying that wordless symbol he omits to mention. No doubt because every educated reader knew it.

The obvious clue to the central meaning of this portrait of the Virgin Queen is her conspicuous Sieve. And since Dionysius of Halicarnassus, Valerius Maximus, and Pliny the Elder all relate how the Vestal Tuccia vindicated her *virginity* by the miraculous feat of *carrying water in a 'captious and intenible' sieve,** modern writers have lightly assumed that the learned Queen's sieve-holding here conveyed by loose association the simple emblematic notion *Virgo Virginissima*, 'Virgin more than the Vestal.' No one, so far as I know, has recognized the painting for what it is: an *impresa*-portrait, a *heroic Device*, complete with its lemma inscribed on the sieve.

And what is more curious, no one in considering this *Siena*

---

* '[Tuccia] Portò . . . al tempio acqua col cribro', Petrarch, *Trionfo della Castità;* 'Tuccia . . . carrying water in a siue', Lyly, *Euphues and his England, Wks.* ed. Bond, 2.209.

portrait seems to have noticed what the Sieve connoted in Siena. For the *Travagliati*, Sienese Academicians, gave for their device a sieve, with the 'word' DONEC IMPURUM, says Ferro (2.260), giving Bargagli as his authority. This meant 'that they would be ever exercised in virtuous actions until they should have sifted out the spots, even the smallest whatsoever, of human imperfection'. (Filippo Picinelli, *Mundus Symbolicus*, 1687, 243*a*.)

A glance moreover at page 86 of Claude Paradin's widely studied *Devises Heroïques* (ed. 1566) again finds the Sieve pictured far from any miraculous vindication of virginity. It is performing its typical ordinary function of *separating the bad* (chaff) *from the good* (flour), with the 'word' ECQUIS DISCERNIT UTRUMQUE? *'Who will separate the two?'* (The device is copied in G. Whitney, *Choice of Emblemes*, 1586.) Similarly, the famous Florentine Academy 'of the Chaff or Bran', dedicated to purifying the Italian language, gave for its *impresa* a Sieve sifting flour, with the elegant 'word' IL PIÙ BEL FIOR NE COGLIE, *'It culls the fairest flower (flour)'.*

And when one looks more than casually at the Sieve in the Siena portrait, at once two features show that here too it presents its usual meaning, and *not* 'Virginity'. First, the Queen holds it dangling *empty*. It contains neither water, nor flour, nor chaff. Second, the 'word' painted on its rim—which must be *answerable* or corresponding to the picture—does not deal with virginity, but (as in the devices of Paradin, Florence, and Siena) *with the result of its function in sifting chaffy flour*: A TERRA IL BEN, MAL DIMORA IN SELLA, *'Down goes the good, the bad remains* [above] *in the saddle.'*

As anyone can see, to *complete* and explain the sense of this 'word', the pictured Sieve is needed. And on the other hand, how is *the meaning of the picture completed* by the 'word'? Answer, *because* the 'word' says *the bad remains*, the ostentatious *emptiness* of Elizabeth's Sieve therefore declares *No bad was there*.

Now since an *impresa*-portrait expresses the sitter's personal thought, the meaning here is to be sought only in Elizabeth's own mind. How this *No bad was there* came to be her personal thought, when—before she had 'swum to the throne through a sea of sorrow'—she was prisoner in the Tower, accused of plotting treason against the Queen her half-sister Mary, was common knowledge at her Court:

> But such was the innocency of that lady, as she wrote in the windows of her lodging in the Tower yet to be seen, and in other places, with a diamond: *Many things have been objected against me, but nothing proved can be. So she gave for her Device a Sieve, for she had been sifted* and fanned with all curious devices, but *no chaff found.**

Clearly, this *impresa*-portrait would be approved by Emanuele Tesauro as a proper or 'popular' one:

> I therefore conclude the 'popular' Device (l'IMPRESA POPVLARE) to be that which offers openly to all, but is above the capacity of the multitude. By wits of middling cleverness and learning it can be interpreted: with the presentment of scholarly features not abstruse, and of circumstances not too hard to be recognized. And on the other hand, if the Device is so superficial that everyone understands it, or so abstruse that no one can make it out, it will be neither 'popular', nor pleasing, nor acceptable.
>
> *Il Cannocchiale Aristotelico*, 1654, ed. 1675, 448

To find that this fairly lucid but today universally misunderstood *impresa*-portrait will at once yield its meaning when looked at from the moderately educated Elizabethan's point of view is not only encouragement but also *direction*. We seem to hear Hugo von Hofmannsthal—*Knowledge is little; to know the right context is much: to know the right spot is everything*. In our CLASPING A HAND, we are first to hunt for *the right context*,

---

* British Library MS. Addl. 11600, f. 48ᵛ, spelling modernized and italics added. Compare Anthony Munday, *A Watch-woord to Englande*, 1584, 29: 'Wherevppon the Lady *Elizabeth*, at her departing out from *Woodstocke*, wrote these Verses with her Diamond in a glasse windowe.

> Much suspected by me: [about, concerning
> Nothing proved can be.
> Quod *Elizabeth* prisoner.'

And in allusion to the well-known meaning of Elizabeth's Sieve, Sir Christopher Hatton (writing in November 1591) bids her 'sift the chaff from the wheat'.

sustained by the hope that that context will point us to *the right spot*.

You will have noticed that the learned Queen's Device conforms to almost all the rules. It conveys no instruction to others; nothing but the personal thought of the sitter. More, her noble mind's hieroglyphic is based on historical truth— her own actual experience. Further, picture and 'word' are each dependent upon the other for completion of meaning, and the 'word' is in a foreign tongue. As for the requisite *wonder*, that emotion will not be stirred by the gesture of holding an empty sieve. But is not this rare sight, both intimate and glorious, of God's chosen vicegerent, able as it stands to hold the mind of 1585 somewhat suspended or astonished? For to that mind her figure was hyperbolical—*heauenborne Elizabeth hath made . . . the worlds eye sight astonied*. As herself, that divine Elizabeth overstepped the common bounds of Nature, striking the beholder with wonder.

Now whether or not Tyndale was right in holding that 'Allegoryes make a man qwick witted', they certainly make him more observant. With eyes somewhat sharpened, another look at our CLASPING A HAND now discovers a startling feature: a feature which I have never seen remarked by any critic of this miniature. Namely, that the joined hands are *not painted skin- or flesh-colour like the sitter's face and neck, and like hands in other Hilliard miniatures*. In each example of this miniature *the hands* are both *painted white*. This abnormality, once you see it, remains so glaring that one can hardly believe it has passed every eye unnoticed. Evidently this unnatural colour is a symbol, carrying a recognized meaning essential to this Device. We cannot as yet see in it the leading clue we need. But we do hear it say, and very distinctly, 'If you haven't seen even *this*, how much else have you failed to notice?'

We are still faced with this formidable little island-fortress of concentrated meaning. Our aim is as simple as it is obvious: to effect a breach somewhere in its wall. It is curious to remember how in 1588—the very year of our Device—the Spanish Dons of the Armada hoped to force successful entry into Elizabeth's England with the magical aid of 'Hieroglliphi-call Simbols, Emblems, impresses and deuises' (Robert Greene,

The Spanish Masquerado, 1589)—painting their black ships' streamers and 'pennons tragicall' with these 'sad ostents of death and dismall feare'. Our present hope is just the other way about: to force successful entry into an enchanting *impresa* of 1588 *by means of Elizabeth's England*. Will such reversal turn an illusory method into an effective one?

To open a breach somewhere in its wall; but where? Should we attack the 'word'? Standing by itself, the lemma as we have learned *must* be unclear, incomplete; and no one has made sense of it. '*The meaning of the inscription is unknown.*' Certainly at this stage of the game *Attici amoris ergo* offers no perceptible point for attack. We are driven back on the figure, the body of the Device.

For a hint, let us look to the distilled counsel of the criminal investigators. Ellis Parker, the most experienced and successful of American detectives, lays it down that 'the thing you want to look for in every case is something unnatural....But you have to learn how to use the unnatural things.' Here is advice even more pointed for our problem than Sherlock Holmes's 'Singularity is almost invariably a clue.' For a claspable, whitened hand reaching down from the sky is not merely singular. It is profoundly *unnatural*. Able to strike any mind with wonder.

Yes. It is this supernatural White Hand from the clouds which clearly emerges as the salient mark for scrutiny. And it poses the instant question, *Whose* hand? Who is it that *behind Was left unseene, save to the eye of mind*? Is it fantastic to suspect that we might recognize the unseen Owner of the Hand before we recognize the fully portrayed Clasper? Yet that is how one might interpret Ellis Parker's counsel; and the possibility, remote as it seems, should be explored. Certainly discovery of that identity might well offer a clue to the 'poetical' or hyperbolical character presented by the Clasper.

We begin with the conviction that this Hand on sight conveyed to the literate eye of 1588 a message as rich as it was unmistakable. When John Donne wrote the lines

> *a hand . . .*
> By Hilliard *drawne, is worth an history*
> By *a worse painter made*

33

it is more than possible that he had in mind this very HAND FROM A CLOUD. What other known hand painted by Hilliard is as likely as this one to embody a story? For we note that both these strangely *white hands* are drawn with careful realism, in contrast to the highly stylized ones usual in his work.

Our first glance into the Elizabethan world of symbol for the meaning of a 'hand from clouds' yields 'a *divine* hand': most frequently '*the Almighty's hand*'. And naturally so, since this symbol of God's omnipotent power and protection, drawn from the Bible (*Ps.* 144:7, *Isa.* 59:1, etc.), is not only universal but of high antiquity. The *manus Dei* appears pictured A.D. 245 in the Synagogue at Dura-Europos on the Euphrates, in the Roman catacombs, in a medal of Constantine the Great, frequently in Christian art of the Dark and Middle Ages, and in the Bayeux Tapestry.*

We also have it in Elizabeth's time. The Emperor Charles V, father of her antagonist Philip II, used the figure of a hand from a cloud, with the 'word' MANUS DEI PROTEGAT ME.† And her brother Edward VI's choice was the globe of the world in a chain, held by a hand out of clouds, with the motto NIL SINE DEO. (Pietrasanta, *ed. cit.*, 204; Typotius, 291–292.) These closely resemble two other published emblems: a hand out of clouds holding a crowned heart (IN MANU DEI COR REGIS), and a hand out of clouds holding the Earth (IN MANU DEI OMNES SUNT FINES TERRÆ).‡

We even find it in 1588 among Queen Elizabeth's jewels, where it apparently means 'God's Scripture' or 'the Power of God's Word': Mr. Chidley had presented the Queen with '*One Jewel of gold, with a hand out of clouds garnished with Opals and*

---

* *The Excavations at Dura-Europos, Sixth Season*, ed. M. I. Rostovtzeff *et al.*, 1936, Pl. XLIX, LI, LIII; J. J. Timmers, *Symboliek en Iconographie der Christelijke Kunst*, 1947, nos. 88–96 and 545; Karl Künstle, *Ikonographie der christlichen Kunst*, 1928, 234–235, 377; C. A. Auber, *Histoire . . . du Symbolisme Religieux*, 1884, 2.401, 534; 3.132, 138, 181, 299, 334; 4.47, 110; for Constantine's medal, see Silvestro Pietrasanta, *Symbola Heroica*, 1634, ed. 1682, lib. 2. c. 2, p. 81.

† Jacobus Typotius, *Symbola . . . Pontificum, Imperatorum, Regum*, 1601–1603), ed. 1690, p. 131, no. XX.

‡ Gabriel Rollenhagen, *Selectorum Emblematum Centuria Secunda*, 1613, nos. 46 and 52.

a pen therein.' And in devising the elaborate crest she granted
to Drake the English Dragon, on knighting him in 1581 after
his circumnavigation, the Queen recalled her brother's emblem
both with the figure and the 'word':

> . . . a Globe terrestrial, upon the height whereof is a Ship
> under sail, trained about the Globe with two golden
> halsers, by direction of an hand out of a Cloud, and a
> Dragon volant upon the hatches, regarding the direction
> with these words, *Auxilio divino.**

Henry Peacham mentions it as 'that deuice vpon Sir *Frauncis
Drake* (which was Q. Elizabeths owne)'. (*The Compleat Gentleman*, 1622, 148.)

Several examples, finally, may be drawn from the drama. In
The Partiall Law (Anon., *ca.* 1615–30, ed. Bertram Dobell, 1908)
1.5, the King describes the knights' devices at a tilt:

A fourth Tilter *passeth by* . . .
KING. An arme from forth a cloud grasping a speare,
And underneath, DAT GRATIA VIRES [*Grace giveth strength*].
. . . *Another* Tilter *passeth by* . . .
KING. A man sunke in the Sea, only his head
Borne above water by a Scepter, which
Is by a hand supported from the skyes,
His word, HINC SOLA SALUS [*The only salvation from this*].

And everyone recalls the familiar symbol from the emblem
books which Shakespeare presents in *Pericles* 2.2:

THAI. The fift, an Hand enuironëd with Clouds,
Holding out Gold, that's by the Touch-stone tride:
The motto thus: SIC SPECTANDA FIDES [*Thus is faith
to be tested*].

On review, three features of this Hand of God stand out.
First, it is typically DEXTRA DEI, a *right* hand, the hand of
power. Second, it is properly a *bare* hand and wrist. As Hum-

---

* William Camden, *Remains*, ed. *cit.*, 379. Cf. Stow-Howes, *Annales*,
1615, 687*b*. The emblem is pictured in Whitney, *op. cit.*, 203. For more
occurrences of God's Hand in emblems, see Henry Peacham, *Minerva
Britanna*, 1612, 1, 12, 15, 43, 44, 98.

phrey Wanley remarks, 'a right Hand, & the Arm, naked, or
. . . clothed in . . . antique sort; for so the Antients used to
express God, & his Power & Providence: as I have seen in
very many old MS.' (British Library MS. Harl. 1422, f. 4.) And
George Chapman corroborates from Shakespeare's time:

> Her naked wrists showde, as if through the skie
> A hand were thrust, to signe the Deitie.
> *Andromeda Liberata,* 137–138

Finally, since it is not a bodily hand at all, but a *mystical sign* of
the All-Powerful, it is not shown touching a mortal's head,
body, or hand.

Turning to our HAND OUT OF CLOUDS, we find none of
these features. In the first place, it is a *left* hand. Second, its
wrist is *clothed in modern dress,* wearing an Elizabethan ruff-cuff.
And third, so far from being incorporeal, the hand is intimately
clasped by the hand of a mortal, a blond young Englishman
of 1588.

As a common article of gentlemen's attire, the ruff-cuff—
always worn to match or suit with the ruff at the neck—
appears at the National Portrait Gallery in the likenesses
(among others) of Sir Nicholas Bacon, Sir Thomas Gresham,
Sir Richard Grenville, The Earl of Leicester, and Sir Philip
Sidney. In Elizabethan plays, the King was recognized by his
always wearing cuffs. (See Jonson, *The Staple of News,* Ind. 42.)

This hand from the sky therefore cannot be the Almighty's.
That is impossible. But it remains a most improbable hand.
And even if, as Sherlock Holmes insists, 'when you have
eliminated the impossible, whatever remains, *however improbable,* must be the truth', we have still to learn what that truth
may be.

Our look through many of the volumes of emblems and
devices widely read by the Elizabethans has so far met no
promising clue. But Samuel Daniel, in the preface to his translation of Giovio (1585), after rehearsing the rules governing
imprese, reminds us of a source more obvious still:

> Have not our Printers also of late honored this profession?
> Have they not bene at emulation for ingenious *Devises?*

Universally circulated, and of most common familiarity, were these devices of printers and publishers. You found them displayed on the title-pages of most of the books you picked up from the bookseller's stall.

Being aimed at a wide public, these devices were usually no more than easily read and generally edifying emblems, drawn from familiar compilations. Few attempted to follow the strict rules of the select *impresa*, and to express a *personal* thought or intent in a puzzle of figure-and-word. Much has been written about this class of device, and Ronald McKerrow gathered and studied the English examples. (*Printers' and Publishers' Devices, 1455–1640*, 1913.) To leaf his pages through is to be spared the labour of examining thousands of Elizabethan books for their title-page devices.

Naturally, almost at once we turn up another familiar example of God's Hand, shown in McKerrow's no. 170, the device of Thomas Vautrollier. At the top a right hand, its wrist bare, emerges from a cloud, holding an anchor by its ring, with the 'word' ANCHORA SPEI. Since this device descended to Shakespeare's Stratford-contemporary-and-publisher Richard Field when he married Vautrollier's widow, we know it well from the title-pages of both *Venus and Adonis* and *Lucrece*. We look farther.

But when we hit upon McKerrow's no. 112β, the device of that very active printer John Charlewood, we give more than 'a start of recognition'. It rivets our gaze; for what do we see? Again a hand from a cloud, but certainly not the Almighty's DEXTRA DEI. This is a *left* hand. And *clothed in an Elizabethan ruff-cuff*. Precisely what is presented in our CLASPING A HAND. Now is there something in the rest of the figure which betrays who this is, who *himselfe behind Was left unseene*?

Let us see. The Hand is here holding out from the cloud a peculiarly constructed *caduceus* or 'charming snaky rod'. One's immediate impulse is therefore to say '*Mercury*'. As for the ruff-cuff, it is to be expected. From the days of the *tarocchi* cards, the Renaissance commonly saw the favourite pagan gods in modern dress. Books, ballets, masques, pageantry, and plays presented their Apollos and their Mercurys in rich costume of significant materials and colours, often fanciful, but essentially *modern*. Approaches to classical nudity or attempts at authentic 'Grecian tires' are exceptional. Just as Hamlet was not presented in the dress of a medieval Dane.

A fresco of the Planets (about 1470) in Ferrara's Palazzo Schifanoia shows Mercury in modern dress: 'The caduceus is his only ancient attribute, since for the rest he appears garbed in rich stylish costume.'* In the illustrated manuscript of Clément Marot's version of Ovid's *Metamorphoses*, presented to the King, Apollo appears in jerkin and hose (Joan Evans, *Pattern*, 1931, 2.23n.); and in Sylvester's Du Bartas his golden dancing-dress is topped with a 'saffron'd Ruffe', while Mercury's is 'How strange a suit', covered with a short dancing-cloak: a 'medly Mantle'. (Joshua Sylvester, *Works* (ed. Grosart), 1.235a.) Further, in Richard Bernard's *Amphitruo*-adaptation entitled *The Birthe of Hercules* (acted at Cambridge 1595–98), Mercury as Prologue tells his audience, 'So perhaps you would take me for a man; but you are deceived, for I am a god.' But since in modern dress and in looks he is so very like the other character Sosia, 'that you may know us asunder, I will wear in my hat a piece of a feather for a difference'.

That ruff-cuff in Charlewood's device, then, might be Mercury's. But another close look at this peculiar caduceus makes us think again. For each of the two familiar knotted snakes shows a striking addition, a Latin phrase issuing from its mouth: (*a*) NOSCE TE IPSVM (*ΓΝΩ^ΘΙ ΣΕΑΥΤΟ′Ν*), *Know thyself* and (*b*) NE QVID NIMIS (*ΜΗ^ΔΕ′Ν ″ΑΓΑΝ*), *Nothing in excess*. These well-known 'words' have nothing to do with Mercury. They are the precepts identified with great *Apollo*, inscribed in gold upon his splendid fore-temple at Delphi. (Pausanias, *Description of Greece*, 10.24.1.) And what is more, just below the serpents the rod rises out of a round or egg-shaped object standing on three legs. This implement is nothing but the far-famed *cortina* of *Apollo*, 'the egg-shaped basin on the Delphian tripod whence the oracles were echoed'.†

---

* B. A. Fuchs, *Die Ikonographie der 7 Planeten*, 1909, 58. For similar Mercurys and Apollos in modern dress, see P. Schubring, *Cassoni*, 1915, Pl. XXXI, XCI, CXXXIII; and ed. 1923, Pl. LIV and LV.

† Lewis Evans, ed. *Satires of Juvenal, Persius, Sulpicia, and Lucilius*, 1872, 310n. And compare Pliny, tr. Holland 1601, lib. 34. c. 3, vol. 2, 489: 'in

Lastly, as for the rod itself, we remember that it was King *Apollo*'s before he gave it to Mercury—just as his lyre was Mercury's own invention and gift-in-exchange:

> the harp of mercurie,
> I mene the harpe most melodyous,
> Geven to this Kyng [Phoebus] by mercurius.
> > Lydgate, Prologue to *The Destruction of Thebes*

Of its snakes, Hyginus (*Poeticon Astr.* 2.7) relates that after Mercury got the rod he pacified with it two fighting serpents, male and female. Whereupon twining about it, says Macrobius, their tails lovingly wreathed in a Hercules or true-love knot, they became henceforth identified also with its magical peacemaking power. In an engraving of 1588, however, Apollo gives Mercury the rod *already fitted with the serpents*. (Principio Fabricii, *Delle Allusioni . . .,* 1588, 277.)

The pointed display of these intimate attributes of Apollo—his rod of power, his Delphic precepts, and his Delphic cortina and tripod—rules out any interpretation but the obvious one. In Charlewood's device, the hand from the clouds is *the royal hand of young Phoebus Apollo*, the beautiful and true-divining god, Prince of Planets, 'Day's King, God of undaunted verse'.

At once we ask, Is this 'Hand of Apollo' our leading clue or our entering wedge into identification of the two men portrayed in our CLASPING A HAND? Before proceeding to test the possibility, we should examine both the background of this device of Charlewood's and its familiarity to Elizabethan eyes. In 1589 and 1590 we see it on the title-pages of three of Tom Nashe's highly popular anti-Marprelate pamphlets—*A Countercuffe giuen to Martin Iunior: by . . . Pasquill of England, The Returne of the renowned Caualiero Pasquill of England,* and *The First parte of Pasquils Apologie.* Though neither author's nor printer's name appears, no one can doubt that all three were

---

old time they were wont to make many large basons, supported with a frame of three feet, knowne by the name of Delphicke basons, for that they were commonly dedicated unto *Apollo* the patrone or god of Delphos, for to receive the gifts and oblations offered unto him'.

Johan Froben

William Baldwin

John Charlewood

written by Nashe and printed by Charlewood. In reproducing their title-pages (*Nashe*, 1.56) McKerrow adds

> Of the device itself I need only say that it was originally Baldwin's, the D in the centre being a remnant of his name the rest of which was cut away, as was also the motto round the frame. See, for facsimile of the device in its original state, Dibdin's *Typographical Antiquities*, III. 503.

Turning to Dibdin, we find that the motto round the frame of William Baldwin's device reads BE WISE AS SERPENTES, AND INNOCENT AS DOVES. MATTHEW. X.

Baldwin doubtless took the suggestion for this New Testament *locus* from the famous device of Johan Froben, the eminent printer of Basel, 1515, who printed the *Utopia* and the *Epigrams* of Sir Thomas More. For Froben's device showed a caduceus—for Wisdom and Peace—held by two opposed left hands-out-of-clouds, one higher than the other, with the heads of what Arnobius called its 'affable serpents' *now enclosing a dove perched on the rod's tip*, in obvious reference to *Matthew* 10:16. Froben's foisting in this supernumerary from the Gospel between the long-pacified, true-loving, and powerfully pacific pagan serpents is a typically Renaissance contrivance or gimmick to secure the best of both worlds, pagan and Christian.

Borrowing this, Baldwin elaborated the Christian side. Better to accord with Gospel, he made it *two* doves; he topped the pagan rod of peace and wisdom with an open Bible, brooded over by the Holy Spirit—a dove with wings outstretched. And as though all this were not ample to assert the superiority of *Christian truth*, he surrounded it with the quite needless quotation, sensibly removed by Charlewood.

But on the other side Baldwin particularized: appropriating the precious *pagan truth* to *Apollo*. This he accomplished by introducing his personal motto LOVE AND LYVE, which brings to mind not the harmlessness of Gospel doves, but the pagan source of love and life, Phoebus Apollo;* by making the wise serpents twisted round Apollo's rod utter Apollo's Delphic

---

* 'O shine still then, our Royall Phœbus! ... the beames of your

precepts; by adding Apollo's Delphic *cortina* and *tripod* (the central D of his name left printed on it for another Delphic note); and by significantly reducing the indefinite plural hands-from-clouds to an *individual hand* from the welkin: *not* the Almighty's, but a *left hand*, dressed in a ruff-cuff—the Hand of King Apollo.

The sharp stimulus of Charlewood's device sends us back to more of the emblem-books, now on a purposeful Apollo-hunt. And not in vain; for in the *Emblemata* of Denis Lebey de Batilly (Frankfort, 1596)*—his Latin verses added to Jean Jacques Boissard's figures-and-verses of 1584—we find pictured by Boissard the very hyperbolical gesture shown in CLASPING A HAND, in Emblem no. LI, *Poetarum Gloria.* Here appears young King Phoebus Apollo, the chariot-driving Sun-god—no longer *left unseene, save to the eye of mind*—, reaching down from the clouds *his left hand, grasped by the human poet's,* to take him up careering in glory on high through heaven's truth everlasting: 'to walk in the *Zodiac* with *Apollo* himself'.

This Apollo-and-poet topos at once points us to Professor Robert J. Clements's illuminating study, 'The Cult of the Poet in Renaissance Emblem Literature' (*P.M.L.A.* LIX, Sept. 1944, repr. in his *Picta Poesis*, 1960). Here the expert

---

Royall hart (the onlie lyfe of love) were ever a warming us.' To King James, Nichols, *Prog. James I*, 3.383.

'Truth . . . is the life and light of love, The Sunne that euer shineth.' *Ben Jonson*, ed. Simpson, 8.393.

'Love is the life of Friendship.' James Howell, Preface to his *Letters*.

'Why, they seem to take the sun out of the universe, when they deprive life of friendship.' Cicero, *De Amicitia* 13.47, tr. W. A. Falconer.

'*That makes thee like* Apollo *in thy lookes . . . For . . . there's . . . the ensigne of true friendship plac'd.*' John Taylor, *Works*, 1630, 2.126*b*.

And Baldwin himself, in the Prologue to his *Treatise of Morall Phyloso-phie*, 1547, writes, 'Reason only was the cause why al the phylosophers haue so extolled philosophie which considered that nothing was so requisite and behouefull for mannes lyfe, as to lyue togyther well and louingly'; and he ends by subscribing both his own *Loue, and Lyue* and Apollo's pagan *Ne quid nimis.*

* See Praz 278–279, who also cites from the Corser catalogue a Heidelberg edition of 1587.

scholar studies this emblem, and gives us the gist of the verses accompanying Boissard's figure:

> *The poet's glory courses throughout the world . . . It is Apollo who initiates him into the holy mysteries . . . the true poet may soar with Phoebus without fearing the tragic fall of Icarus.*

Also—which crowns the identification—Plutarch explains why the hand which Apollo extends in honouring the poet is his *left*. In his *Moralia* (tr. Holland 1603, 1253) he gives Apollo's

> very image . . . in his right hand a bow, and in his left the Graces; and euery one of them hath an instrument of Musicke.

And the extremely popular medieval *Libellus De Imaginibus Deorum* declares, 'In his right hand, indeed, he had arrows, bow, and quiver. In his left, however, he held his lyre.'*

By this gesture Apollo Loimios the dread Slayer showed himself also god of Music and of 'that Musicall part of humane knowledge, Poetry', which belonged to him as Apollo Paean, the Healer. As Henry Peacham points out, Music 'is the best Physick for many melancholly diseases'. Thus Apollo is both Destroyer and Healer: his right hand for the Bow, and his left hand for the musical, healing charms of Poetry.

Further, our MAN portrayed is showing the fingers he clasps as pressed *to his palm*. By this he gives another pointer, for *the palm of the hand* is consecrated to *Apollo*: 'And as the heathen haue consecrated . . . their tongue to *Mercurie*, . . . their secretes [*i.e.*, privy parts] to *Venus*, their palmes to *Apollo*.' (Dr. Adam Hill, *The Crie of England*, 1595, 7).

Full ocular corroboration carries conviction. The left HAND in our miniature is the royal HAND OF APOLLO honouring the poet. Now at length we are learning *how to look*. We are beginning to assume something of what the lookers of 1588 assumed. And if we knew more of what they knew about Apollo, perhaps we might augment the evidence by recognizing

* See H. Liebeschütz, ed. *Fulgentius Metaforalis*, 1926, 118. Similarly for the Elizabethans: 'APOLLO . . . in his left hand an Harpe, and in his right hande, a Bowe.' Stephen Bateman, *Golden Booke of the Leaden Goddes*, 1577, A2ᵛ.

a further item or two of the meanings packed into our *impresa*.
What of *number symbolism*? Recent brilliant studies have sur-
prised the scholarly world by revealing how pervasively the
Renaissance employed this art of the ancients.*

Almost any good handbook of symbols will tell us that
'Apollo's number is Seven'. And H. J. Rose, in the *Oxford
Classical Dictionary*, with 'Seven is Apollo's number' cites
Hesiod's *Works and Days*, line 771. But for Apollo Hebdoma-
getes in full and fascinating detail we turn to A. W. Mair's
edition and translation of Callimachus:

> Apollo was born on the 7th Thargelion . . . Phœbe gave
> the oracle at Delphi as a birthday gift to Phœbus . . . The
> Delphians celebrated the seventh day of the month
> Bysios—the birthday of Apollo—when he was supposed
> to revisit his temple, and the seventh of the holy month
> . . . was celebrated by the Delians when Apollo was sup-
> posed to return to Delos from the land of the Hyperbor-
> eans.   W. Schmidt, *Geburtstag im Altertum*, 86

And Mair translates Callimachus on the birth of Apollo:

> . . . *with music the swans, the gods' own minstrels . . . circled
> seven times round Delos, and sang over the bed of child-birth . . .
> Hence that child* [Apollo] *in after days strung the lyre with just
> so many strings—seven strings, since seven times the swans sang
> over the pangs of birth.*
>   Loeb Classical Library, 1921, 62, 49, 105

Apollo's number was not forgotten by the Elizabethans. In
1575, as last and best of the gods offering gifts to the Queen
arriving at Kenilworth, Elizabeth found Apollo with his
identifying *seven*: 'On the seventh Posts, last and next to the
Castle, were . . . the presents of *Phœbus* the God of Music.'
(R. Laneham, qu. Nichols, *Progr. Eliz.*, 1788 1. *sub* 1575. Spelling modernized.) Having tuned to this reiterated note, we
recall for good measure that Phoebus Apollo is God of the
Seven Arts, and—as Sol—is King of the *Seven* Planets as well.

---

* See A. K. Hieatt, *Short Time's Endless Monument*, 1960; M.-S. Røstvig,
The Hidden Sense, 1963; Alastair Fowler, *Spenser and the Numbers of Time*,
1964; *Triumphal Forms*, 1970.

Looking again at our HAND OUT OF CLOUDS, and observing the carefully drawn plump white cumuli (best shown in the *Howard*), we now hardly need to count them. For we know they will be *seven*, to sign young Apollo Hebdomagetes, *deified King Of that unshorn and everlasting spring.*

But is this all? The rule of concentrated meanings in miniatures forbids premature satisfaction. Scipione Ammirato tells us that such paintings 'concealed in themselves many fine secrets'. A fact about Apollo already mentioned may reveal something more. For busied with poetry we sometimes forget that the Hippocratic Oath begins, 'I swear by Apollo the Physician'; that 'Appoloes cunning extendeth it self aswel to Phisick, as musick or Poetrie':

> Great *Apollo,*
> That know'st to heale with thy sweet harmony
> The fierce rude minds of men, as well as bodies
> With thy try'd medicines . . .
>
> The King and Queenes Entertainment at
Richmond, 1636, C3

Aristophanes and Callimachus told of Apollo's original skill in restoring health long before Ovid in his *Metamorphoses* (1.521) gave Apollo the line *Inventum medicina meum est*—'Of Phisicke and of surgerie I found the Artes' (Golding). 'Apollo first founde Physicke, the repayrer of health.'* For Spenser (*F.Q.* 4.12.25), Phoebus was '*Apollo* King of Leaches'. Lyly's paean to Apollo Paean (the Healer) runs,

> *Iô* Pæans let vs sing,
> To Physickes, and to Poesies King.
>
> Midas 5.3.135–136

And Heywood's too:

> Phœbus *unto thee wee sing,*
> *Oh thou great* Idalian *king:*
> *Thou the God of* Phisick *art,*
> *Of* Poetry, *and* Archery . . .
>
> Love's Mistress 3.2

* William Cuningham, *The Cosmographical Glasse,* 1559, B1ᵛ. The Apothecaries' Society of London bore for their arms *Apollo in his glory.* Richard Wallis, *London's Armory,* 1677, 21.

—putting his healing first, before his poetry. *Paean*, then, in Greek. In Latin, *Apollo Medicus, Apollo Salutaris.*

With this fresh in mind, we turn back to his white LEFT HAND FROM SEVEN CLOUDS in our miniature. And this time we look more closely at this hand 'worth an history'. Although we know that the human hand is celebrated as *organum organorum*, 'The instrument of instruments . . . Psyche's great secretary, the dumb's eloquence,'* we are not much more proficient in its powers of communication than Donne's 'Ideot' was before he instructed her—

> Foole, thou didst not understand
> The mystique language of the eye nor hand.
> *Elegie VII*, 3–4

For what do we know of *chironomy*—the old-time actor's and orator's traditional art of speaking gesture, the richly expressive art of signs? Rudiments only.

But again recalling Ellis Parker's advice, we ask, Is there— beyond its *white colour*—something *unnatural* about this HAND clasped by the MAN? And at once we see it. From the other fingers *its index or forefinger is strangely and ostentatiously divaricated or held out.* Without a word, that pointedly isolated index proclaims, 'I am the sign.'

Apollo displaying his 'foremost finger' was no new thing to Elizabethan eyes. John Gower had long ago described a marvellous golden image in Rome,

> *The which was clepëd Apollo. . . .*
> *Forth right he straught his finger out . . .*
> *Confessio Amantis*, 1554, lib. 5, fo. 122*b*

And Chapman shows that it was his *left*—for *healing Music*:

> the God of light . . . pointed out . . . with his harmonious
> finger. *Byron's Tragedy* 1.2.89–92

On looking up *forefinger* in Jean Nicot's sixteenth-century French–Latin dictionary, we find that it is *Digitus salutaris*, the

---

* Tomkis, *Lingua* 4.6; Sidney, *Poems*, ed. Grosart, 2.157; 'The hand. beyng . . . the organ of organes, and an organ before all other organs.' John Banister, *The Historie of Man*, 1579, 108.

healthful finger. And again, in Littleton: 'Salutaris digitus, *The fore-finger.*' Also in G. C. Capaccio's work on *Imprese*, 1592, 147, we read 'Of the Finger': '*Indice, detto . . . Medico*'—'the Index, called . . . the Physician.' Evidence, finally, both ocular and convincing is presented by Professor Seznec's reproduction (Jean Seznec, *The Survival of the Pagan Gods*, 1953, 28, fig. 3) of a tenth-century drawing of APOLLO MEDICVS, holding up his hand (the right, since as a gowned physician he has neither bow nor lyre), its *forefinger separated from the other three*, precisely as in our clasped HAND: where, pointedly indigitated by the held-out index of his HAND FROM SEVEN CLOUDS, we recognize the physician-god, Apollo Medicus, King of Leeches.

In brief, this wonderful left hand from the sky, like the similar one in Charlewood's title-page device taken over from Baldwin, is the hand of the beautiful young King, Phoebus Apollo. It was identified in that device by the repeated Delphic features; and here, not only by Apollo's number in the Seven clouds and the marked display of his Physician-finger, but also by Boissard's complete emblem-scene of the royal charioteer Phoebus Apollo in the clouds, reaching down his left hand to the poet's.

Although some in describing Hilliard's CLASPING A HAND have supposed the hand's slimness to indicate a woman, there is no longer any question. We understand its delicacy as proper to the stripling Apollo, *Phœbus ephebus*, 'of wondrous beauty and of freshest years'; fairer than woman; 'never on the girl cheeks of Apollo hath come so much as the down of manhood'. (Callimachus, *Hymn to Apollo*, 37, tr. A. W. Mair.) And from *Philaster* one recalls the description of the fair maid Euphrasia, disguised as a page: *His form is angel-like . . . this is he that must . . . Sit by your pillow, like young Apollo, with His hand and voice binding your thoughts in sleep. . . . 'Tis a sweet boy.*

To mistake the figure of Apollo for a woman is not only a modern error. 'Anselmus de Boodt, in his explanation of the devices in the third part of Sadeler, [mistakenly] identifies [Apollo] as Diana; perhaps because the sight of him young, without the mark of Man, makes him take him for a Woman.' (Ferro, *op. cit.*, 2.79.)

If in our miniature it is astonishing to see the royal hand of

Apollo reaching down from the heavens in an Elizabethan ruff-cuff, it is hardly less marvellous to see it clasped by the hand of a *human* figure clad in a doublet. At sight of someone thus closely joined to the great Apollo, the viewer of 1588 might well ask, 'But soft, what man or God is this?' For on referring to the precepts laid down for *portraits* in *imprese*, we find that Torquato Tasso, prince of Italian poets, admits only portrayals of *Men either feigned as Gods or Deified; others, not.* (Ferro, 1.62.) And we have noted that Luca Contile, that prime authority, likewise allows human portraits *only* where presented poetically as 'Mars', 'Apollo', 'Venus', 'Mercury', 'Neptune', 'Pallas', 'Jove', 'Saturn'.

Already we have seen portrayed one god, Apollo. If our portrait-Device would merit Tasso's approval and conform to Contile's identical requirement, this 'Apollo' *must be an Elizabethan youth of 1588, feigned as a god.* And *so also must the MAN.* His 'poetical character' likewise is *a god.*

By consulting Elizabeth's England, we have opened a breach in the wall confronting us. Remains the shrewd question, Can we make it wide enough to admit *the head*? We can only hope so. For as Giordano Bruno—that witty Italian of Nola welcomed by cultivated Elizabethan London—pointed out, 'In all affairs the difficulty consists in getting the *head* through; because after *that*, the trunk and the whole body easily follow.' (*Candelaio* 5.16.)

At all events, we have made a clear aperture. A man may see day through a little hole. We have seen King Phoebus Apollo, Day himself. Is he perhaps the glorious centre of the high poetical intent upon which our MAN founded his Device?

4

In a Poetical Character

OUR strong sense of drawing closer to this MAN—the poet whose purpose in his *impresa* (like Queen Elizabeth's in her Siena portrait) is *autobiographical*, 'to acquaint your eyes with my mind'—can be no illusion. For we have now joined him in getting a firm hold on the HAND, which *Stood for the whole to be imaginëd.*

Looking back, we remember that our list of 'features presented' began *First comes the cardinal sign of the* MAN's *poetical intent: the supernatural action, symbolizing a fact known in 1588 upon which the Device is founded.* Although that fact known in 1588 is still to find, we have identified the supernatural action. It is *clasping the royal hand of Apollo.*

Joining hands. What gesture could be more common, more simple? Here, however, that familiar gesture's importance is clearly central. If we have learned any elements of detection, we should be foolish to let it pass unscrutinized.

No one needs reminding that the symbol of *joined hands*— meaning Faith or Truth, Concord or True Love—is 'not merely a pictorial contrivance or invention of the picturer, but an ancient tradition and conceived reality': one of the oldest and commonest in the world, from classical times to the present. Roman finger-rings show it. Frequent throughout the sixteenth century, the *joined hands* in Philip II's emblem mean CONCORDIA; and in Henri III's, they signify LOVE: his motto is AMOR VINCIT OMNIA. (Typotius, *Symbola*, 1601, ed. 1690, 208, 272; Ferro, 2.9.) And for our day, a *New York Times* illustrated article (10 October 1961) on tattooing-parlours in New York gives, as one of four most popular designs, *joined hands* with TRUE LOVE lettered beneath.

In England this familiar symbol was known as the Handfast or the Hand in Hand. And since the gesture was used to plight faith, friendship, or true love, it readily became associated with the four-looped true-love knot:

> Your fingers tie my heart-strings with this touch
> In true-love knots, which nought but death shall loose.
>
> Massinger, *The Fatal Dowry* 2.2

> Then you love us, we you, and we'll clasp hands.
> When peers thus knit, a kingdom ever stands.
>
> Shakespeare, *Pericles* 2.4

> Let's join hands;
> This knot of true-lov'd peace . . .
> Beaumont & Fletcher, *The Faithful Friends* 3.3

This close association vividly meets the eye in a printer's device, McKerrow's no. 372. Here the hands join through one of the four bows of the Bowen or true-love knot.

So much for the Hand in Hand, true-faithful or true-loving. Now for the colour *white*, which unnaturally and significantly sets off both the hands in our miniature. Do we need Henry Peacham's assurance that *white* stands for 'Innocency, or Purity of Conscience, Truth, Integrity'? For John Donne gives us 'white sincerity', 'white integrity', and 'my mindes white truth'; Joseph Hall (*Characters*), 'Hee hath white hands, and a cleane soule'; and Robert Tofte (*Laura*), 'White as thy hands, so white thy faith . . .'

A favourite gift to the Queen was a gold bodkin with the royal *main de justice*: one 'with a white hande ennameled', another 'with a white hande holding a long Jacinte', another with 'a white hande pendaunte garnished . . . with very small opalls', and yet another 'with a white hande & a pendaunte of a Diamonde'. (MS. Royal App. 68, ff. 31ᵛ and 32.)

Should any remaining Thomas demand palpable evidence of other Elizabethan hands *painted white*, it is given by the heraldic painters. Among the arms of members of Gray's Inn with which they adorned the Society's Hall appeared the bearings of the family named *Purefoy*: In a field *Sable*, *three paire of hands joyned hand in hand argent**—that is, *white*; with

* MS. Harl. 1042, f. 63. And see MS. Addl. 18594, f. 111; MS. Harl. 2089, f. 130; R. Holme, *Academy of Armory*, 1688, 399*b*.

the canting motto *Pure foy ma joye*, 'Faith white, my delight'. And for the name *Truelove*, we find two painted coats of arms. One Truelove bore *white hands—On a chief or, two hands conjoined argent*—while the other bore four-leaved *true-loves* of gold: *three quaterfoyls or.**

The *white* of joined hands therefore exhibits the 'true faith' or 'true love' as sound, sincere, and spotless. Their owners are *amici candidi*. But in addition there is a specific reason why *this particular identified* HAND FROM SEVEN CLOUDS of ours is white *par excellence*. For the young Sun-god Phoebus Apollo was venerated as the god of *truth*. 'Apollo, *veritas*.' 'Truth's symbole, the bright sunne.' 'As true . . . As Sunne.' 'All *Apollo* saieth is soothe.' 'The great *Apollo* suddenly will haue The Truth of this appeare.'†

And there is likewise special reason why *the hand which clasps Apollo's must be white*. For Apollo personified 'the ideal of fair and manly youth—a pure and just god, requiring *clean hands* and pure hearts of those that worshipped him'. (C. M. Gayley, *The Classic Myths*, 1911, 27. Italics mine.) His word is, '*Pure am I and may I be the care of them that are pure.*' (Callimachus, *Hymn IV (To Delian Apollo)*, 98, tr. A. W. Mair.)

By such eloquent details of the poetical story they present we begin to understand why each of these white hands *By* Hilliard *drawne, is worth an history*. And beyond what we have only now been enabled to read, how much more have they to recount? That is still to be seen; but 'knowledge on one point flashes illumination on another'. Knowledge that the HAND is Apollo's should help us to recognize the MAN, here represented not as his familiar ordinary self, but *in a 'poetical' character, feigned as a god*. And the essential clue to the identity of that character is *his clasping 'Apollo's' hand*. With these white hands

---

* Holme, *ibid.*, and MS. Harl. 2089, f. 186. The marriage-emblem of Emperor Ferdinand I and Anna of Hungary combined the two symbols: two hands clasped, holding a branch of three four-petalled primroses or 'true-loves', with the motto SIC IN PERPETUUM, '*Thus for ever*'. Typotius, 137–138.

† Liebeschütz, *op. cit.*, 56; T. Middleton, *The Triumphs of Truth*, 1613, 133; Shakespeare, *Troi. & Cres.* 3.2.185; G. Gascoigne, *Works*, ed. Cunliffe 1910, 2.484; *Winter's Tale* 2.3.200.

joined he declares his spotless true-loving friendship with 'pure Apollo'.

* * *

Who is the Friend of Apollo? That immediate question answers itself. Who could he be but *Hermes–Mercury*, his dear devoted half-brother, called *the companion of Phoebus*? (*Phoebique comes Cyllenius*. Claudian, *On Stilicho's Consulship*, lib. 2, 22.440.)

At Olympia Pausanias reports an altar to Apollo and Hermes in common; and a part of Apollo's Delphinion at Athens was called 'Hermes'. (*Description of Greece* 5.14.7; Plutarch, *Theseus* 18.) 'On Mount Helicon were statues of Apollo and Hermes striving for the lyre. . . . In Megalopolis there was a common sanctuary to the Muses, Apollo, and Hermes.' (W. F. Otto, *The Homeric Gods*, tr. M. Hadas (1954), 124.) Every Athenian house was guarded by the two symbols of Apollo and Hermes (B. B. Rogers, tr. & ed. Aristophanes, *The Wasps*, 1915, 125); and as Callimachus sings to Artemis, 'There in the entrance [to the house of their father Zeus] Hermes and Apollo meet thee.' (*III Hymn to Artemis* 142, tr. A. W. Mair.)

In the calendar following the Manilian system they are side by side, two handsome youthful gods at the height of the young year's beauty: 'Apollo protects the Twins and May, Mercury the Crab and his June-month.' (Aby Warburg, *Gesammelte Schriften*, 1932, 2.470.) And the Elizabethans saw them inseparable: 'we have *Apollo* and *Mercurie* for Goddes of wisdome.' (John Grange, Ep. Ded. to *The Golden Aphroditis*, 1577.) 'What godds but those of arts, and eloquence? *Phœbus* and *Hermes*?' (*Ben Jonson*, ed. Simpson, 8.395.)

How their eternal true-loving friendship was founded is told in the *Homeric Hymn to Hermes*. Apollo longed to add to his own piping the music of Hermes' sweet song enhanced by the harmony of his magical invention, the stringed lyre. As a peace-offering, Hermes gave him both instruction and the instrument: 'taking this gift from me, and do you, my friend, bestow glory (*kudos*) on me' (tr. H. G. Evelyn-White, Loeb 1936, 399)—which the Elizabethan Chapman renders, '*Take thou my Lute (My Loue) and giue thou me, The glorie.*' Apollo in

return bestowed on Hermes not only the art of wisdom or
divination but also his pastoral pipe and his rod of power.

'Then wise Zeus was glad, and made them both friends.
And Hermes loved the son of Leto continually, even as he does
now'—or, as Chapman has it,

> Whom *Ioue* much ioi'd to see; and endlesse stay [*duration*
> Gaue to their knot of friendship. From which date
> *Hermes* gaue *Phœbus* an eternall state
> In his affection . . .

and ending,

> Thus King *Apollo* honor'd *Maia's* Sonne
> With all the rights of friendship: all whose loue
> Had Imposition from the Will of *Ioue*.

Thus we see these two—the only Athenian gods intimate
and equal in friendly love. In other respects, of course, they
are far from equal. For King Apollo is (after Zeus) 'the mightiest
of the gods', and, like a king, withdrawn: 'he always abode
for part of the year in a remote and secret place'. (Otto, *op. cit.*,
63.) A god wise and true, and also pure and holy: as befits a
Phoebus above the clouds in the clear mysterious heavens.

Our familiar Hermes–Mercury, by contrast, 'the friendliest
of the gods to men', with his caduceus bringing peace, concord, and gain, is a far humbler figure, unhampered by dignity.
He is not only gentle, but also witty, ingenious, and most
approachable. As much at home when resourcefully helping
men like you and me as he is while running errands, devising
entertainment, or doing housework for the divine court on
Olympus. Quite natural for Mercury to remark, 'So perhaps
you would take me for a man; but you are deceived, for I am
a god.'

Now is this in fact what the MAN clasping King Apollo's
honour-giving hand is telling us? 'Note me well in all my
particulars. You will find that the poetical person I present is
Mercury, and no other'? Is our MAN, like another in an *impresa*
described by Ferro (2.5), *Un' Huomo significante Mercurio*?
Certainly a hypothesis to be tested; and tested by every means
our miniature affords.

To begin with the HAND, which already has told us so much. Since Apollo was identified with the element AIR, his hand must come from the heavens above; and the humbler Mercury, identified with EARTH, would clasp it from below.* What is more, the MAN clasps Apollo's *left* hand with his own *right*. This shows without question that he is stationed *at Apollo's left*, in deference giving his dear friend King Apollo the 'upper hand' or 'better hand' of greater dignity. We turn again to the *Homeric Hymn to Hermes*, and precisely there is where we find Hermes–Mercury: 'Then the son of Maia ... took courage and stood at the left hand of Apollo'—which Chapman renders 'he gave him still the upper hand'.

Good so far. Now if we move from hands to *fingers*—and once more to that pointedly separated Physician's index which declares the hand of Apollo *Paean* the Healer, what do we find? We see that held-out forefinger clasped *by the* MAN's *similarly separated little finger*. The little finger, called by Spaniards *merguerite*—Mercury's.† '... his *mercurial* finger.' 'Which finger's that?' 'His little finger.' (Jonson, *The Alchemist* 1.3.49–51.) In palmistry, 'the swelling or monticule at the base of the little finger is called *the mountain of Mercury*'. And in Jonson's *Gypsies Metamorphos'd* acted before King James, the chief Gypsy comes out to read the royal palm:

> Here's a Gentlemans hand ...
> Your *Mercuries* hill too a witt doth betoken,
> Some booke crafte you have, and are prettie well spoken.

To clinch the identification, the little finger is also the finger of *lovers*; and to Renaissance eyes Mercury is *divinus amator*, the adoring *divine lover of Apollo*. (E. Wind, *Pagan Mysteries in the Renaissance*, 1967, fig. 24.)

'The mystique language of the ... hand.' In what the

---

* Apollo is shown with an Octahedron, formed of 8 equilateral triangles, signifying the element AIR, in pageantry of 1603/4 (Nichols, *Prog. James I*, 1.348); Mercury's is the Cube, signifying EARTH: see G. Pierio Valeriano, *Hieroglyphica*, App. by C. A. Curione, lib. 2. c. 22, from Plato, *Timaeus* 53c. Cf. '*Terra* is but ... a *punctum* squared'—that is, 'a point cubed'—Greene, *Friar Bacon and Friar Bungay* ix.33.

† John Minsheu's enlargement of Percivale's *Dict.*, 1623, 168c.

3 Hilliard: *Unknown Man Clasping a Hand issuing from a Cloud*
(*Howard*)

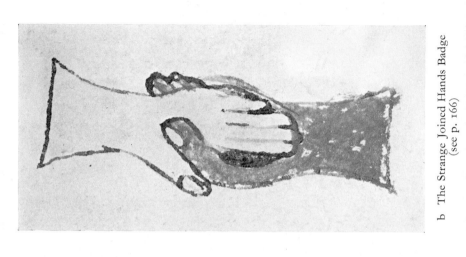

b The Strange Joined Hands Badge
(see p. 166)

4a Hermes as *divinus amator* (Achille Bocchi)
Mercury kisses his hand in loving adoration of
Phoebus Apollo

speaking gestures of these joined white hands and fingers communicate, our hypothesis passes the test. Their evidence holds that here the hand of 'Apollo' is clasped by the hand of 'Mercury'.

Now for the face and the head which might present 'Mercury'. What do we know of Mercury's looks? The first certainty is that he is a young man, but not so youthful as the perpetually 'beardless and young-year'd' Apollo. For Apuleius —like Lucian—gives Mercury's cheeks a comely growth of down ('decenter utrinque lanugo malis deserpat' *Apol.* 63), and Martianus Capella sketches a slight beard: 'on his chin certaine young haires of a yellowish colour'. (R. Linche, tr. of V. Cartari's *Imagini* as *The Fountaine of Ancient Fiction*, 1599, Q4ᵛ.) 'Mercury to be seen with rod, swift wings, mantle, and beard.'* Our young MAN's pickedevant, trimmed 'short and sharp, amiable like an Inamorato', is of the same fair colour as Mercury's.

As for Mercury's hair, both Virgil and Apuleius describe it as *flavus*—golden or bright auburn; and Apuleius adds that the golden locks are *curls*. (*Aen.* 4.558; *Metam.* 10.30; and Linche, *loc. cit.*) This distinguishing colour the Renaissance exactly preserved. 'Mercury ... the hair of gold ... as he is found depicted by the Painters, and described in many books by the Poets, and in particular ... Apuleius.' (Cesare Ripa, *Iconologia*, ed. C. Orlandi, 1764–67, 1.296.) 'Mercury ... they describe with ... curled yellow haire.' (Peacham, *Compleat Gentleman*, 1622, ed. 1661, 161.)

They identified the gods with the planets; and since of the major planets Mercury is both smallest and *nearest to the golden Sun*, they ingeniously traced his golden hair to his keeping such close company with Phoebus–Sol: 'The rayes of the sonne make the heer of a man abourne or blounde.' (Caxton, *Myrr.* II.xvii.103, qu. *OED s.v.* Blond.) 'Mercury. .. is described by the Poet as red or yellow haired to signify his vicinity to the Sun.' (Alexander Ross, *Mystagogus Poeticus*, 1647, 266.) Again our young MAN with blond curls answers the description of Mercury, companion of Phoebus.

* G. Harvey, *Gratul. Valdin.*, 1578, lib. 2. And to the *comas* ('his head') of Ovid's *Met.* 2.733 Golding adds 'his beard'.

In looks, Mercury may not match Apollo's surpassing beauty, but he is decidedly comely. Together, they are 'Two handsome youthfull Gods, and light [*i.e.*, gracefully agile, quick], and strong'. (William Basse, *Works*, ed. R. W. Bond, 1893, 273.) Marco Girolamo Vida sees them *Insignes ambo facie, & florentibus annis**—which an Elizabethan renders 'both young in yeres, and beautifull in face'. Lydgate saw Mercury 'wonderful of cheer'; Spenser speaks of his 'faire face, and that Ambrosiall hew'; Robert Greene's Cloris 'thought none so faire as Mercurie', and Giordano Bruno brings him before us as *il bel numo Mercurio*, a handsome god. Any impartial judge would, I submit, without hesitation pronounce our young MAN's fine countenance 'handsome'.

So much for the testimony of gesture and physical features. Still to explore remains the ample field of *costume*: the articles of dress and ornament which the MAN displays. In any such *impresa*, every aspect of costume was employed to communicate ideas or concepts, which the Elizabethans called *conceits*. 'Arras ... wrought With liveliest colours of conceipt-full thought.' Masquers' costumes—the 'court hieroglyphics'— as Ben Jonson's descriptions amply show, were always 'rich conceited'. And similarly in painting. The Italian critic Malvasia approved paintings of gods or personified virtues if the subjects were *eruditamente vestiti*, costumed learnedly.

Our MAN has chosen the details of his dress and his ornaments for two specific purposes: first, to declare the identity of the poetical character he presents; and second, to manifest his poetical intent. We shall come to the second in its turn, but first we must carry on with the possible proofs of identity. Does this apparel proclaim *Mercury*? And if so, how?

We begin with the hat. Why should the sitter for this *impresa*, a young man adorned with such handsome golden curls, hide most of them under a hat, just like Mercury in Apuleius?† Obviously because his poetical character in the Device requires it. The *hat* is Mercury's distinguishing attribute: 'your hatted *Mercury*'. (C. Gesner, *The Treasure of Euonymus*,

---

* *Scacchiæ ludus* 178. Διὸς περικαλλέα τέκνα. Hom. *Hymn* 5.397, 504.
† 'crispatus capillus sub imo pilei umbraculo appareat'. *Apol.* 63.

tr. 1559, Preface.) No other god wears a hat. But Mercury always has his hat on, even when he has almost nothing else.

To be proper for Hermes in ancient times, it should be a low, broad-brimmed *petasus* or travelling-hat, furnished (for him) with small wings. Yet even the Greeks are far from consistent in this shape. A red-figured vase-painting in the Berlin Museum shows Hermes wearing a narrow-brimmed winged hat with an eye-shading peak, the rather high crown conical, resembling a beehive or a pointed sugarloaf.* And on a *lekythos* or oil-jar in the Jena Museum he wears a brimless 'beehive' or 'sugarloaf' even taller. (See F. J. M. de Waele, *The Magic Staff*, 1927, Fig. 3.)

In the Renaissance we find the modern-dress Mercurys with similarly narrow-brimmed conical headgear, sometimes with a peak or visor, sometimes without wings.† To this, the nearest thing in sumptuous dress of 1588 was the stylish beaver called 'copatain' or 'copintank' which our MAN has selected: a sugarloaf.

Now here we recall Samuel Daniel's conclusion about portraits in *imprese*: 'but yet when the human form shall be in a strange & unaccustomed manner, it beareth a great grace'; and remember also that following this rule in dressing the part, the MAN would identify his chosen poetical character by *strange or unusual features of his articles of costume*. Accordingly we ask, Is there something strange or unaccustomed about the MAN's hat? Let Percy Macquoid remind us of the Elizabethan's hat:

> The hat was a great asset in a well-dressed man's attire: he fought in it, and with it, using it as a parry; he sat at church [and in the House of Commons] and at meals with it on, and only removed it with most profuse ceremony on meeting a lady, instantly replacing it: he remained uncovered only at court and *in the presence of royalty*.
>
> *Shakespeare's England*, 1916, 2.109. Italics mine

* *Greek Mythology*, F. Guirand, *Mythologie Générale Larousse*, tr. D. Ames, 1963, 52.

† Cf. Guy de Tervarent, *Attributs et Symboles dans l'Art Profane, 1450–1600*, 1, 1958, col. 70; 2, 1959, Pl. XXXI, fig. 54. Idem, *Les Enigmes de l'Art*, 3, 1947, Pl. II, fig. 1. And Schubring, *Cassoni, loc. cit.*

Here is Custom. In the presence of royalty, Elizabethans invariably went bare-headed. 'That's the Prince; the rest are bare.' And here in our portrait-Device is the *strange & unaccustomed manner*, striking any Elizabethan on sight. For this MAN, holding the hand of King Apollo, is in the presence of royalty. Yet *he strangely does not uncover*. Therefore he *cannot* be seen as his familiar everyday self, nor even as the hatless poet clasping Apollo's hand in Boissard's emblem. He is presenting *a peculiar person who wears his hat in the presence of King Apollo*. What conceivable person could this be but *Mercury*, inseparable companion of Phoebus?

> . . . a thick beuer, which he [Mercury] vs'd to weare . . .
> That did protect him from the piercing light
> Which did proceed from *Phœbus* glittring sight.*

So much for what *wearing the hat* implies. Can we gather anything more from this 'copatain' itself? At least four features of this hat are presented: *colour, feather, jewelled brooch*, and *ornamented hatband*. Leaving *colour* for attention at the close, let us begin with the *feather*.

A small feather or tuft in a stylish, expensive Elizabethan beaver presents nothing unusual:† here an aigrette or egret—of the Lesser White Heron, strangely called 'Osprey' by the milliners (*OED*). But our miniature is a Device; and in *imprese* a feather carried meaning, as Camden tells us:

> The victorious Black Prince . . . used sometimes one Feather, sometimes three, in token . . . of his speedy execution in all his services, as the Posts in the Roman times were Pterophori, and wore feathers to signifie their flying post-haste.   *Remains, ed. cit.*, 369

And the three plumes of Charles, Prince of Wales, similarly 'signifie . . . *velocitie*'. (H[enry] G[oodere], *Mirrour of Maiestie*, 1618, B3ᵛ.)

---

* Anon. (F. Beaumont?), *Salmacis and Hermaphroditus*, 1602, lines 515, 517, 518, recalling Statius: '[Hermes] obnubitque comas et temperat astra galero.' *Thebaid* 1.304–305.

† C. Willett and Phillis, Cunnington, *Handbook of English Costume in the Sixteenth Century*, 1954, 135–140.

For Shakespeare, the feather is not only the sign of speed, as

> In feather'd briefness sails are fill'd . . .
>
> *Pericles* 5.2.15

It also conjures up Mercury, 'swiftest of the planets seven', who is *Thought* or *Reason*:

> Be Mercurie, set feathers to thy heeles,
> And flye (like thought) *King John* 4.2.174

> . . . fleet-wing'd duetie with thoghts feathers flies
>
> *Lucrece* 1216

> If he do set
> The very wings of reason to his heeles:
> And flye like chidden Mercurie from Ioue
>
> *Troi. & Cres.* 2.2.43–45

> . . . and all things thought vpon,
> That may with reasonable swiftnesse adde
> More Feathers to our Wings *Henry V* 1.2.305–307

(For 'reasonable swiftness' meaning *swiftness of reason or thought*, compare *Tempest* 5.1.81: 'reasonable shore', meaning *shore of reason or thought*.) Similarly Robert Greene, in his lines of 1588 —*Verses under a carving of Mercury throwing feathers into the wind*, figuring the swiftness of Wit (that is, Thought or Reason).

In the MAN's hat-feather all eyes can read the speed of Mercury, swift as reason or thought in his 'flying hat'. And since 'Words (sayth *Mænander*) hath wings',* many will catch the allusion to the wingëd words of Mercury's all-persuading eloquence—to which not only poetry but also painting aspired: 'Poets and Painters ought to have their conceites fethered with *Mercuries* plumes.' (Greene, *Ciceronis Amor, Tullies Love*, 1589.) Here in his poetical character 'like feather'd Mercury' the MAN passes us Mercury's familiar word in Plautus, 'I will wear a piece of a feather in my hat.' ('Ego has habebo usque in petaso pinnulas.' Prol. to *Amphitruo*.)

* Greene, *Penelopes Web*, 1587. And Linche (*op. cit.*, Q4): 'unto those feathers . . . so placed upon Mercurie . . . is compared . . . the nature of . . . words; in that they are no sooner pronounced . . . but they doe . . . flie away . . . Homer oftentimes called them winged or feathered words.'

Elizabethan eyes would particularly scan the next feature, the jewelled brooch, for 'significance'. For as *A Lover's Complaint* (printed with Shakespeare's *Sonnets*) implies, they read *deep-brain'd sonnets that did amplify Each stone's dear nature, worth, and quality. . . each several stone With wit well blazon'd.* The hat-jewel was customarily chosen to show the wearer's intent: '*Impresa* . . . Also a iewell worne in ones hat, with some deuise in it,' says Florio. Such devices have been recently studied.*

As to the precise form or shape of the jewel at the base of our MAN's feather, could anyone speak confidently? But about *the stone* of which it is made, there can be no question. Since its colour is unmistakably purple-violet or violet, the stone is clearly an *amethyst*.†

And the Amethyst announces 'Mercury'. According to Sir John Ferne in 1586 (*The Blazon of Gentrie*; cf. R. Borghini, *Il Riposo*, 1584, 2.240), the colour Purple 'signifieth in Plannets, Mercury; in Pretious stones, Amethist; in Flowers, the Violet'. Sir Henry Spelman gives the same: 'Purpureus—Pourpre—Mercury—Amethistus.' (*Aspilogia*, ed. with the work of Nich. Upton, by E. Bysshe, 1654, 75). As G.-B. della Porta further reports in his *Magia Naturalis* (Antwerp 1560, c. XXIIII, 133ᵛ–134),

> Carved in an Amethyst is frequently found a young man, with caduceus, hat, and on his feet winged shoes, sometimes holding a cock in his left hand, whom all know at sight to be Mercury; nor does he differ in power from the stone, by which its wearers are promised wisdom and wit; and more besides, since his nature is versatile.

Such a Græco-Roman amethyst ringstone, carved in the likeness of Hermes, is among the gems of the New York Metropolitan Museum of Art. (Gisela M. A. Richter, *Catalogue of Engraved Gems*, 1920, No. 155, reproduced in Pl. 41.)

First among the amethyst's Mercury-like virtues stands the

---

* C. R. Beard, 'Cap-brooches in the Renaissance', *The Connoisseur* 104, December 1939. See also Praz, 52–53.

† Cf. *OED*: 1398 Trevisa, *Barth. De P.R.* XVI. xi (1495), 557, Amatistus is purpre red in colour medelyd with colour of uyolette.

one given in the (pseudo-Aristotle) *Lapidary* which gives it its name: αμεθυστ-ος, 'not drunken' (*OED*)—and familiar in Shakespeare's time. 'The amethist staieth drunkennesse.' (Lodge, *A Margarite of America*, 1596, 79.) *The purple colored Amatist, 'Gainst strength of wine prevailing.* (Drayton, *The Muses Elizium*, The Ninth Nimphall 127–128.)

Mercury is Reason, Prudence, Temperance, as well as Wit. Friend of Apollo, he takes wine for 'the true Phœbeian Liquor, Clears the Brains, makes Wit the Quicker'. ('Over the Door at the Entrance into the Apollo', qu. *Ben Jonson*, ed. Simpson, 8.657.) He drinks to be merry, witty, and wise; not to make himself a blind or babbling fool. Mercury, in short, since too much 'drink makes virtue useless in a man', drinks *in reason*. There was a temple dedicated to Mercurius Sobrius; and Plutarch tells of the virtue of 'the stones called Amethysts, which some take before and hang about their necks, to keepe them from drunkennesse as they sit at bankets, drinking wine merily'. (*Morals*, tr. Holland, 1603, 18.) Since Mercury Caducifer is also the bringer of peace, concord, and friendship, he loathes what Jonson calls 'the wild Anarchie of Drink, subject to quarrell only', in which the mindless debauchee lives, his wits lost, his reason drowned.

Again like Mercury—the alert, helpful, witty, keen-eyed, nimble, and diligent teacher of letters and arts—, the amethyst 'aids literary work . . . makes a man vigilant, and lends its wearer a good understanding' (Porta, c. XXII); 'an *Amatist*, whose force was to . . . sharpen his vnderstanding at his booke'. (Melbancke, *op. cit.*, G5.) And Cleandro Arnobio, after rehearsing all these virtues of the amethyst, adds Camillo Leonardo's report that the amethyst makes its wearer 'nimble or dextrous, and full of care and speed in his actions'. (*Tesoro delle Gioie*, 1602, ed. 1676, 92–93.) And the amethyst similarly 'is said to help hunters, and it makes them lucky in hunting'. (Nich. Upton, *De Militari Officio*, ed. E. Bysshe, 1654, 112.)

Lastly, and of special importance to the MAN as 'Mercury' clasping *a royal hand*, the amethyst is also said to 'cause men to be gracious with princes . . . by the means thereof they shall find easie accesse to their presence, and favour in their eyes'. (Qu. Pliny, lib. 37. c. 9. Tr. Holland, 1601, 2.621.)

For modern illustration, lovers of Sherlock Holmes will recall that in *A Case of Identity* the keen sleuth 'held out his snuffbox of old gold, with a great amethyst in the centre of the lid. . . . "It is a little souvenir from the King of Bohemia in return for my assistance in the case of the Irene Adler papers."' His creator Conan Doyle (who makes no parade of his learning) was evidently well read in gem-lore. What conceivable stone will suit his Sherlock Holmes but the King's amethyst? For it makes a man vigilant, dextrous, and sharp-witted. It helps the hunter detect and run down his quarry. And it causes men to find favour with princes.

With the language of symbol, and in no uncertain voice, the hat, the feather, and the jewel all say 'Mercury'. This brings us to the *hatband*. Readers of Elizabethan works will agree both with T. M. Parrott that the hatband 'was a special mark of the young gallant in Elizabethan days' and with Ronald McKerrow that it 'seems to have been a somewhat important article of attire'. So important, indeed, that to wear your hat *without a band* made you conspicuous. Its absence was the recognized sign of melancholy—whether a lover's melancholy, the melancholy of a malcontent, a fool's melancholy, or the dangerous bad-melancholy of the Damned Crew.

For mourning, you properly swathed your hat in sad 'Cypresse blacke as ere was Crow':*Enter the Lady* Widow-Plus [and others], *with her sonnne and heyre Maister* Edmond, *all in moorning apparell*, Edmond *in a Cypresse Hatte*. (Middleton, *The Puritaine* 1.1.) Awareness of this custom would have spared us a critic's wandering notion, that our MAN—who wears a gallant's hatband strikingly ornamented—might be a mourning widower, clasping the heavenly hand of his dear departed.

Elaborate hatbands worn on costly beavers were both ensigns of gallant style and fields for the exercise of ingenuity. Dekker counsels his Gull 'to put off to none, unless his hatband be of a newer fashion than yours, and three degrees quainter'.

In dealing with any Device the only safe rule is, *Leave no place unsought, no corner unrifled*. And since the MAN's hatband offers a *locus* as much inviting attention as his feather or his jewel—'your [hat]band is conceited too!' (Jonson, *Cynthia's*

Revels 1.4.156)—we realize that it also must carry a meaning both consonant and personally apposite.

True, to the casual glance it presents nothing extraordinary:

> HAT-BAND A length of gold, silver, coloured silk or ribbon bound about the base of the crown of the hat as ornament. In the late 16th c. very elaborate, often goldsmith's work and enamelled, set with gems and pearls, or formed of a string threaded with buttons of precious metal.
>
> C. W. & Phillis Cunnington & Charles Beard,
> *A Dictionary of English Costume*, 1960, 103b

The band in our miniature is of this style, but clearly not so excessively precious: a long ribbon, tape, or string, wound round and round, *thickly set or stuck full with glistening white black-centred eyelets* very like the spangles known as *Oes*: 'metal eyelets tacked or clinched to the material in designs . . . or powdered over the whole surface'. (M. C. Linthicum, *Review of Engl. Stud.*, 7.198–200.) And two passages quoted by the OED tell us that such *Oes* were typically worn in masques and theatrical shows: 'Oes, or Spangs, as they are of no great Cost, so they are of most Glory' (Francis Bacon on Masques), and 'Divinity will cast a far more radiant lustre . . . than the Stage presents us with, though oe'd and spangled in their gawdiest tyre' (Feltham, *Resolves*). Peacham's *Compleat Gentleman* offers a third: 'Thalia . . . in a Robe of Carnation . . . and Gold spangles: . . . ornaments belonging to the Stage.'

Since our MAN is personating or presenting a poetical character, he may be expected to choose ornaments associated both with the stage and with *poetarum gloria*. But carrying here *particular significance for his 'person'*. Now with these shining black-pupilled *eyelets*, we ask, what can he be exhibiting but *eyes*? Shakespeare's Lysander calls heaven's glorious stars 'oes and eyes of light'. And here the MAN has some hundred eyes, bound all round his head.

No one needs to have read in Ovid's tale (*Met.* 1.625) of Mercury, Io, and Argus the line *Centum luminibus cinctum caput Argus habebat*—'Argus had a head engirdled with a hundred eyes'—to catch our MAN's pointed allusion to the far-famed

Circumspectator. Elizabethan theatregoers saw Argus on the stage. Among the properties of the Admiral's Men was an 'Argosse head'. Lady Diana Primrose praises Queen Elizabeth's provident rule—*With Argus' eyes foreseeing every houre All dangers imminent*. And in imitation of a sonnet by Ronsard, Sir Arthur Gorges entreats Nicholas Hilliard as a supernatural portraitist to mount the heavens, *With Argus' eyes there view the shapes divine*, and therefrom paint *one perfect face*: his mistress's. In Shakespeare's *Troilus and Cressida* Ajax is seen as 'a purblind Argus, all eyes and no sight'. Another playwright mentions the peacock, 'Queen Juno's bird, Whose train is spang'd with Argus' hundred eyes' (Robert Wilson, *Three Lords and Three Ladies of London*, Hazl. Dods. 6.467)—which recalls Milton's cherubim, *Spangled with eyes more numerous than those Of Argus*. But why quote the poets? Those eyes were proverbial. '*Pain d'Argus*, Spungy or light bread . . . full of eyes' (Cotgrave); 'If cheeses in dairie haue Argusses eies' (Tusser).

The MAN wears Argus's eyes obviously not to intimate either vain peacock, spongy bread, or ill-pressed cheese, but as *a property or trophy of Mercurius Argeiphontes* the Argus-slayer, *more vigilant than the all-eyed Argus*. As Mercury remarks in Bernard's version of the *Amphitruo*, 'for there is the credit: to put a man down at his own weapon'. In a *poetic* Device the Argus-eyes were pointedly apt: since a poet is 'a son of Mercury', Thomas Churchyard sees him exploiting the spoils of victory: 'A poet is no common man: He looks with Argoes eies.' (*Churchyards Charitie*, 1595, G2ᵛ.)

Among the common Renaissance playing-cards (*tarocchi, tarots*) the Mercury-card shows the god with the head of Argus, full of eyes, between his feet. In the Schifanoia fresco already mentioned, all-eyed Argus is pictured as Mercury's attribute. Stephen Bateman's *Golden Booke of the Leaden Goddes*, 1577, presents 'Mercurie . . . close by his side . . . headlesse Argus'. In the masque of 1527 at Greenwich Palace, when there 'entred a person clothed in cloth of golde, and ouer that a mantell of blew silke *full of eyes*', no one had to wait for his oration celebrating the peace between the listening King of France and Henry VIII before recognizing this eloquent herald of peace as *Mercury* the vigilant Argus-slayer.

As one would expect, the all-eyed Argus was frequent in *imprese* or Devices. Giovanni Ferro (2.10) describes four such. Samuel Daniel had borrowed one of these to illustrate his translation of Giovio. William Drummond saw another embroidered on the Bed of State of Mary Stuart—'The *Impressa* . . . of *Mercurius* charming *Argus* with his hundred eyes.' (*Ben Jonson*, ed. Herford and Simpson, 1.209.)

The symbols we recognize presented here in our portrait-Device were familiar ones. Their familiarity appears in the detailed description of 'Devices . . . by way of masking' planned to be shown at Nottingham Castle in May 1562 as peace-propaganda for the meeting of Elizabeth Tudor and Mary Stuart. Here are the lovingly *joined hands*: 'Pallas . . . in her hand a standard, in which is to be painted 2 ladies' hands, knit one fast with the other, and over the hands written in letters of gold, FIDES.' Here is 'the jailor Argus, otherwise Circumspection'; and here, sent down with a properly pacific message from 'Jupiter the god of heaven', is wise Mercury, called 'Discretion'. (British Library MS. Lansd. 5, ff. 126–127ᵛ. Spelling modernized.)

To recapitulate, except for its colour still to be studied, we have read the message of the hat. Strikingly and strangely kept on in the presence of the King, great Apollo, its wearer can be none but *Mercury*. And the feather, the amethyst, the Argus-eyes trophy, all alike present *Mercury*.

Next comes the turned-down, flat-lying collar of white lace. Known as a *falling-band, fall*, or *French fall* (Fr. *rabat*), it came in about 1580, doubtless one of the French styles adopted during Alençon's courtship of Queen Elizabeth.

What first strikes the eye is its complete contrast to the familiar showy Elizabethan wheel-ruff, stiff-set high under the chin. And what that ostentatious ruff brought to mind is easily guessed. Even in those days of costly excess in all articles of attire, the rich ruffs were singled out as symptoms of *pride*. Stubbes calls them 'cartwheels of the devil's chariot of pride'; another speaks of 'the deadlye sinnes of pride . . . their sterched ruffes'; and Taylor the Water-Poet describes 'the ruffe, Which into foolish mortals pride doth puffe'.

To that ruff, high-standing in pride, the low falling-band

naturally presented the contrasted opposite: modest humility. Fynes Moryson says it was favourite neckwear with the Italians, who called it the smooth, plain, or simple collar: 'Whatsoever they [the Italians] weare, they desyre to have it rather commodious and easy then fyne and rich, as falling bands rather then Rooffes.' With the Spaniards, as John Minsheu tells us, it was specifically the humble clerical collar, *cuello de clerigo*, 'because the Priests and religious men in Spaine weare these bands, and all the rest ruffe bands'. And humbled by Cupid, a character in Heywood's *The Fair Maid of the Exchange* muses, 'Shall I fall to falling-bands, and be a ruff-an no longer? I must.'

The High *vs.* Low of ruff *vs.* fall is brought out by Sir William Cornwallis in writing *Of Vanitie*. After quoting a Florentine rabble-rouser's seditious speech—*clothe us with their garments and them with ours, and doubtless we shall look like noblemen, they looke like vassals*—Cornwallis comments, 'It is like a face used to look through a ruffe, when put in a falling band, lookes as if looking through a halter.' (*Essayes*, 1601, no. 43. Ed. D. C. Allen, 1946, 177.) John Davys similarly employed the association of the fall with 'underfortune'. Among his 'lots' for the ladies of Elizabeth's court in 1602, Lady Cumberland's was a *Falling bande*, with the couplet

> *Fortune would have you rise, yett guides your hande*
> *From other lotts unto a falling bande.*
>
> Qu. Bond, ed. *Lyly*, 1.503

The fall's contrast with *pride* gave the wit his opening both for a moral and an equivoque—

> A question 'tis why women wear a *fall*?
> The truth on't is, to pride they're given all;
> And pride, the proverb says, will have a *fall*.
>
> *Witts Recreations*, 1654.
> Nares, *Glossary*, 1832, 1.293*b*

For a time, Fashion allowed these two contraries to be worn together—proud ruff above, humble fall below; and the satirical Marston had underlined their symbolism of the proverb:

Nay he doth weare an Embleme bout his necke.
For vnder that fayre Ruffe so sprucely set
Appeares a fall, a falling-band forsooth.

Satyre III with *The Metamorphosis of
Pygmalion's Image*, 1598

As we have noted, the ruff-cuff of our 'King Apollo's' clasped HAND implies that his unseen neck is matchingly encircled by a ruff. But for our 'Mercury', humbly giving his beloved King 'still the upper hand', no ruff of pride. He will clothe his neck in a vesture of humility—as becomes his Prince's ministering servant.

So much for the significance of *wearing* a falling-band. Now for the *figures* which this particular fall presents. The choice Italian *reticella* lace pictured, known to the Elizabethans as *cutwork*, 'was made by cutting away the material in squares, and filling the spaces with geometrical designs of needlework'. (M. C. Linthicum, *Costume in the Drama* . . ., 1936, 139.)

Geometrical designs are of course imbued with symbol. To take only one, the *circle*—which still today means 'eternity', in the posy *Like to this circle round, No end to Love is found*. In Elizabethan times, since 'the perfect'st figure is the round', it was also *perfection*. Chapman describes his love for Sir Thomas Walsingham as 'entirely circular'. As Donne says, circles are 'types of God' (eternal perfection), and the circle *par excellence* is the Sun: 'How glorious is God, as he looks down upon us through the Sunne!'

As 'God's vicegerent' and 'very Type of God's Majesty', the King was also universally seen as the Sun, of which his crown —'the golden circuit', 'the circle of my glory', 'Glory is like a circle'—presents the figure.

With this in mind, what geometrical design should one expect to find in the cutwork collars worn by royalty? We turn up the half-length portrait of King James,* and observe the lace of his collar. Its figures are all *circles* or '*suns*'.† Again, we

---

* National Portrait Gallery, Edinburgh, repr. D. H. Willson, *King James VI and I*, 1956, Frontispiece.

† King James was so often called 'the Sun' that we need mention only John Davys's 'this rising Sunne' at his accession, 'the Sun' in the Preface

consult the Bodleian portrait of Henry, Prince of Wales (repr. Bodleian Picture Books, *Portraits*, 1952, Pl. 11), and examine the lace of his stiff collar or *rebato*. Once more the design is nothing but circles or 'suns'. And in repeated miniatures of King James and Prince Henry we find the same.*

Finally, in the sumptuous oil-painting of Queen Elizabeth, celebrating her defeat of that *mortal moon* the deadly crescent-shaped Spanish Armada,† the Queen's elaborate lace collar is made up of twenty-four radiating white *sets* or pleats, to intimate the hours of the full or 'natural' Day. And each of them ends in an ornamented circle, figuring the majestic glory of 'Elizabeth our Sun'—Spenser's 'Sun of the world . . . great *Gloriana*'. And, upon her defeat of the Spanish *mortal moon*, Hellwis's Sun-Woman of the Apocalypse—'clothed with the Sunne . . . and having the Moone . . . placed under her feete'.

Such experience of geometric emblem in dress reminds us again that here too we must strive *to descry Each beauteous part, not letting overslip One parcel of his curious workmanship*. The deviser of our *impresa*-portrait would neglect no available means of identifying his 'poetical character' to the educated eye. And the choice of a cutwork *design* presents a ready means. Although in comparing the two examples of CLASPING A HAND you will have noticed that in the *Howard* the lace is more elaborate than that in the *V&A*, both in falling-band and in matching cuff, in each miniature the emphasis in the design is obvious. It is on the *squares*, and the '*fours*' which those squares enclose. What does one read in the *four* and the *square*?

'Four is Hermes' number, being his birthday (*Hymn. Hom. Merc.* 19).' (H. J. Rose in *Oxford Classical Dict.*, 1949, 614.) Or, for Elizabethan readers, 'unto *Mercurie* is consecrated of all numbers, the quaternarie especially . . . borne he was upon the

---

to the 1611 Authorized Version, and Heywood's Prologue at Court, 'this glorious Sunne'.

* See Auerbach, *op. cit.*, Plates 134, 154–156 of King James, and Plates 143, 160c of Prince Henry.

† Auerbach, Pl. 77, the Woburn; and in Roy Strong, *Portraits of Queen Elizabeth I*, Pl. XIII, the Tyrwhitt-Drake.

fourth day of the moneth'. (*Plutarchs Morals*, tr. Holland, 1603, 614.) This consecrated *four* of his is seen repeatedly emphasized in Agostino di Duccio's famous bas-relief of Mercury in the Malatesta Temple at Rimini. (Tervarent, *Attributs*, 2, 1959, Pl. XXXI, fig. 54.) The columns flanking him are topped with *quatrefoils*—meaning Luck and True Love; his rod's two serpents show *four* heads, one at each end, as *amphisbaenae*; and his lute, the *tetrachord* he invented, is strung with *four* strings. The heralds (under Mercury's patronage), giving colours for blazon in proper order, list Mercury's Amethyst or Purple as the *fourth*. (Nich. Upton, *De Militari Officio, ed. cit.*, 111.)

Mercury's day, Wednesday (*mercredi, mercoledì, miércoles*), is the *fourth*, the 'mediator' of the week. And since Mercury not only brings lovers together but also gives them luck, for wedding-days (so the folklore runs) 'Wednesday is the best day of all.' 'Wednesday for good fortin.' (Lean, *Collectanea*, 2.268.) *Solomon Grundy . . . Married on Wednesday*. Wednesday is the day first named by Capulet for Juliet's wedding. On Wednesday Mary Tudor married Philip of Spain; on Wednesday Henri IV of France married Maria de' Medici; on Wednesday James VI by proxy married Anne of Denmark; on Wednesday his son Charles married Henrietta Maria. And beyond Mercury's *fourth* day of the week, also lucky for weddings was his birthday, the *fourth* of the moon-month: 'The fourth day celebrate thy nuptial-feast.' (Hesiod, *Works and Days* 800, tr. G. Chapman.) The *Faerie Queene's fourth* book, of *Amity*, featuring the spousal of Thames and Medway, is the Book of Mercury. (See Alastair Fowler, *Spenser and the Numbers of Time*, 156f.) And among William Basse's *Pastorals*, the best, in 'worthy Memory' of Two Friends, is *Wednesday*, Eglogue *4*. Hadrian Junius, hymning Mary Tudor's Wednesday wedding in his *Philippeis*, represents Mercury as 'persuading the marriage'. And in the Oxford play *The Seven Days of the Week*, 'Wednesday's'—that is, Mercury's—skill in gluing hearts together in concord is underlined: 'By trade he's a *joyner*.'*

Mercury's notorious identification with *four* is another of

* From *The Christmas Prince* (St. John's College Oxford 1607/8), Malone Soc. Repr. 1922, 146. Italics mine.

those bits of common knowledge familiar to Shakespeare's audience and quite unknown to Shakespearean critics. Editors have noticed nothing but nonsense in the speech of that sly Autolycus, 'litter'd under Mercury',* in which—in Scene *Four* of Act *Four*—he makes the following *four* points with *four*:

> Here's another ballad of a Fish, that appeared ... on wensday [*fourth* and Mercury's] the *four*escore of April [*fourth* month], *for*tie thousand fadom above water ...
>
> *The Winter's Tale* 4.4.279–282

What is a *godsend* but a *hermaion*, a happy windfall sent by the god of luck? Besides being luck-giver in the marriage-lottery, Mercury was also god of luck in gaming, both with the *four*-suited cards (sometimes called 'The History of the *Four* Kings') and as Deus Tesserarius with the dice—'the *square* rattling bones'—invoked for luck in the throw: *Mercurio dextro*. Accordingly, in the fable *Jupiter's Lottery* 'Mercury was employed to preside at the drawing', and in every lottery the Greeks named the winning first lot drawn *kleros Hermou*: Hermes' lot. Leonidas the epigrammatist called Hermes *tetraglōchin*—O Thou Four-square (*Anthologia Graeca ad fidem cod. Palatini*, VI.334, 3), like the Greek fabulist Babrias who called him *Tetragonos*—and Constantin (*Lex. Græcolat.* 2nd ed. 1592) cites for illustration the Athenians' favourite and ubiquitous *herms*: *square* pillars topped with the head of Hermes. In his *Marriage of Mercury and Philology*, Martianus Capella tells us, 'this quadrate or four-square number is consecrated to Mercury himself, because he alone is accounted the four-square god'.

The Elizabethans had Hermes Hidrumenos pictured before their eyes in Alciati's celebrated Emblem no. 98 (eds. 1542, 1605), seated steadfast on his four-square cube, in triumphant contrast to fickle Fortune on her ball, rolling at the edge of the abyss. And Francis Thynne gave Sir Thomas Egerton this free pedestrian version of Alciati's Latin:

* Chione 'bare by *Mercurye* A sonne that hyght *Awtolychus*', Golding's tr. of Ovid's *Met.* 11.312; '*Autolycus* [son] of *Mercurie*', Greene, *Planetomachia*, 1585; Burton, *Anat. Mel.* 1.2.1.2.

Art, the antidote against fortune

On rolling ball doth fickle Fortune stand;
On firm and settled square sits *Mercury*,
The god of Arts, with Wisdom's rod in hand:
Which covertly to us doth signify
That Fortune's power, unconstant and still frail,
Against Wisdom and Art cannot prevail.

For as the sphere doth move continually,
And shows the course of fickle fortune's change,
So doth the perfect square stand steadfastly,
And never stirs, though fortune list to range.
Wherefore learn Arts, which always steadfast prove,
Thereby hard haps of fortune to remove.

Emblemes and Epigrames, 1600, 6

And since the virtue of both wisdom and art lies in their *truth*, Pietro Bongo (following Macrobius and Valeriano) writes

> The ancients used to set Wisdom on a square or cube, to show her firm and unshaken. And since with them Mercury was held the God of Wisdom, therefore the Athenians made those square figures, Herms, naturally for the firmness and constancy of the true word; because truth from every side whatsoever is like itself.
>
> *De numerorum mysteria*, 1585, ed. 1618, 459 & App. 49.
> Cf. Ferro, 2.321–322, and Ripa, *ed. cit.*, 2.127

For ocular demonstration the Elizabethans saw wise Mercury *true* on his four-square cube not only in Alciati's but in Geoffrey Whitney's *Emblemes* of 1586 as well; and *constant* or *steadfast* on his four-square pillar both in Cartari's *Imagini* and in the device of the Parisian publisher David Douceur. In an Elizabethan military code-book, the too-transparent symbol for 'peace' was the *square* of Mercurius Pacifer. (See C. G. Cruikshank, *Elizabeth's Army*, 1966, 74.)

We have seen enough to realize by now that the FOUR or the SQUARE is Mercury's indelible trade-mark. The idea of Mercury is saturated with FOUR. And since this *impresa*-portrait is to be his form, his *idea*, it should be similarly crammed with FOUR. Has our scrutiny of it left no place un-sought, no corner unrifled?

We look once more, this time with attention focused. And the results make a list as long as it is surprising:

1. Examining the MAN's white or *silver hand of peace*, we now mark the significant *unusual* or *strange*. In every ordinary handclasp, the thumb is employed, bent and clasping. But *here it is not*: both thumbs are straight or turned outwards, in the Roman sign of *peace*.* In this *peace*, the MAN is clasping FOUR fingers with his own FOUR; and of these the FOURTH, clasping his Friend Apollo's Physician-finger, is Mercury's: FOUR for *Friendship*, like Spenser's Book FOUR of Friendship, of Mercury.

2. In the more carefully painted *Howard*, the points of lace he shows on his cuff are FOUR.

3. Again in the *Howard*, of his falling band he shows FOUR descending strips of the linen—one on his right, three on his left—marking off FOUR SQUARES.

4. The figure displayed on each of the black buttons down the central front of his doublet (five at least are plainly shown) is FOUR light spots or points, arranged in a SQUARE.†

5. The *soul* of his picture, his choice 'word' or *reason*‡ ATTICI AMORIS ERGO, ends with a FOUR, the tetragram ERGO; and also with a built-in pun to drive it home: ERGO *means* FOR.

6. This 'word' or *reason* is made up of *sixteen* letters: the SQUARE of FOUR. Mercury's SQUARE signifies Reason, the 'perennial fount of virtues' (Bongo, *op. cit.*, 195).

7. Mercury the Peace-bringer's luck extends even to the *date* inscribed on his *impresa*: the Wonderful Year of victory over the Spanish Armada, when *Peace proclaims Olives of endless age*. A.D. 1588 is Leap Year, the multiple of FOUR. Had the date been 1587 or 1589, he would have left it out.

---

* 'pollice deorsum verso pendente', O. Scarlattini, *Homo . . . Symbolicus*, 1695, 2.74, 1.221; G. P. Valeriano, *op. cit.*, lib. 36. c. 7, *Pacificatio*.

† Precisely as shown on Mercury's long-sleeved garment in pl. 172 of F. W. E. Gerhard's *Auserl. griech. Vasenbildern* III; and in a 10th c. miniature (J. Seznec, *op. cit.*, 74) his robe is powdered with quatrefoils.

‡ Cf. *OED* Reason 14.b. A motto, posy. *Obs.*

We descend finally to the MAN's black satin doublet. This principal garment is clearly 'rich, not gaudy'. For *humble black* could disguise even Pride clothed in costly satin:

Hides all his haughtie thoughts in humble blacke ...
With Silke of poorest colour [*note*, Blacke], deerely bought.

And what the fabric *satin* signifies, Marin Sanuto pointed out long ago: '*dimostra* il raso *summa gentilezza*'. *Gentilezza*, says Torriano, is 'gentility, nobility ... of birth or of mind, also gentlenesse, affability, courtesie, mildnesse'. In his satin our MAN has chosen the very cloth which denotes Mercury—the ever gentle, affable, and courteous.

*　　　*　　　*

From what we have found, it is evident that this main garment, adorned in detail with rows of quilted figures, must contain some essential identifying message beyond Mercury's *humility* and *gentleness*. But can that message be read today? In the *V&A* many of the doublet's details are lost, since sun or damp has dimmed much of its chief side, the MAN's left. The *Howard* has however luckily preserved most of them still clear, though still—even if seen—unrecognized and unread.

How often did I seem to inspect these ranks of forms paraded in black satin in the *Howard*! But viewing vacantly, 'the careless eye had seen nothing but accident'; neglecting the warning—*all the figures work to the intent: nothing useless.*

Then at last my good angel urged me to an alert scrutiny of the row *across the MAN's heart*; and under a strong light I made out several capital *letters*, establishing them as

YZ[ ]EST

'What should that alphabetical position portend?' Everyone knows, except some Malvolio. Only *the end of the A B C*, followed by a sign or character and the Latin verb *est*. And for me it rang a far-off bell in memory. For this is part of the first print confronting every English child: his *horn-book*, Shakespeare's *Absey booke*, the leaf mounted 'Beneath a pane of thin transparent horn' (Cowper) upon a wooden battledore, from which he learned A B C, the cross-row, his letters.

We turn to McKerrow's *Nashe*, 4.205. Here he quotes from Thomas Morley's *Practical Music* 1597 the text of the horn-book as read, set to be sung; ending, with a line added—

> y. ezod. & per se. con per se. tit[t]le tit[t]le. est Amen,
> When you haue done begin againe begin againe.

And Nashe (3.45) gives the horn-book's 'A per se a's . . . *the* est Amen *of valure*' and '*A per se, con per se, tittle, est, Amen!*'. The pregnant *est* ('be it so', 'so it is') equals Heb. *amen*. Greg referred McKerrow to Andrew Clark's *Shirburn Ballads*, 1907, no. VIII—dated 1624, and probably first printed 1564/5: *A right Godly and Christiane a. b. c.* And the first lines of its closing stanzas begin as follows:

> **Y**ong folke, be sober . . .
> **Z**aché the Publican . . .
> **&** plainly *Luke* doth specifye . . .
> **Est** in *English* doth specifye in speech, a *latine* verbe . . .
> **Amen**! God graunt we slacke no tyme . . .

Thus the character following Y Z on our MAN's doublet must represent the sign & ('and-per-se-and', ampersand); and after EST I fancy I can make out ā, standing for a*m*[en].

Discovery here called for sharpest scrutiny of the whole garment; and I list its results.

Body

1. *Top of his left shoulder:* (?) αβγδε
2. *Right and left upper breast, line 1, partly covered by the points of lace:* Characters I cannot identify.
3. *Right breast, line 2:* HER[or MER[, with a final character too dim for my eyes.
4. *Left breast, line 2:* Y Z & EST followed by (?) ā.

Sleeve

5. *Line 1 near cuff:* Three letters of (?) Hebrew.
6. *Line 2:* z & EST
7. *Line 3:* Three letters I cannot read.

Expert linguists will, I trust, throw light on items 2, 5, and 7. But already the sign manual of Hermes–Mercury stands unmistakable: the *horn-book* in 4 and 6, and HER[or MER[in 3. For here the Lord of Language displays his immortal achievement as Numen Literarum—original, basic, the genesis of all literature: his invention of LETTERS.

> Mercurius ... dicitur ... Ægyptiis ... litteras tradidisse.

> Letters, ... the treasure of memory, ... were founde by Mercury in Egypt. [Bruno therefore names him THECA MNEMOSYNES.]

> *Mercurie*, the first god who found out letters in Aegypt.

> *Mercury* [found out] letters, [prompted by] Love.

> > Till *Hermes*, secretarie to the Gods,
> > Or *Hermes Trismegistus*, as some will,
> > Inuented letters . . .*

In his *second* lines, for our *Second* Age—of '*Mercury, wherein we are taught and instructed*'—the Teacher bears his gift, tool of his mystery, the Alphabet; peculiar to him ever *Since minde at first in carrecter was done* (Son. 59.8)—which Malone rightly glossed '*after the first use of letters*'. It is his attribute, and his alone: divine Inventor, Founder, and Patron of all Literature, the Poet Mercury.

And in 1588/9 our MAN would win approval for a 'conceit acute and fit' set in Mercurial characters on his satin doublet; for Puttenham, defining the Device in 1589 (*Arte*, (N) 1), calls it

> such as a man may put into letters ... in any bordure of a rich garment to giue by his noueltie maruell to the beholder.

*   *   *

Now for his identifying costume-colours. Chief and most striking here is the *purple* or 'murrey' of the hat: more reddish-purple in the *Howard*, and more violet-purple in the *V&A*. We have already seen it, displayed in the matching Amethyst of the brooch. Hilliard himself in his *Arte of Limning* declares 'ammatist orient for murrey'. Ferne says Purple 'signifieth in

---

* Cicero, *De natura deorum; An abridgement of* P[olydore] *Vergile*, 1546, b5; *Plutarchs Morals*, tr. Holland, 1603, 789; Burton, *Anat. Mel.* 3.2.3.1; Nashe, *ed. cit.*, 3.273.

Plannets, Mercury'; and in royal heraldry Purple is 'Mercury'. This colour had long identified the god. In a fresco surviving at Pompeii he appears dressed in 'a short violet mantle'.* And centuries later in Shakespeare's time without a change: 'Mercury [in the ballet] was accoutred altogether as the poets describe him . . . his mantle was of violet cloth-of-gold.'†

Mercury's colour was evidently no item of recondite learning. Familiar to all, it gave folk-names to flowers: 'Mercury's violets'—an Elizabethan name for Canterbury bells, and 'Wild Mercury' for the purple snapdragon or foxglove. (*OED s.v.* Mercury 10.d. and 11.)

So much for Mercury's prime identifying hue—Purple, Violet, Murrey. But from ancient days he is also widely identified or associated with the combined and contrasted Black and White: the two 'original' or 'natural' colours, which our MAN displays in feather (White), hatband (Black and White), doublet (Black), and falling-band and cuff (White).

Young persons in eighteenth-century England found Mercury described in François Pomey's attractive handbook, translated 1784 by Andrew Tooke as *The Pantheon, Representing the Fabulous Histories of the Heathen Gods.* Opening to Chapter VII, they read a dialogue—its details drawn chiefly from Conti and Cartari—beginning as follows:

> *Paleophilus.* Who is that young Man, with a cheerful Countenance, an honest Look, and lively Eyes; who is so fair without Paint; having Wings fixed to his Hat and his Shoes, and a Rod in his Hand, which is winged, and bound about by a Couple of Serpents?
>
> *Mystagogus.* It is the Image of *Mercury,* as the *Egyptians* paint him; whose Face is partly black and dark, and partly clear and bright; because sometimes he converses with the *Celestial,* and sometimes with the *Infernal* Gods.

But how a face pied black-and-white like Anubis can still be *so fair* remains an Egyptian mystery. Alberic the Englishman

---

* B. Combet Farnoux, 'Mercurio', *Encicl. Dell'Arte Antica,* 4.1034.

† B. de Beaujoyeulx, *Balet Comique de la Royne,* 1582, qu. P. Lacroix, *Ballets et Mascarades de Cour,* 1868, 1.46.

(*Libellus de Imaginibus Deorum*) more credibly reports the Black and White as adorning Mercury's *hat*: as symbols not however of his unique frequenting of both Hell and Heaven,* but of his miraculous transformations: 'Whites he made black, and blacks white, which is shown by his hat, half white and half black.'† And George Gascoigne joins those for whom Mercury's power of black-into-white is the force of his *eloquence*:

You know that in his tongue consists his chiefest might:
You know his eloquence can serve to make the Crowe seeme
white.   *Works* (*ed. cit.*), 2.118–119

Mercury's identification with these colours is more than symbolical. Legend affirms that he actually appeared in black and white. When the Olympian gods were pursued into Egypt by the hell-hound Typhon, they eluded him by assuming forms of animals. Apollo turned himself into a Raven or Crow, and Mercury 'lurked under Ibis' wings'. (Ovid, *Met.* 5.331. Cf. Hyginus, *Poet. Astron.*, lib. 2. c. 38.) This Ovidian passage is given by Golding as '*Mercurius* hid him in a Bird which *Ibis* men doe call.' He went about as a Sacred Ibis: his body white, his head, neck, and legs black.

Our Greek Hermes is identical with the Egyptian Thoth, the Ibis-headed god of Eloquence. On this topic Sir D'Arcy Thompson notes that 'the opposed white and black of the Ibis' plumage, as sometimes of Mercury's raiment, suggested various symbolic parallels, the opposition of male and female, of light and darkness, of order and disorder, of speech and silence, of truth and falsehood'. (*A Glossary of Greek Birds*, 1895, 1936, 114.) Among these, the one drawn by Aelian is of special interest:

They say that the Ibis is beloved of Mercury the father of speech because it bears the form and likeness of speech; for its black feathers may be compared to the tacit and

---

* 'deity that sharest hell and heaven, thou alone hast the right to cross either threshold, and art the intermediary between the two worlds'. Claudian, *Rape of Prosperine* 1.89–91, tr. M. Platnauer, 1922.

† Qu. Hans Liebeschütz, *op. cit.*, 60–61. 'Mercurie was portraicted . . . wearing an Hat of white & blacke colloures'. Stephen Bateman, *op. cit.*, A4.

not-yet-uttered, and the white to speech brought out, the declarer of the inward thoughts.

De animal. nat., lib. 10. c. 29

And in Plutarch:

> . . . speech is two folde; the one interior or inward, the gift of *Mercurie* surnamed *Hegemon*, that is, Guide; the other pronounced and uttered foorth, which is instrumentall, and a very interpreter to give notice of our conceptions.
>
> *Morals*, tr. Holland 1603, 290

We have Mercury again with black and white as both discoverer and dispenser of the precious 'Moly, the Gods most soveraigne hearbe divine': magical antidote against spells and sorcery. Homer's Ulysses 'went to Circe with moly, which he had received from Hermes, and throwing the moly among her enchantments, he drank, and alone was not enchanted'. (Apollodorus, *Epitome* tr. J. G. Frazer, Loeb, 2.288.)

Littleton gives the English names of moly as *Hermal* and *Wild Rue*; and Homer says that the herb had a black root and a white flower. Ovid, in Golding's translation, writes

> The peace procurer *Mercurie* had given too him a whyght
> Fayre flowre whoose roote is black, and the Goddes it *Moly* hyght.

In the black and white of Mercury's hermal, the Renaissance persisted in seeing his magical *eloquence*. Emblem 195 (ed. 1550) of the widely read Alciati, entitled *Eloquence is Difficult*, points a moral in Latin verse to this effect:

> *Although Mercury's moly has a charming white flower which like his shining eloquence wins everyone, yet the black root which produces it is hard to pull up. To achieve eloquence is a work of much labour.*

In no. 93 of Achille Bocchi's *Symbolicæ Quæstiones* we have it again; elaborated also by G. C. Capaccio in his *Il Principe*; and Ferro (3.395) tells us that in Mercury's divine gift of black-and-white moly 'is figured Eloquence; which [the poet] Tasso

appropriated to himself with the words DEORUM MUNUS' —
'*the Gift of the Gods*'.

The might of Mercury's Eloquence was also seen figured by
the irresistible music of his pipe, which 'lullabyed asleepe' the
all-eyed Argus. Gabriel Harvey noted 'many Strategemes and
mysteries in that Arcadian Pipe' of Mercury's. We have mentioned the *impresa* on Mary Stuart's Bed of State, showing
Mercury piping Argus to sleep. Its lemma reads, ELOQUIUM
TOT LUMINA CLAUSIT, '*Eloquence closed so many eyes*'. So
familiar was this metaphor that Marlowe and Nashe could use
it for the public stage, of the all-too-persuasive Sinon,

> Whose ticing tongue was made of *Hermes* pipe,
> To force an hundred watchfull eyes to sleepe.
>
> *Dido* 2.1.145–146

With the pied black-and-white bewitching eloquence of the
Piper Mercury before us, we are tempted to see him at the
bottom of the tale of the Pied Piper. Natale Conti's popular
Mythologiæ (1551, etc.) held that

> the ancients pictured Mercury [*as a young man handsome
> without cosmetics or trimming*], attached to men's ears by
> golden chains, accustomed to draw mortals whither-
> soever it pleased him, as it is said of Hercules [*e.g.* by
> Lucian].

That is, Hercules Gallicus or Ogmios, Type of Eloquence. In
describing Hans Franck's woodcut of this Celtic god drawing
crowds after him with his tongue, Arnold von Salis brings us
close up to Hamelin by styling him the 'Rat Catcher' (*Antike
und Renaissance*, 1947, 173.); and brings *Mercury* by reproducing
Dürer's famous drawing (Vienna, Kunsthist. Museum L. 420),
in which it is not Hercules but *wing-footed Mercury* whose tongue
is pulling the multitude along.

According to Hyginus (Fable 201), Mercury passed on to
his son Autolycus not only his supreme skill in stealing un-
detected but also his magic of transformation. 'He could
turn what he snapped up into whatever shape he wished, from
white into black, or from black into white.' And Golding, in

his version of Ovid, symbolizes this hereditary black and white by calling Autolycus 'a wyly pye':*

> shee bare by *Mercurye*
> A sonne that hyght *Awtolychus*, who provde a wyly pye . . .
> He was his fathers owne sonne right: he could mennes eyes
> so bleere,
> As for too make yᵉ black things whyght, and whyght things
> black appeere.

Little wonder therefore that Shakespeare pleases his audience by having his 'wily pie' Autolycus—that *mercularius* or 'Haberdasher of small Wares', that snapper-up of unconsidered trifles—come in singing

> *Lawne as white as driuen Snow,*
> *Cypresse blacke as ere was Crow* . . .

but some surprise that no commentator has seen the obvious.† And the lottery-god's colours enrich the proverb's wit: *In Lotteries men mourn in white* (=blank) *and laugh in black* (=prize).

We may leave this topic on a graver note of symbolic ceremony. The whole tribe of human heralds, steeped in symbol, was dedicated to Mercury, eloquent Herald of the Gods: 'Praeconum genus Mercurio sacrum est' (Pollux, *Onom.* IV. § 91). How religiously Shakespeare's contemporaries preserved their patron's identifying white and black is evident by Gerard Legh's report of the solemn creation of a herald. It was accomplished with a *white and black* chain: by putting 'about his necke a coller of SS. The one S. being argent, the other S. Sable.' (*The Accedens of Armory*, 1562, ed. 1576, 42.)

To sum up this portrait's significant costume-colours, from looking into it we have learned, first, that Purple or Violet declared *Mercury* to every discerning eye. Later on we shall be

---

* 'now like a *Pye*, all clad in blacke & white'. I. M., *The Newe Metamorphosis* vol. 1, pt. 2, f. 77ᵛ.

† In Dryden's *Amphitryon* Act V, Mercury wittily calls himself 'black and white'. Phædra, before she will become his Succuba or 'lawfull Concubine', exacts signed, attested Articles—'that I may have him under black and white'. *Merc.* 'With all my heart; that I may have thee under black and white hereafter.'

finding a topically personal meaning as well in this colour of his. Second, that Mercury's too is the ancient antithesis of Black and White: the colours which intimate, among other things, his power to *transform*, his Chaos and Order, his Hell and Heaven, his Female and Male, his Falsehood and Truth, his Sleep and Waking, his Silence and Speech, his Moly or magical Eloquence.

If you prefer Mercury Purple or Violet, our MAN gives you his brooch and his hat. If Mercury Black and White, you shall have the rest of his dress. Friend of man, our gentle 'Mercury' knows how to please all.

When we look back over the profusion of pointers to his 'poetical character' given by our MAN, we are struck as much by their precision and their concinnity as by their rich variety of reference. He shows himself *so quaint in array, so conceited in all points*, that in almost every conceivable manner he silently proclaims 'Hermes–Mercury'. And he does it without bare breast and scanty chlamys, without winged hat and winged heels, without snaky rod, pipe, sword, or trumpet—those hackneyed properties which would reveal him to every rustic.* Here, as David Piper rightly says of Elizabethan portraiture, 'Each part has its significance; pose, costume, and attributes establish the subject precisely.'

Not only has he left no possible stone unturned, but as Hermes, of the stone-heap', the *Sorites*, he has piled them up into a hilltop cairn conspicuous to guide the literate Elizabethan eye. Could he be expected to foresee that posterity's ignorance of his world's mental heritage, an ignorance spreading with the years, would creep up like a mist to conceal it?

Or, to come down to our modern jargon, can anyone upon review of our MAN's heap of indicators imagine an Elizabethan

* Authors of Devices presenting *poetical characters* treated them just as Ben Jonson did those in his masques, 'wherein the garments and ensigns deliver the nature of the person; . . . to have made themselves their own decipherers, and each one to have told, upon their entrance, *what they were*, . . . had been . . . utterly unworthy any quality of a *Poem*: wherein a *Writer* should always trust somewhat to the capacity of the *Spectator*; . . . so to be presented, as upon the view, they might, without cloud or obscurity, declare themselves to the sharp and learned.' (*Ben Jonson*, ed. Simpson, 7.91, 287. Spelling modernized.)

Identikit more complete in every feature than his harmony of Hermes clasping his too-dear Apollo's *kudos*-bestowing hand, executed for him by *this time's pencil*, the age's master-limner Nicholas Hilliard? Or one in its scale more gem-like?

Here is no imperfect *portrait parlé*, to be eked out with conjecture. This *work of art contains within itself all that is necessary for its comprehension*. For we have heard the picture. Here to the educated eye is Virgil's *omnia Mercurio similis*. Our MAN offers a superb *portrait parlant*, a speaking iconism eloquent of Mercury in every feature, gesture, object, number, letter, form, and colour. And all of them—in Pindar's words— 'vocal to the wise; but for the crowd they need interpreters'.

5

The Unequal Gods of Friendship

ON reconnoitring, it now seems clear that our sustained
Elizabethan attack has enlarged the breach made in this small
citadel's wall—wide enough at least to admit the head. A
wealth of concurring evidence has made the presence here of
a '*Mercury' joined in True Love with an 'Apollo*' virtually a foregone
conclusion. And for testing its soundness our *impresa*-portrait
presents the decisive means, in the soul of this picture's body:
our MAN's 'word of high intention', exposing what Henri
Estienne calls his 'rare conceipts and gallant resolutions'.

> *Inscription there allured the eye*
> *With many a wondrous mystery*
> *Of ancient things made novelty*
> *That never man did yet descry.*

Attici amoris ergo. What do we know about this baffling
Latin, inscribed close by the handclasp? Two things. That its
sense is purposely dark and incomplete, that only the true
meaning of the picture, applied to it, will make it clear. And
reciprocally, that something in the phrase, when properly
understood, will add what the picture lacks for its complete
comprehension.

The expression *amoris ergo*, meaning 'for love' (*i.e.*, *because of*
love), is a phrase—like *amicitiæ ergo*—commonly used for
inscriptions by Elizabethan Englishmen. In the *album amicorum*
of Johannes Le Maire of Antwerp, we find some Greek and
Latin extracts written out for him by Bodley's future librarian,
and subscribed '*Hæc scripsit Oxoniæ, Thomas James amoris et
benevolentiæ ergo 23 Julij 1598.*' (The Hague, Royal Library.
Handschr. IX. 11, no. 75.I.2.) And writing in Captain Segar's
album, that 'Priest of Apollo and the Muses' Ben Jonson
closes with this: 'D. Fran: Segar. Amoris & Amicitiæ ergò

Beniamin Ionsonius Londinensis Apollinis & Musarum Sacerdos subscripsit.'* A cursory look through the scores of such albums surviving would be rewarded by many further examples of the phrase.

Nothing difficult, therefore, and certainly no sneaking allusion to 'Greek love', in the friendly expression *amoris ergo*. The puzzle in our inscription lies in the single word *Attici*.

Now when a phrase in a foreign tongue has baffled all critics, it is no good resorting to lexicons already combed by those critics. The hopeful course is to consult a native speaker, or an expert saturated with that language's peculiar idiom. Only such a mind will know instinctively both what that phrase *could not* mean, and what it *might* mean or *does* mean. For lack of a Tully, I took *Attici amoris ergo* to the man who in the course of his long life had, I suppose, read and remembered as much Latin of all sorts as anyone you could name: my friend the late Professor Sir Frank Adcock of Cambridge.

One glance, and he pronounced it a 'sticker'—which is precisely what its composer meant it to be. Then I tried on him the various guesses I have seen. 'Could it mean "Because of Attic love" or "For the sake of classical love"?' 'Certainly *not*.' 'What about "For love of Atticus"?' 'No. Of course not,' said Sir Frank. 'In this construction *Attici* cannot be a genitive singular. *Attici* here can be nothing but a *nominative plural*. All that the phrase can be made to say is "Athenians for love" or "Athenians because of love". And what is meant by *that* is more than I can tell you.'

Thanks to Sir Frank, the long-standing fog of doubt is dissipated. The riddling lemma which met the eye of 1588 conveyed *Athenians for love* or *Athenians because of love*.† Armed with this certainty, we now look for the next step. What was it that William Camden told us about the lemma?

* Henry E. Huntingdon Library, HM 743, qu. *Ben Jonson*, ed. Simpson, 8.664–665.

† Many readers would also catch the presented association, *viz.*: among the Romans (see Nepos), the rich, disinterested *Atticus*, impartially devoted and generous to warring partisans in their need, earned the loving veneration of all as the perfect Friend, Friend *par excellence*; his name thus enriching this Device of Two Athenian Friends with the association *Atticuses for love*.

. . . the body must be of fair representation, and the word in some different language, witty [*i.e.*, full of meaning], short, and answerable thereunto.

Answerable means 'corresponding to the body or picture'.

Athenians thus answers to these young Elizabethans of 1588 feigned as those true-loving *Athenians* Apollo and Mercury, their *Attica fides* shown in their joined white hands: *ancient things made novelty*, the 'Greekish scene' in English guise.

For Apollo was *the original Athenian*, the Athenian *par excellence*: worshipped in a temple to Apollo Patrous near the Areopagus, as well as in the Delphinion and the Lyceion. Plutarch (in *Demetrius*) says that the games sacred to Pythian Apollo were 'kept and solemnised at Athens . . . because he was patrone of the citie, and . . . the Athenians maintained that he was their progenitor'. Conti quotes Aristophanes' commentator: 'This God was believed by the ancient Athenians to be the Father-God and defender of the city.' (*Mythologiæ*.lib. 4. c. 10.)

And as for Hermes–Mercury as an Athenian old-timer, he is commonly shown already on hand at the birth of Athena. Though far less impressive than his loving half-brother, mighty King Apollo, no god was more popular with the Athenians. Their favourite oaths show it—'by Apollo!' 'by Hermes!' And now we realize only belatedly that our MAN–Hermes has presented an *Athenian* association also by wearing a hat with a *violet crown*. For 'the violet was the favourite and distinguishing flower of the Athenians, who took pride in being called the *io-stephanoi*, or *violet-crowned*'. (Thomas Mitchell, tr. Aristophanes' *Knights*, 1820, 1329 *note*.)

What sight as common in ancient Athens as Hermes' statue? So common indeed that the term for 'a carver of images' was *Hermoglypheus*. Pierio Valeriano writes,

And since with the ancients Mercury was held the God of wisdom, among the Athenians there used to be made those Herms: that is, squared stones . . . to signify that reason and truth, just like forms four-square, stand ever straight upright. lib. 39. c. 32

And the *Encyclopædia Britannica* (14th ed., 13.365) illustrates our own age's view of those images:

In the oldest times Hermes . . . was worshipped in the form of a heap of stones or of an amorphous block . . . which afterwards took the shape of a phallus, the symbol of productivity. The next step was the addition of a head to this phallic column, which became quadrangular (the number 4 was sacred to Hermes . . .), with the significant indication of sex still prominent. In this shape the numbers of herms rapidly increased . . . In Athens they were found at the corners of streets; before the gates and in the court-yards of houses, where they were worshipped by women as having the power to make them prolific; before the temples, in the gymnasia and palaestrae.

But the Renaissance, not bound by our modern animalizing sex-obsession, joined Plutarch in seeing Hermes' potent phallus standing to signify *vis patratura*, the *efficient power of Eloquence*. As Valeriano says, 'If the ancients wished to show the effective force of speech and persuading, they would make an image of Mercury' *most strongly ithyphallic*.* And they typically made the ithyphallic Herm a bearded old man like a Nestor, type of the power of Prudence and Eloquence. One recalls Sir John Davys 'Of the Soule of Man':

> But most [old men], euen to their dying howre,
>   Retaine a mind more liuely, quicke, and strong,
>   And better vse their vnderstanding power
>   Then when their braines were warm, and lims were
>   yong. . .
>   . . . when we heare that halfe-dead body speake,
>   We oft are rauisht to the heauenly *spheares* . . .

—as by the deep harmony of the dying Gaunt's *this England*.

*   *   *

* 34.26, & 35.24. Cf. *Plutarchs Morals* tr. Holland 401, and Conti, lib. 5. c. 13. Some Neoplatonists (*e.g.*, Plotinus, cited by Ficino) saw Hermes Logios as '*Semen Ideale*: that *Vis Prolifica*' whose generative power gives the mind's ideas embryonic form, maturing to be born *expressed by words*. See John Sadler, *Masquarade du Ciel*, 1640, 37; and Wind, *op. cit.*, 27*n*.

Since we believe we have recognized those two *Attici* in the picture as 'Apollo' and 'Mercury', we are now at length prepared to put our conjecture to the proof, by the decisive tests prescribed for any *impresa*: tests which will show whether our proposed solution is correct or not.

First, then, Does the picture as we have interpreted it *complete* the lemma and make it intelligible?

Answer, Yes: the *supernatural* in the picture shows us that these young Englishmen are not figuring any mortal Athenians, but *divine* ones: *the only two gods of Athens who were joined in loving friendship.* The picture thus supplies the lemma with the missing concept *gods*, completing it to read (*Divi*) *Attici amoris ergo*, '*Athenians* (*Apollo and Mercury*) *because of love.*'

Again, Does the lemma as we have read it *complete* the picture and make it clear?

Answer, Yes: it completes the picture by supplying the guiding concept *Attici*; telling us that these two young Englishmen of 1588 hyperbolically pictured in friendly love are 'shadowed' in the Device as *Athenians*—as those unique divine Athenian friends Apollo and Mercury. And with *amoris ergo* it explains the astonishing scene. The magical power which makes them like unto gods is their *love*.

Picture and lemma: each purposely imperfect and baffling by itself, when put together they reciprocally complete and make clear. Will not an impartial mind allow that our solution passes the verifying test?

If the representation of these two friends as gods still seems an idea strange or bizarre, we need to remember the fact: that to the sixteenth-century mind it was not strange at all. To that mind, no high experience of the heart could approach the sublimity of *friendship*. As C. S. Lewis put it, 'This alone, of all the loves, seemed to raise you to the level of gods.' (*The Four Loves*, 1960, 89.) *Homo homini Deus*, 'Man is to man a God'. is Erasmus's version of the Greek proverb "Ἄνθρωπος ἀνθρώπῳ δαιμόνιον; and Tottel's *Miscellany* (1557) has

In wealth and wo thy frend, an other self to thee;
Such man to man a God, the proverb sayth to be.
Both in M. P. Tilley, *Dict. Prov.*, M241

In a translated passage about love and friendship published
1576, James Sanford again gives 'the Greeke Prouerbe',
Englished as 'man is to man a God'. (*The Mirrour of Madnes*,
STC 17980, A3.) And an anthology of 1607 translates an
apposite line from a Greek drama as *Honora amicos tanquam
honorares deos*, 'Reverence friends as you would reverence gods.'
(*Polyanthea*, D. Nani Mirabelli, ed. J. Lang, 1607, 65*b*.) Everyone recalls familiar passages of Shakespeare with the same
thought. In one, the friendship between the Venetian Antonio
and Bassanio is a *godlike* amity; and in another, *Twelfth Night*'s
Antonio says of his friend Sebastian,

> And to his image, which me thought did promise
> Most venerable worth, did I deuotion . . .
> But oh, how vilde an idoll proues this God!

If then—as these and other sixteenth-century speakers repeatedly aver—true friendship makes each friend a god to
the other, is it strange to show them in a picture as such?

It may not be realized how widely this ideal deifying was
practised in those days. Remembering the Renaissance's
poetic revival of the ancient cult of royalty, most of us are
prepared to find the apotheosis of kings. We do not pause over
Pontus de Tyard's calling Henri II 'Apollo', or over an *impresa*
showing Philip II as Phoebus driving his chariot. In another
Henri IV appears as Hercules Gallicus; and again, in a medal,
as Mars—with Maria de' Medici as Minerva. And his mistress,
Gabrielle d'Estrées, was actually painted as Diana. Du Bartas
hails Queen Elizabeth as Pallas, and King James is held up as
Phoebus Apollo well nigh *ad nauseam*.

But perhaps not equally familiar is the fact that they accorded
this apotheosis also to poets: not merely associating the poet
with Apollo, as in the emblem *Poetarum Gloria* already mentioned, but deifying him. This was done most frequently, of
course, after a poet's death. Five years after Christopher Marlowe was killed, Henry Petowe apotheosized him as Phoebus:

> this suppos'd *Apollo*
> Conceit no other, but th'admired *Marlo*: . . .
> *Marlo* late mortall, now fram'd all divine.

And Henry Coventry, elegizing Ben Jonson—

> *Poetry* shall know
> No *Deity* but *Thee* . . .   *Jonsonus Virbius*, 1638

Yet similar 'godding' of a *living* poet was far from unknown. Ronsard's admirer Mary Stuart offered him a 'Parnassus' made of silver, inscribed *A Ronsard l'Apollon de la source des Muses.* Ronsard not only accepted it, but publicly 'assumed the god'. For as Sun-King Apollo Genitor, he sternly told all the insolent reformers of religion—Calvinists, Lutherans, etc.—to *know themselves*:

> Vous estes tous yssus de la grandeur de moy,
> Vous estes mes sujets, je suis seul vostre Roy.
> *Responce aux Injures*, lines 1037–1038, text of 1587

And Spenser, in his *December* eclogue—since 'Onely *Pan* . . . seekes to compare with *Apollo*'—says that when young he foolishly believed Harvey, who identified him with Apollo:

> And if that *Hobbinol* right iudgement bare, [Gabriel Harvey
> To *Pan* his owne selfe pype I neede not yield.
>   For if the flocking Nymphes did folow *Pan*,
>   The wiser Muses after *Colin* ranne.

And John Davies of Hereford's address to William Browne on his second book of *Pastorals* is similar:

> So, all in both will make a *God* of thee,
> To whom they will exhibit *Sacrifice*
> Of richest *Loue* and *Praise* . . .

This *deifying* recalls the Renaissance view of the poet as a *divine creator*—Scaliger's *alter deus*, followed by both Sidney and Tasso—a view commonly held also of the painter.*

And on classical precedent, the poets confidently claimed another divine power: the power of 'eternizing', of *making immortal*. According to them, they created *immortal* verse. And with it they also *bestowed immortality* upon the fortunate subjects of that verse—'Verse, that immortalizes whom it

---

* D. C. Allen, 'Herrick's "Rex Tragicus" ' in *Studies in Honor of DeWitt T. Starnes*, 1967, 219; E. Panofsky, *Idea*, 1924, tr. 1968, 125, 248 *n*.37.

sings!' (Cowper). They held its eloquence equal in power to the gods' own nectar, that *whosoever drinks thereon Immortal shall be made*. Marlowe and Chapman's *Hero and Leander* (1598) on its title-page spreads the claim of the poet's invention to that immortalizing power: *Ut Nectar, Ingenium.*

As Père Le Moyne says, a Device is a poem; and in the convention a poet is a god. We have noted the requirement of *deification* in Contile's and Tasso's rules for the *impresa*-portrait. In considering our CLASPING A HAND, we may reasonably take the two human figures to be *feigned as gods* not only following this rule, but also on two further recognized grounds, namely (*a*) the *godlike* amity of the Friendship shown, and (*b*) the *divinity* of the immortalizing poet.

6

Hilliard's *A Youth*: 'Apollo W H'

FROM what has gone before, the reader has seen how much my curiosity about CLASPING A HAND has taught me of the peculiar nature of the portrait-Device: how the noble thought of its sitter is drawn from the historical truth of actual experience; how the sitter should be feigned as a god, striking the beholder with wonder; how figure and lemma must reciprocally complete and explain each other.

None of this was in my grasp at the poet's fourth centenary, when in writing *Mr. W. H.* I identified Hilliard's masterpiece A YOUTH LEANING AGAINST A TREE AMONG BRIER-ROSES (*ca.* 1588) as *my love's picture*: Shakespeare's Friend, Master William Hatcliffe. Fortunately I had found leading facts about Hatcliffe—his election late in 1587, aged 19, as Prince of Purpoole for the revels at Gray's Inn, the quatrefoil-primrose or 'True Love' of his ancestral arms furnishing the badge and theme of his reign, his family's lion-crest borrowed from Pompey the Great, with Pompey's story recalled in the portrait's lemma from Lucan *Dat pœnas laudata fides*—enough to make that correct identification.

But from the wealth now revealed in CLASPING A HAND, everyone will realize that there must be much more in Hatcliffe's portrait-Device—'by general consent one of the prime masterpieces of English painting'—than I was able to get from it in those days.

Before attacking it afresh, however, there is a point which should be made about the sitter represented. A subjective guess unsupported by evidence has been offered, to the effect that the YOUTH portrayed is the same as the sitter in another Hilliard miniature (Auerbach, Pl. 81) in the Metropolitan Museum, New York, dated 1588 and giving the sitter's age as 22. That guess I believe to be mistaken; and in support I would quote Shakespeare's Warwickshire countryman Michael Drayton:

> *Within the compasse of Mans Face we see*
> *How many sorts of severall Favours bee;*
> *And in the Chin, the Nose, the Brow, the Eye,*
> *The smallest Diff'rence that you can descry*
> *Alters Proportion, altereth the Grace,*
> *Nay, oft destroyes the Favour of the Face:*
> *And in the World, scarce Two so like there are,*
> *One with the other, which if you compare*
> *But being set before you both together,*
> *A judging Sight doth soone distinguish eyther.*

On comparing the two, it is at once obvious that both sitters exactly follow a style of hair-dressing fashionable in 1588. But this is hardly enough to make them identical. To my eyes, the two faces are otherwise so markedly dissimilar, both in features and in expression, that to imagine them two contemporaneous attempts by Hilliard to represent the same man is out of the question. The length and contour of the chins and the shaping of the eyes alone are much too disparate. To admit the possibility, one would first have either to forget or to deny the master's known excellence at catching the distinctively personal likeness, the individual's *hæcceity*.

Now to take up Hatcliffe's portrait-Device from where we left it in *Mr. W. H.* There we had recognized his figure as presenting True Loving Friendship, as described in Allot's *Wits Theater of the Little World*:

> The Romaines . . . Shadowed [Friendship] in the shape of a young man whose heade was bared . . . putting his finger to his harte.

The figure and its pose made it unmistakable. But we have now learned that the rules of the portrait-Device leave no place for simple personified abstractions. This human figure must therefore be presenting *a known god who is also True Loving Friendship.* Now which god is that?

In Chapter 3 we have already seen him. It is that unique

Hilliard:
Unknown Youth among Roses

source of life and love, *Phoebus Apollo*. Cicero, prime authority on Friendship, says 'They seem to take the sun out of the universe, when they deprive life of friendship.' And John Taylor, *'That makes thee like Apollo in thy lookes . . . For there's the ensigne of true friendship plac'd.'* 'Friendship . . . the Sun of all the World.' (Melbancke, *op. cit.*, Aa2.)

It is striking to mark how this identification at once illuminates and defines the background of this individual Device. For we now realize that if the YOUTH presents King Apollo, called in Homer *greatest of the gods*, the particular personal tie which occasioned his *impresa*-portrait must therefore be that rare precarious bond, *a friendship between a superior* (himself) *and an inferior*. Here is a new and specific fact about the YOUTH: a clue of central importance.

As we noted, the *tree in the briers* declares that the True Loving Friend is *constant in adversity*; not one 'that hath left his friend in the briers' as in Joseph Hall's lines—

> Your friends all weary, and your spirits spent,
> Ye may your fortunes seek; and be forwent
> Of your kind cousins and your churlish sires—
> Left there alone 'midst the fast-folding Briers.
> *Virgidemiae*, 1597, 2.2.35–38, spelling modernized

'True Love is recognized in adversity.' As Ralegh writes, 'Love, that only shineth in misfortune': when one's summer 'friends' have all fallen away, leaving for comfort only the faithful beams of Apollo's True Loving 'Royall hart'. And the *roses* again show the YOUTH to be *Love* and *King* Apollo. For as Prince Will's friend Campion sang, *Roses . . . Are flowers for loue and flowers for Kinges*.

The *tree* against which the YOUTH leans should have given us another familiar pointer, as it gave the Elizabethans. In the entertainment at Sudeley Castle 1592, 'her Maiesty sawe APOLLO with the tree'. 'APOLLO was portraicted beardlesse, standing by a Bay tree' (Bateman). Both *oak* and *bay-laurel* were sacred to Apollo. Has anyone noticed that the YOUTH almost duplicates the pose of Apollo shown in Benedetto Montagna's engraving of the god? 'A young curly-headed man (beardless) . . . his head bent slightly right (towards the strong trunk of a tree at his right) . . .' (A. M. Hind, *Cat. of Early Italian Engravings*, 1910, 481.) Apollo Sauroktonos (after Praxiteles) leans against a tree. Remember Apollo Agyieus with his pillar, conspicuous before the Athenians' house-doors (Valeriano, 49.39). And compare Lucian's *Anacharsis* § 7: 'Lyceian Apollo; you see his statue, the figure leaning against the pillar.'

Again, to make it obvious that his head is the head of King Phoebus the glorious Sun, the Prince of Purpoole does precisely what we have seen Queen Elizabeth do at this same date: he surrounds it with a great wheel-ruff, presenting the majestic circle of the sun, made up of twenty-four radiating white *sets* or pleats to intimate the hours of the natural day. And the white of his ruff, of his long stockings and his pumps—on his right, the East—is set against the black of his short cloak —on his left, the West—similarly to denote Phoebus: his white figure emerging from the black like the God of Day from Night. Pointing out that both *white Swan* and *black Raven* are sacred to Apollo, Martianus Capella (9.894) says that their combined colours witness to the succession of Day and Night.

> The snow-white Swan betokens lightsome Day,
> The coal-black Crow, of darky Night is sign.
> R. Tofte, *Laura*, 1597, 3.22. Spelling modernized

As we noted (above, p. 51), Phoebus Apollo is *Veritas*: 'Truth's symbole, the bright sunne.' 'Lay thy hand on thy heart, and speak the truth.' And he is not only *Truth* (Light) but also *Love* (Heat). 'The seate of truthe is in our secret harts' and the heart is 'the seat where Love is enthroned'. By placing his hand on his *heart* the sitter gives the essential Phoebus-sign; *Apollo . . . was called Heart of Heaven*, says Cartari. And Burton names 'the *Heart* . . . the Sun of our body, the King'. In astrology, 'The Sunne gouerneth . . . the Braynes . . . the heart.' 'Sol, caput & Cor.'*

Chapman versifies a passage, one of the many he lifts from Plutarch's *Moralia*:

---

* *Anat. Mel.* 1.1.2.4; John Maplet, *The Diall of Destiny*, 1581, A2; J. Ravis Tixier (Textor), *Officina*, 1588, 79ᵛ.

The sunne, doth with the heart analogise,
And through the world, his heate and light disperse:
As doth the heart through mans small vniuerse.*

To the contemporary unriddler of Devices the meaning of that gesture *to the heart* is patent.

So far we have met nothing difficult. But now we strike a snag. Why in presenting 'Apollo', we ask, does he *stand with one leg across the other*? This is a question we cannot smoothly evade 'as slyly as any commenter goes by hard words, or sense'. And not to realize that it requires an answer is to disqualify ourselves as critics. For in a Device 'no place . . . figured nought', and every why hath a wherefore. The particular crossing of Will Hatcliffe's leg is no idle gesture. Like his hand on his *heart*, it is there to say something: something which an Elizabethan could read. But what? Does that oblique leg underline the diagonals multiplied on his doublet? Where shall we find *light for the right understanding of decayed knowledge herein*?

That slim silken leg slanted into my thoughts and settled there, amused to see me trot about mystified, ransacking shelves for every Apollo-description I could lay hands on—and gleaning not a hint. Not the ghost of a hint; tempting me to give up this Message of the Leg unread, as 'a speaking such As sense cannot untie'.

I might well have gone ignorant to the grave but for the helping hand of Tom Randolph—that brilliant Son of Ben 'nighest his throne of all his men' (Swinburne). Randolph earns our thanks by revealing the illuminating answer in his play *Hey for Honesty*, translated in his Cambridge days about 1628 from the *Plutus* of Aristophanes. There in the first scene the slave Carion growls, '*O, how I could cuff Apollo! I have a quarrel to Apollo, that wry-legged, riddling, fiddling god.*' Here at last is our eureka. *Wry*, says the *OED*, is (*adj.*) 'Inclined or turned to one side'; (*adv.*) 'In an oblique manner, or direction; awry'.

* *De facie in orbe Lunae*, 928B; pointed out by F. L. Schoell, *Etudes sur l'Humanisme Continental en Angleterre*, 1926, 243. Chapman, *Eugenia*, Vigilia Secunda, 212–214.

Randolph's *wry-legged god* is his translation of Aristophanes' term *Loxias*, which Henry Fielding's version of the *Plutus* gives as *that oblique deity*. For the explanation we turn to Littleton: 'Apollo was called *Loxias*; who in his replies was *loxos*, that is, *oblique*, and speaking ambiguously, so that he may be taken divers ways.'* *Obliquus* is Englished in Calepino-Passerat 1609 as 'Acrosse, awrie, or overthwart'; the verb *obliquo*, as 'To sett awrie, to crosse'; and the bird *Loxia* is 'a crossbill'.

Randolph's expression shows that in images of Delphic Apollo Orthos, the *crossing of his leg* was a recognized symbol of his *oblique* or 'riddling' oracles— *vaticinia obliquis . . . ambagibus* (Martianus Capella 1.56)—, of the truth which 'Apollo Hath clouded in hid sense' or 'wrapp'd up in cross doubtful terms'. And Prince Will's learned portrait-Device as 'Apollo' did not fail to include it, as one of the silent messages vocal to the wise.

With this (I told myself) one might reasonably leave the matter as solved. Yet before long I found my mind teased by the thought of pictures *showing* the Delphic Apollo standing in this significant pose. If such drawings were evidently familiar to Randolph and his fellows at Cambridge, where had they seen them? Why not in illustrated volumes of emblems and devices? As far back as Gabriel Harvey's time those undergraduates had been neglecting Aristotle to study Claude Paradin and Paolo Giovio,† and Sir Philip Sidney had pored over Ruscelli. But nowhere in such collections of the period had I seen any appearance or mention of the *wry-legged* Delphic Apollo. And from the detailed studies of modern scholars I could recall nothing of the sort.

Into one richly illustrated work listed by Mario Praz I had looked briefly: Principio Fabricii's six books of allusions, devices, and emblems on the life, works, and actions of the late Pope Gregory XIII (Ugo Buoncompagno), reformer of the Calendar. In this, as its engraved title-page announces, 'under the allegory of the Dragon—the arms of the said Pontiff—is described both the true form of a Christian Prince,

---

* 'Loxias Apollo dictus est, qui in suis responsis λοξος, i. *obliquus* & flexiloquus erat.' Cf. Schol. Lycophron. 1476; St. Jerome, *Epist.* 84.4; Macrobius, *Saturnalia* 1.17.31.

† E .N. S. Thompson, *Literary Bypaths of the Renaissance*, 1924, 63.

& other things . . . Rome . . . 1588'. A glance at some of its 256 excellent copperplates by Natale Bonifazio left me marvelling at the author's tireless ingenuity in dragging the Dragon of the Buoncompagni into good company of the most astonishing variety, while I sent the volume home to its shelf in the Yale Library.

Now what drew me back to Fabricii's book in search of Apollo Loxias? Was it the unforgettable date of its printing— *1588*, that terrible *octogesimus octavus* of bale-threatening world-prophecy, that *annus mirabilis* of the deadly Armada-Moon's eclipse, and the very year of our two portrait-Devices executed by Hilliard? Was it a hunch?

Well, whatever it was, with this book my luck was in. For on its page 112 I found Bonifazio's engraving of Apollo's temple: suppliants kneeling before the god's oracular cortina, while in the background on a pedestal is great Apollo radiant in glory, standing *with his legs crossed.*

And for good measure on page 132 we are given a similar scene at Trophonius' Cave. There in its gloom the deified and oracular Trophonius stands like Will Hatcliffe *with crossed legs* in flattering imitation of wry-legged Apollo's. Further, since Apollo is the type of *Veritas* or truth, it seems to me that his peculiar distinctive 'Loxias' stance was borrowed for the female figure of naked Truth, standing *cross-legged* in Bartolommeo Delbene's *Civitas veri*, 1609, 151.*

It takes no more than a glance at some of the Greek coins portraying Apollo to discover the authority which Fabricii and Bonifazio could show for the peculiar pose that presents the god as *Loxias*. For the McClean Collection at Cambridge alone affords at least two examples:

No. 8701 Lydia, Saitta. *Apollo standing . . . right leg*
Pl. 305.10.   *crossed over left.* (B.M. Cat. Lydia, p. 217, 28.)
No. 9062 Cilicia, Epiphaneia. ?A.D. 244/5. *Apollo, nude,*
Pl. 326.11.   *standing front, . . . legs crossed.*†

* Repr., with no notice of this extraordinary feature, by F. A. Yates, *The French Academies . . .*, 1947, Pl. 11a.

† S. W. Grose, *Fitzwilliam Museum. Catalogue of the McClean Collection of Greek Coins*, 1929, Vol. III.

Experts will point out more figures of Apollo Loxias. But here already is ocular proof. Young Hatcliffe's chiastic 'thwarted leggs' did not baffle the educated eye of 1588.

Before leaving those adminicular legs, we note that some critics have supposed them elongated in the painting to serve a purpose of the artist's in the design. Is it not more likely that the sitter desired them lengthened to serve his purpose of presenting 'Apollo'? For as Algarotti remarked,

> the legs and the thighs of the Apollo Belvedere, somewhat longer than just proportion would allow, contribute not a little to give him that light grace (*sveltezza*) and agility which suit so well with the comely motion (*movenza*) of that God.　　　　　*Saggio sopra la Pittura*, 1762, 44

Thus far, then, to add to the Hatcliffe-signs of True Loving Friendship shown in *Mr. W. H.* 208–215, we have now recognized him as *Apollo leaning against his Tree*; *Phoebus*, in the Sun-like ruff and the Day-and-Night of his white and black; *True Loving Apollo*, *Heart* of the World; that Delphic *oblique* deity *Apollo Loxias* both in his oblique crossed leg and in the oblique lines adorning his doublet and sleeves; and *Apollo's active grace* in the graphic lengthening of his legs. Plutarch quotes Heraclitus on Apollo's oracular communication: he 'doth neither speake, nor conceale, but signifie onely and give signe'—as Will Hatcliffe does here. (See Wind, 13 *n*.42.)

In such exquisite dress he is evidently not presenting 'a lovesick lover'. That common unthinking assumption of modern criticism is at once ruled out by Rosalind's list of the familiar requisite signs of love:

> . . . your hose should be ungarter'd . . . your sleeve unbutton'd, your shoe untied, and everything about you demonstrating a careless desolation. But you are no such man: you are rather point-device in your accoustrements.

But it is not really comfortable to reflect that, in studying this masterpiece of the great Hilliard's, not one of us has recognized the obvious character and purpose of the Prince of Purpoole's dress. If one were to mention to any Elizabethan his great ruff, his short cloak and doublet, his long white stockings and his white pumps, and then inquire *what it is that their wearer is dressed for*, the eyebrows raised at such ignorance would not be flattering.

He is dressed for the ballroom, for the *dance*. These garments are his *Inns of Court revel tire*. First, for the great ruff and the short cloak. In *Christmas his Masque* (1616), Ben Jonson presents 'MIS-RULE' in *a short Cloake, a great yellow Ruffe like a Reveller*; and Sylvester shows Apollo dancing at his own wedding in a 'saffron'd Ruffe'. (Queen Elizabeth loathed yellow. These quotations are Jacobean, after the introduction of yellow—saffron—starch.)

> I shall shortly   [*i.e.*, 'an Inns
> Be one myself. I learn to dance already,   of Court man']
> And wear short cloaks. I mean in your next masque
> To have a part.   Jasper Mayne, *The City-Match* 1.5

> Then came the [Nine] Maskers [of the Middle Temple, 1599]
> in their short cloaks and doublets.
>   Sir Benjamin Rudyard, 'Noctes Templariae'

> . . . in the capring [capering] cloake
>   Marston, *Scourge of Villanie*, 1598, F5ᵛ

Next, for the 'high paire of silke netherstocks that couered all his buttockes and loignes'—Lord Leicester's fashion:

> Or if you had but your long stockings on, to be dancing
> a galliard . . .   Jonson, *Every Man Out* . . . 3.9.53

> Why, I haue beene a reueller, and at . . . my long stocking,
> in my time.   Jonson, *Poetaster* 3.1.175–176

> I cannot revel in long stockings, frisk
> To please your wanton eyesight.
>   Shirley, *The Humorous Courtier* 2.2

And for the white pumps:

> Last night which did our *Ins* of court men call
> In silken sutes like gawdy Butterflies
> To paint the Torch-light sommer of the hall [*main roof-beam*]
> And shew good legs . . .

He passing from his chamber through the Court
Did spoile a paire of new white pumps with durt.
E. Guilpin, Skialetheia, 1598, B4

. . . the Orbes celestiall
Will daunce Kemps Iigge. They'le reuel with neate iumps
A worthy Poet hath put on their Pumps.
Marston, The Scourge of Villanie, 1598, H3^v

John Davys avers that Dancing is 'of Man's fellowship the true-love knot' and that 'true love . . . dancing did invent'. It is therefore most fitting that Prince True-love, leader of Purpoole's revels, presents himself in his Device as True Loving Apollo Terpsichoros. Phoebus Apollo's crowning musical grace was his *dancing*.

> At last the golden Orientall gate
> Of greatest heauen gan to open faire,
> And *Phœbus* fresh, as bridegrome to his mate,
> Came dauncing forth . . .
Spenser, Faerie Queene 1.5.2.1–4

> For that braue Sunne, the Father of the Day,
> Doth loue this Earth, the Mother of the Night;
> And like a reuellour in rich aray,
> Doth daunce his galliard in his lemman's sight,
> Both back, and forth, and sidewaies, passing light;
>   His princely grace doth so the gods amaze,
>   That all stand still and at his beauty gaze.

> When the great Torch-bearer of Heauen was gone
> Downe in a maske vnto the Ocean's Court,
> To reuell it with Thetis all alone . . .
John Davys, Orchestra, 1596, 39 &7

The *Homeric Hymn to Pythian Apollo*, as Chapman translates it, presents a heavenly dance:

> Phœbus-Apollo toucht his Lute to them
> Sweetely and softly, a most glorious beame
> Casting about him as he danc't and plaid . . .

In the Pitti Gallery at Florence is Giulio Romano's painting, *The Muses dancing with Apollo on Parnassus*—as Ronsard writes,

> Et Phebus qui conduit des neuf Muses le bal . . .
> > *Œuvres*, ed. Laumonier, 6.262

John Day, similarly,

> Apollo and the Muses daunce:
> Art hath banish'd Ignorance.
> > *The Parliament of Bees*, Char. 12

and Michael Drayton,

> vpon that very day
> *Phœbus* was seene the Reueller to play . . .
> > *Endimion and Phœbe*, 183–184

The dramatic dances performed at Florence 1589, to celebrate the wedding of the Grand Duke, featured importantly both the choreography of Apollo's fight with the Python and his dance of joy at having freed the Delphians from that frightful monster; and a few years later both were included in Rinuccini's *Dafne*. (A. Warburg, *op. cit.*, 1.275, 288, 295.) And for England, Lord Falkland presents 'mighty *Charles*' as King Apollo, dancing in Ben Jonson's masques:

> And oft hath left his bright exalted *Throne*,
> And to his *Muses* feet combin'd His owne.
> > *Jonsonus Virbius*, 1638

Perhaps at this point we should pause to consider a modern suggestion which has been offered more than once. Namely, that the YOUTH in Hilliard's masterpiece might be the Earl of Essex. But (apart from the utter dissimilarity of the two faces) when we reflect that the 'poetical character' assumed for the Device is True Loving Delphic Apollo Terpsichoros, King of Dancers, we recognize the extreme implausibility of the suggestion.

Everyone knows that Essex thirsted for glory in war, and reasonably aimed at excelling as a soldier. Shortly after Hilliard's miniature of the YOUTH (*ca.* 1588), the handsome portrait in oils of *Robert Devereux Earle of Essex 1590* (National

Gallery, Dublin) shows the Earl harnessed in steel, girt with sword and dagger, and holding the truncheon of command. Another of this date owned by the Earl of Jersey presents him similarly accoutred. In 1594 Saviolo dedicated his manual of swordsmanship to Essex as 'the English Achilles'; in 1598 Chapman addressed him as 'Most true Achilles'; and after his death William Browne recalls him as 'A brave, heroic, worthy Martialist'.

We know too that he aimed (less reasonably) also at excelling as a politic statesman. But never as a *dancer*—such as the well-graced Sir Christopher Hatton, 'who came to the Court by the galliard, for he came thither as a private gentleman of the Inns of Court in a masque'. For Essex's secretary and intimate Sir Henry Wotton, after recalling the Earl's astonishing carelessness of his dress, observes 'he was so far from being a good Dancer, that he was no graceful goer'. Essex did not even *walk* with grace.

Now in a portrait-Device 'the garments and ensignes deliver the nature of the person'; or, again, 'the habits must be proper to the . . . humour of the person'. Essex, in short, might conceivably present himself in a Device as 'Mars' or as 'Achilles'. But Essex as 'Apollo the all-graced Dancer'? A question not to be asked.

To return to our sitter. When writing *Mr. W. H.* and identifying the YOUTH as Will Hatcliffe, Prince of Revels at Gray's Inn, I failed to see the unmistakable corroboration displayed by his conspicuous Inns of Court revel tire. This failure shows, first, that I did not know how to look with eyes at all like the eyes of 1588; and second, that if I could not see a thing so obvious as that, there must be *more* still hidden from me.

Since his portrait is the 'body' of Hatcliffe's Device, 'to be understood by some but not by all', Hilliard naturally did not inscribe it with the sitter's name, or even with his age. But such Devices by definition 'concealed in themselves many fine secrets'—such as the one which Peter Paul Rubens later incorporated in his portrait-group called 'The Four Philosophers', seated under a bust of Seneca (Pitti Gallery, Florence).

Beside the bust he painted an unobtrusive vase of tulips. Was this mere ornament? A needless grace? Only in 1964 could we read the note made before 1941 by Ernst Friedrich von Monroy,* revealing its lost significance. Like the persons portrayed, the tulips are *four*. And *two of the four* blooms *have faded*, to intimate that *two of the four* 'Philosophers' shown (Justus Lipsius and Philip Rubens) *had died* before Rubens painted the picture. Here, at length re-seen by modern eyes, is a typical 'fine secret'. And now we shall find that Hilliard earlier had not failed to insert a similar secret to please the connoisseur.

The story is this. Among those more experienced than I in unravelling symbolic art there was luckily one who read *Mr. W. H.* He was Professor Stillman Drake of the University of Toronto, the eminent interpreter of Galileo. And though Mr. Drake did not get round to reading the book until 1967, he then promptly and most generously passed his discovery on to me.

It was the *unnatural* feature which Hilliard imported into this masterpiece that caught Mr. Drake's practised eye; and he at once scrutinized it. He noticed that (set off against the black cloak near the YOUTH's mid-thigh) there is *one branch* which—in striking contrast with all the normal, acute-angled branches of the brier—*unnaturally* grows out from the stem *almost at a right angle*. And that thereby, *as a crossbar* between the vertical stem and the vertical section of another branch, *it forms a capital H*. And what is more, immediately above that capital H four acute branches free of leaves form *a capital W*.

> So true it is that most often we need someone to show us that which should, as it seems, have leapt to the eyes of all.   Algarotti, *Saggio sopra l'Architettura*, 1784, 8

For of course when once you have seen it, that stylishly growing *W H* stands out conspicuous whenever you glance at the painting—just as the *white hands* in CLASPING A HAND and the *tulips* of Rubens now do. But only eyes such as Stillman Drake's, trained to the Age of Symbolism, were able to notice it in the first place.

* Died 17 September 1941, aged 27. His *Embleme und Emblembücher in den Niederlanden 1560–1630* was edited with commentary by Frhr. H. M. von Erffa in 1964. See its page 110.

Before that unlooked-for discovery reached me, however, the YOUTH's *tree*, his *crossed leg*, and his *revel tire*, when added to the *True Loving Apollo* and *Prince Will Hatcliffe* features we have seen displayed in his portrait-Device, had for me already placed the keystone of the arch. For from the *Gesta Grayorum*, Campion, Chapman, and others, we knew that the 'Grayans' were commonly played upon as *Graii*: Greeks. Also that Gray's Inn, by choosing for its arms—still borne today— *Apollo's emblem* the golden Griffin (*Knowledge*),* had blazoned its Delphic claim; that therefore Henry their Prince was *ex officio* their Apollo, and of course *presented Apollo* by his crest, 'the glorious planet *Sol* . . . supported by two . . . *Griffyns*'; likewise, that the boy-orator of St. Paul's School must necessarily exhort this Apollo to 'return to your Palace of Purpoole, Oracle of the Graii [its gate pointedly distinguished by Apollo's Tree],† by which as by the soothsaying voice of *Delphic Apollo* all disputes are ended'.

Here we had the unmistakable equation *Prince of Purpoole* = *Delphic Apollo* repeatedly stated. And our knowledge that *publicly in 1588* (reigning privately for several years thereafter) *the only known Prince of Revels in London was William Hatcliffe of Gray's Inn* clinched the identification. We hardly need to recall the other clincher which Gray's Inn found in Hatcliffe's family arms to display him as their Phoebus Apollo—*his crest*, the *Lion*: for 'The Signe of the *Lion* (in Heaven) is by all Astrologers made the proper Palace of the *Sun*, and the *Device* of PHEBVS.' (Sadler, *op. cit.*, 8.)

---

* 'The griffin, emblem of the Hyperborean Apollo.' D. Osborne, *Engraved Gems*, 208; 'The two Griffins and the Tripos are the Symbols of Apollo.' R. Cowdry, *Curiosities of Wilton House*, 1752, 30; Apollo is All-Knowing: at Chartres his Griffin symbolizes *Knowledge*. J. J. M. Timmers, *Symboliek en Iconographie*, 1957, no. 1257; and like Apollo's fabulous wise *Grifo*, 'il Drago, presa communemente per la sapienza'. Principio Fabricii da Teramo, *Delle Allusioni* . . . , 1588, 138; 'Nel Grifo . . . significauano Apolline'. Capaccio, *Delle Imprese*, 1592 108ᵛ; 'Huic Deo [Apollini] gryphes . . . dicati sunt.' Conti, *Mythologiæ*, lib. 4. c. 10. And it was not beyond the learned Graii (Greeks) of Gray's Inn to point to the identity of *Greeks* and *Griffons*. See the *OED*: Griffon[1] *obs. rare.* (OF griffon, grifon) A Greek.

† 'hoope it about like the tree at *Grays-Inne* gate'. Nashe, *Have with you* . . . , 1596, F2ᵛ.

Having found more conclusive evidence than any detective could have expected, I was satisfied. But Stillman Drake's totally unforeseen gift of those initials, standing with their owner in these thorny briers, seems a notable case of 'whosoever hath, to him shall be given'.

I now look back with no pleasure at a passage I set down in *Mr. W. H.* about this portrait:

> Indeed if Hilliard had added to it a name beginning with the initials W and H, it would long since have been claimed as a painting of Shakespeare's hero.

For I wrote this while blind to the plain ocular evidence that Hilliard *had* at least added to it those famous initials. As soon as the picture was painted, any discerning eye would see that this graceful Master of the Revels of 1588, presenting himself with his Pompey-lemma from Lucan as 'Delphic Apollo, the True Loving Friend', was *labelled* 'W H'.

*   *   *

We are now equipped to subject our proposed solution of this second portrait-Device to the tests prescribed.

First, then, Does the lemma *Dat pœnas laudata fides* (*sc.* dum sustinet . . . Quos fortuna premit)—'*Faith, though praised, is punished* (while it supports those whom Fortune crushes)'— *complete* the picture and make it intelligible?

Answer, Yes: it does this by revealing that the figure shown *punished* is not some unfortunate abandoned in the thorny briers, but *the faithful Friend, who willingly stands constant among them, as if by his Fortune-crushed friend.*

> Hee that is thy friend indeede,
> Hee will helpe thee in thy neede; . . .
> These are certaine signes, to know
> Faithfull friend, from flatt'ring foe.
> *The Passionate Pilgrime*, 423–424, 429–430

> That's *Love in earnest*, which is constant found,
> When Friends are in *Affliction* . . .
> George Wither, *Emblemes*, 1635, 237

Apollo saith Love is a relative,
Whose being only must in others be.
Fulke Greville, *Caelica* LXX

For the *true love* white roses say, 'I am not where I am, but with my love.'

Again, Does the picture as we have read it *complete* the lemma and make it intelligible?

Answer, Yes: it does this by adding that the true *faith* which *is punished* for its loving loyalty to Fortune's victim in Lucan's phrase is no abstract virtue, but *the faithful god, True Loving Delphic Apollo*.

*   *   *

Such encouragement emboldens us to a fresh look at this *impresa*-portrait. And recalling Albani's rule, drawn from a close study of Raphael, *it behoves a painter to express by every attitude more circumstances than one*, we ask, May not the learned deviser have conveyed something more by this *Apollo against his Tree among White Roses and Thorns* besides 'True Loving Apollo Constant in Adversity'?

Only now are we equipped to understand Shakespeare's repeated hint: 59.7 *Your image in some antique booke* and 68.9 *In him those holy antique howers are seene*. With the Elizabethans, eager to appropriate the glories of classical antiquity, not only was London (*Augusta Trinovantum*) called *Troynovant* (Spenser) or *Nue rearèd Troy* (Peele) but her proud heraldic badge or cognizance was '*Troy*' (British Library MS. Addl. 14919 f. 53^V; Bodl. MS. Ashm. 337 f. 138^V.); and *Troy's builder and defender* was *Apollo. Pro Troia stabat Apollo*. Query: Is there something here obvious to the Grayans of Delphic Purpoole marking Hatcliffe as 'our *Apollo of ancient Troynovant*'?

Where had lovers of antiquity *with a back-ward looke, Euen of fiue hundreth courses of the Sunne* (59.5–6) seen 'our New Troy's Apollo'? We turn to Stow's *Chronicles of England*, 1580, 98:

> *Sebert* [King of the East Saxons *ca.* 602] . . . embraced Christianitie, and (immediately to shewe himselfe a Christian,) builte a Churche to the honour of *Saint Peter*, on the West side of *London*, in a place whiche bycause it

was ouergrowen with Thornes and enuironed with Waters, the Saxons . . . called it *Thorney*, and nowe of the Monasterie and West scituation is called *Westminster*. [Preserved today in *Thorney Street*, Horseferry Road to Millbank.]

In this place long before was a Temple of *Apollo* (as *Sulcardus* writeth) [*ca.* 1075, the Abbey's historian *500 years before*].

'Moreover . . . if *London* of old had her Temple of *Diana*, *Westminster* had one to a greater Deity, which was *Apollo*.' (James Howel, *Londinopolis*, 1657, 346.)

Here in Thorn-ey, the *Isle of Thorns* by New Troy, *of yore*, in *daies out-worne*, stood our British Apollo. Now in 1588, presented with a British Apollo standing *among thorns*,* if (even when prompted by the Sonnets) you fail to recognize him, either you've neglected your *antique book* of local history, or you've forgotten the fleet-foot *holy antique Hours*, faithful attendants of their King, Apollo.

And Shakespeare, in adapting the lines of Ovid's Apollo (*Met.* 1.509) to describe a painting of Daphne, made it more British than we have realized. Unlike Ovid, he presented her already *lacerated and bleeding* before a weeping *Apollo in a thorny wood*:

> Or *Daphne* roming through a thornie wood,
> Scratching her legs, that one shal sweare she bleeds,
> And at that sight shal sad Apollo weepe,
> So workmanlie the blood and teares are drawne.
>
> *The Taming of the Shrew* Ind. 2.59–62

This striking feature appears nowhere in the scores of 'Apollo-Daphne' drawings reproduced in Stechow's exhaustive iconographical study. He finds it only in this same *thorny wood* passage from Shakespeare. (Wolfgang Stechow, *Apollo und Daphne*, 1932, 40 *n.*3.)

*　　*　　*

* *Thorn* or *Canker* was a common name for the Brier-rose: 'this Thorne, this Canker' 1 *Hen. IV* 1.3.176; and Sonnet 54.5, 7: *The Canker bloomes . . . Hang on such thornes.*

'A most beautiful Device, certainly', like those of Marcantonio Epicuro; and we speculate as to its deviser. We cannot
exclude the possibility that Will Hatcliffe may have thought it
out for himself. After all, he had been chosen Sovereign of
Purpoole, one of the 'noblest nurseries of humanity and liberty
in the kingdom'; and among its rules we read that

> ... every Knight of this Order shall endeavour to add
> conference and experience by reading; and therefore shall
> not only read and peruse Guizo [Guazzo], the French
> Academy, Galiatto [*Galateo*], the Courtier, Plutarch, the
> Arcadia ... but also frequent the Theatre ... whereby
> they may not only become accomplished with civil con-
> versations ... but also sufficient ... to make epigrams,
> emblems, and other devices, appertaining to [the Prince
> of Purpoole's] learned Revels.

Among Will's Purpoole-subjects were numbered both Abraham Fraunce, the poet from whose work of 1588 on the Device
we have quoted, and the painter and herald William Segar,
afterwards chosen Garter King of Arms and later knighted,
who contrived the devices presented 1594/5 at Court by the
Knights of Will's successor as Prince, Henry Helmes.

But I incline to think that his *Dat pœnas* betrays the learning,
the skill of a high expert. And if so, Will Hatcliffe had an
eminent craftsman of *imprese* at hand, upon whose affectionate
favour and interest he could count. This was his father's first
cousin, the celebrated William Skipwith, already described
on p. 24. Skipwith's learning, more than equal to planning
all the 'Apollo' features we have noted, including the crossed
leg, is evidenced by his surviving translation of Juvenal. In
1582, when the fourteen-year-old Will went up a freshman to
Jesus College Cambridge, he was welcomed to the high table
by his experienced cousin Will Skipwith, already in his third
year as a fellow-commoner of Jesus.

A few years later, when young Hatcliffe had achieved great-
ness in London by being 'instated in his throne' of Purpoole
as Apollo of the *Graii*, and desired a portrait-Device supremely
appropriate to give to his humble 'renowner' and poet-friend
—one *made lame by Fortune's dearest spite*—he could not have

done better than to turn to that leading expert in *impresa-*
making, his cousin Will Skipwith.

*   *   *

We know that Hilliard limned the poet Ralegh and also
Penelope Rich, the poet Sidney's Stella. Experts hold that he
painted the poet Donne as well. Our present discovery, that—
and as perhaps his greatest masterpiece—he painted *my loues
picture*: Prince Will, 'Apollo W H', the *Sun, Sovereign, God,* and
Friend of the Sonnets, at once brings Hilliard very close to the
poet Shakespeare. Dr. Otto Kurz has shown that John Davies,
who familiarly reminds 'good *Will*' that he might have 'bin a
companion for a *King*', was also an intimate friend of Hilliard's
leading apprentice Rowland Lockey. We now realize that this
painter-friend of Shakespeare's Davies was living with Hilliard
—and soon to be taking up his indentures—at the very time
when his master painted the poet's Friend as 'King Apollo the
Faithful Friend'.

Now we have already seen the honour-giving royal Hand
of 'Apollo' clasped in friendship by 'Mercury' in Hilliard's
execution of that other portrait-Device of 1588: our MAN's.

The fact that these two works of Hilliard's are contemporaries, and the fact that they share not only *the figure of 'Apollo'*
but also *the singular theme of True Friendship (fides) between a
superior and an inferior*—which was held by all (*Mr. W. H.*, 300)
to be impossible or at best impermanent among mortals—
argue that these Devices belong together; that the 'Apollo' in
both is the same man: indicating that these *imprese* of 1588—
like the *sigilla, little images of the gods* which Roman friends gave
each other at the Saturnalia—were exchanged as New Year's
gifts* by the two young friends 'Mercury' and 'Apollo'; and
each was based upon the fact known to the London of 1588:
the True Friendship joining those Unequals, the humble

---

* 1 January 1588/9 was still '1588' (and Leap Year 1588 ran from 29
February 1587/8 to 28 February 1588/9). It was 'the general, if not
invariable, custom to carry on the old year to 24 March, while observing
1 January as New Year's Day.' A. F. Pollard, in *The English Historical
Review*, April 1940.

eloquent poet-and-renowner suffering *the spite of Fortune* and his glorious *sovereign* who *honours him with public kindness*.

And since the Sonnets of Shakespeare's pupil pen belong to the period from late 1587 to 1589, and since the painted 'Apollo W H' is the 1588 Prince of Purpoole Will Hatcliffe, the plebeian poet's *Sun, King, God*, and his dear Friend *Will*, every piece of evidence points one way. Namely, to an inkling that the poet 'Mercury' clasping the hand of 'King Phoebus Apollo' in our miniature may be *Nicholas Hilliard's portrait of the young William Shakespeare*.

This tremendous surmise has already been forecast. Reviewing Dr. Auerbach's *Nicholas Hilliard* (*Sunday Times*, 28 May 1961), that perceptive critic Raymond Mortimer recognized in her half-tone reproduction of the *Howard* that Hilliard's *'wide-eyed man grasping a hand could be Shakespeare himself'*.

Our present study has thrown fresh revealing light from his own time upon his figure. With identifying features unnoticed hitherto now manifest to all, has our Invisible Man under our opened eyes emerged into view, at last *effectually seen for what he is*? Have we in fact here before us the only known living likeness of the master poet of the modern world?

These are grave questions. They cannot be answered without more evidence—including the relevant personal testimony presented by young Shakespeare himself. And we shall consider that capital evidence in its proper place.

7

Shakespeare, that Nimble *Mercury*

IN Chapter 4 we saw the multiplied and unmistakable signs of Mercury displayed by the MAN CLASPING A HAND of his royal 'Apollo' of 1588 in friendly love: an act strongly recalling Shakespeare's own sonnet-theme of that date. Could this 'Mercury' be the poet Shakespeare? In weighing the possibility, one's natural first question would be *Did men of his own time think of him as Mercury?* I have never seen this question raised by any Shakespearean. Here however this question is imperative. It must be both asked and answered.

For us, Shakespeare is the supreme Poet. And if with him in mind we turn up *Mercury* and *Mercurial* in the *OED*, we read as follows:

> *Mercury* I. 1. A Roman divinity, identified from an early period with the Greek Hermes (son of Jupiter and Maia), the god of eloquence and feats of skill, the protector of traders and thieves, the presider over roads, the conductor of departed souls to the Lower World, and the messenger of the gods . . .
>
> *Mercurial* 3. Of persons: Born under the planet Mercury; having the qualities supposed to proceed from such a nativity, as eloquence, ingenuity, aptitude for commerce.
>
> 4. Volatile, sprightly, and ready-witted.

The terms *poet* or *poetical* do not appear; and certainly the modern connotations of 'eloquence' and 'ingenuity' are not enough to bring the thought of *poetry* to our minds.* What we

* Again from the *OED*:

Eloquence 1. The action, practice, or art of expressing thought with fluency, force, and appropriateness so as to appeal to the reason or move the feelings . . . Primarily of oral utterance, and hence applied to writing that has the characteristics of good oratory.

need for that is the missing term *imagination*, found nowhere in these definitions.

But on examination it seems that this might be another case of 'decayed knowledge' which has escaped the historical lexicographer. The question here of course is not what *we* think about Mercury, but what Shakespeare's contemporaries thought about him. And on inquiry it amply appears that if for them *Apollo* was the far-off god of poets and poetry, the one at hand was *Mercury*, the *Poet*.

Hermes Logios, Lord of Language and Wisdom, was fabled as the one *immortal god* among the four most ancient *poets*: 'Orpheus, Musæus, Mercurius, Linus, antiquissimi poetæ';* and L. A. Cornutus (*De Natura Deorum*) says that Mercury was held to be *mantis* or *vates*—'a true divining poet'. In Dürer's drawing, Vienna, MANTIS is one of Hermes' names. Astrology affirms that Mercury's planet 'is the governour of imagination, fantasie, and cogitation'.† Eloquent poets in the sixteenth century were *Mercurians*:

> Mercuriens deserts poetes   [*i.e.*, *diserts*
> Enfans des neuf muses cheris.
>
> > Marseille d'Altouvitis, qu. F. Godefroy,
> > *Dict. de l'Anc. Langue Fr.*, 1938, 5.256

And the admirer's praise of the poet Pontus de Tyard is his supreme *Mercuriality*:

> Ce grand Pontus en sa grandeur assemble
> Tout le plus grand des grandeurs de Mercure.
>
> > Qu. *Œuvres de Pontus de Tyard*
> > J. C. Lapp, 1966, 126

Ingenuity 6. Capacity for invention or construction; skill or cleverness in contriving or making something (material or immaterial) . . . (The current use.)

* Conti, lib. 1. c. 6. And G.-B. della Porta, *De Occultis Literarum Notis*, 2nd ed., Strassburg 1603, 20.

† D. Origanus, *Ephemerides*, 1633, 52. Compare Jean Le Maire de Belges (16th c.): 'le noble Dieu Mercure, duquel la planette est . . . maistresse de vertu imaginative, fantastique et cogitante'. Qu. Ludwig Schrader, *Panurge und Hermes*, 1958, 102.

Tom Nashe, apostrophizing the dead poet Sidney as 'Astrophel', sees him deified and supplanting Mercury: 'thy diuine Soule, carried on Angels wings to heauen, is installed, in *Hermes* place, sole *prolocutor* to the Gods'. And Gabriel Harvey for once agrees with him: 'Astrophill . . . an other Mercury at all dexterities, and how delitious a Planet of heauenly harmony.' (*Astr. and Stella*, 1591, Pref.; *Pierces supererogation*, 1593, X3.)

Renaissance art represented poets and painters as *children of Mercury* (Jean Seznec, *op. cit.*, 70f.); and William Rankins called poets '*Hermes* lawful sonnes in wit', while John Marston addressed them as *Mercurys*: 'Ye sacred spirits, *Mayas* eldest sonnes.' In the Cambridge *Parnassus* plays, the foolish Gullio boasts himself '*tam Marti quam Mercurio*; insomuche that I am pointed at for a poet in Pauls church yarde, and in the tilte yard for a champion', and the swaggering windbag Furor Poeticus makes his fustian vaunt—'I am the bastard of great *Mercurie*, Got on *Thalia* when she was a sleepe.' For Richard Brathwait, England's poets are '*Albions Mercuries*'. Addressing William Browne as a born poet, John Davies of Hereford concludes,

> *Hermes*, it seemes, to thee, of all the *Swaines*,
> Hath lent his *Pipe* and *Art*.

Robert Burton (*Anat. Mel.* 1.3.1.3) lays it down that '*Mercurialists* are . . . Poets', and Tom Randolph in his *Jealous Lovers* 3.5 offers two poets '*personating two Mercuries*'. The anonymous sonneteer of *Zepheria* (1594) declares—

> Ye moderne Lawreats famous'd for your writ, . . .
> On your sweet lines eternitie doth sit; . . .
> . . . nay *Hermes* tunes the praises
> Which ye in sonnets to your mistresse giue.

Already we have noted the claim of classical and Renaissance poets to *godlike* faculty. And they obtained that endowment by *Mercury's* means. For as Conti states, it is Mercury only who brings 'that divine power from God which is poured into the minds of men'. Further, it was not Apollo's lyre, but *Mercury's moly* (*Eloquence*) which Tasso, prince of Italian poets, appropriated with the word DEORUM MUNUS, the Gift of the Gods. To Gabriel Harvey the poet Sidney was 'the secretary of *eloquence*'; and to William Basse the poet Spenser was similarly 'a swaine profound and *eloquent*'.

After hearing such a flood of testimony, it is only natural to find that epithets which English writers employed to describe 'Poem', 'Poesie', 'Poetrie', 'Poet'—such as *divine, powerful, intrancing, sweet, sugred, ingenious, witty, artful, lying, facetious, pleasant, sprightly, well-drest, brisk, nimble, lively*—describe *Mercury*, and none but Mercury. (Joshua Poole, *English Parnassus*, 1657, ed. 1677, 151.)

In the *New York Times* of 22 January 1967, I find Walter Kerr using the phrase 'to create an illusion of poetry, of mercury ...' Perhaps I relied too much on the *OED* in supposing the identity of Mercury and Poetry possibly 'decayed knowledge' today. And H. J. Rose in the *Oxford Classical Dictionary* does mention that the god 'became in time the general patron of literature', quoting Horace's epithet for literary men, *Mercuriales viri*. But whatever the case today, the passages I have cited leave no doubt of the fact: namely, that to look with the eyes of 1588 at a man painted in a poetical *impresa* as 'Mercury' is at once and infallibly to see *the Poet*.

*   *   *

Nothing could be more imperatively called for here than a fresh scrutiny of Shakespeare's figure in the minds of his contemporaries: of Shakespeare's image as painted in their praise of him. They will answer our question, Did *you* see him as Mercury?

Let us begin with two eulogies of Shakespeare alive, published 1614. First, Thomas Freeman of Magdalen College Oxford writes

To Master W. Shakespeare.

Shakespeare, that nimble *Mercury* thy braine,
Lulls many hundred *Argus*-eyes asleepe,

So fit for all thou fashionest thy vaine,
At th'*horse-foote* fountaine thou hast drunk full deepe . . .
    Epigr. 92 in his *Runne and a great Cast*, qu. Chambers,
                       William Shakespeare, 1930, 2.220

—that is, at the Muses' *Hippocrene* on Mount Helicon, 'that *Well*
Whence gurgle streames of Art, and sacred Skill.' (H[enry]
G[oodere], *The Mirrour of Maiestie*, 1618, Emb. 24.)

Freeman sees Shakespeare's brain as Mercury, supremely
quick and resourceful: Marston's 'quick braynd MERCVRY'.
Further, so all-pleasing is his great poetic power, that when
success draws upon him jealous 'Hundred-eyed Envy' (Barnes,
Parthenophil and Parthenophe, 1593, dedicatory sonnet), *it can
charm even that Envy to sleep*. With Shakespeare (as Nashe had
said of Sidney) it is now 'Sleepe *Argus*, sleep Ignorance, sleep
Impudence, for *Mercury* hath *Io*.'

The other eulogy of 1614 presents C[hristopher] B[rooke]'s
Ghost of Richard the Third, declaring

To him that impt my fame with Clio's quill;   [*reinforced*
Whose magick rais'd me from Obliuion's den;
That writ my storie on the Muses hill;
And with my actions dignifi'd his pen:
He that from Helicon sends many a rill;
Whose nectared veines, are drunke by thirstie men:
   Crown'd be his stile with fame; his head, with bayes;
   And none detract, but gratulate his praise.

Yet if his scænes haue not engrost all grace,
The much fam'd action could extend on stage.
                      Qu. Chambers, 2.219–220

Again Shakespeare is Mercury. In his conjuring up the spirit
of the long-dead Crookback he is seen as Hermes Psychagogos,
Marston's 'Mercury, the god of Ghosts'; his *magick* is

               this awefull Wand,
    With this th'Infernal Ghosts I can command.
        Mercury in Dryden's *Albion and Albanius*

Mercury–Shakespeare, god of poetic eloquence, is properly 'on
the Muses hill', and the immortalizing nectar of his poetry
inspires men.

In the lines of *I.M.S.* written for the Second Folio 1632,* this image of Shakespeare as swift Mercury, the god stronger than Fate, reappears—now drawn in full lively detail:

On Worthy Master Shakespeare
and his Poems.

> *. . . To out run hasty time, retrive the fates,*
> *Rowle backe the heavens, blow ope the iron gates*
> *Of death and Lethe . . .*
> *In that deepe duskie dungeon to discerne*
> *A royall Ghost from Churles; By art to learne*
> *The Physiognomie of shades, and give*
> *Them suddaine birth . . .*
> *To raise our auncient Soveraignes from their herse . . .*
> *Enlive their pale trunkes . . .*
>   *This, and much more which cannot bee exprest,*
> *But by himselfe, his tongue and his owne brest,*
> *Was* Shakespeares *freehold, which his cunning braine*
> *Improv'd by favour of the ninefold traine*

—the Muses, who 'woo'd him', 'lov'd as a brother'. Again Shakespeare's 'cunning braine' is Mercury's; the Muses love him as a brother; and his caduceus gives England's royal ghosts 'sudden birth', as in the Edinburgh pageantry for Charles I in 1633: 'Mercury, with . . . his caduceus, with an hundred and seven Scottish kings, which he had brought from the Elysian fields.'

But quoting from the Second Folio 1632 has drawn us ahead of our investigation, which began with two eulogies of Shakespeare as Mercury in 1614, two years before he died. And the dates of our next illustrations need to be determined before being presented.

To reflect upon Shakespeare's death is to stir a query in our minds about epicediums: that is, *elegiac verses written on the occasion of his loss,* like those poured out at the deaths of Sidney and of Jonson. Such verses are of course at once distinguishable from retrospective praise (written years later) by their ex-

* The unknown *I.M.S.* I identify as Sir John Suckling, and am preparing to publish the evidence of his authorship.

pressions. When these present the shock of sudden loss, tears, fresh grief, funeral, burial, 'now you are gone', etc., no matter how long they may have waited for publication they betray the date of their composition: *shortly after the sad news was broken in April 1616.*

If we now look through *The Shakspere Allusion-Book* (1909) applying this obvious test—which is something I have never seen done—we at once recognize three such timely elegies or epicediums.

First, and most familiar, we have William Basse's 16-line 'Elegie upon the death of Mr Wilyam Shakespeare',* beginning *Renownëd Spencer, lye a thought more nye* . . . Edmond Malone was convinced that it was 'written recently after Shakespeare's death'. For Basse writes of 'this day', urging that the poet should sleep (in the Abbey) either as a *fourth* with Spenser, Chaucer, and Beaumont, or in a marble tomb by himself. Although Jonson pointedly refers to it in his tribute to Shakespeare for the Folio 1623, Basse's elegy did not get into type until 1633. Its only noticeable allusion to 'Mercury'– Shakespeare is its emphasis on *fourth.*†

Second, there is the moving lament of the poet Hugh Holland (1571–1633), not printed until the appearance of the First Folio seven years later:

Vpon the Lines and Life of the Famous
Scenicke Poet, Master WILLIAM
SHAKESPEARE.

Those hands, which you so clapt, go now, and wring
You *Britaines* braue; for done are *Shakespeares* dayes:
His dayes are done, that made the dainty Playes,
Which made the Globe of heau'n and earth to ring.
Dry'de is that veine, dry'd is the *Thespian* Spring,
Turn'd all to teares, and *Phœbus* clouds his rayes:
That corp's, that coffin now besticke those bayes,

---

* The title of a copy in British Library MS. Addl. 15227 f. 77, not mentioned either in the *Allusion-Book* or by Chambers.

† '*Mercury* . . . was reckon'd the fourth of the *Samothracian* Gods . . .' Dr. William King (1663–1712), *An Historical Account of the Heathen Gods*, 2nd ed. 1722, 99.

Which crown'd him *Poet* first, then *Poets* King.
If *Tragedies* might any *Prologue* haue,
All those he made, would scarse make one to this:
Where *Fame*, now that he gone is to the graue
(Deaths publique tyring-house) the *Nuncius* is.
   For though his line of life went soone about,
   The life yet of his lines shall neuer out.

Holland is clear: now that the Poet Mercury–Shakespeare—
Heaven's *Nuncius* or Herald, Horace's *magni Iovis et deorum
Nuntium*—is gone to the grave, his goddess-daughter, ever-
living *Fame*, fills his place, triumphing—like him—over Fate.*
And third, there is the least-known but most impressive
unsigned Elegy following, which had to wait till 1640 to be
published by Benson, *Poems . . .,* L-L^v:†

*An Elegie on the death of that
famous Writer and Actor,*
M. William Shakespeare.

I Dare not doe thy Memory that wrong,
Vnto our larger griefes to give a tongue;
Ile onely sigh in earnest, and let fall
My solemne teares at thy great Funerall;
For every eye that raines a showre for thee,
Laments thy losse in a sad Elegie.
Nor is it fit each humble Muse should have,
Thy worth his subject, now th'art laid in grave;
No its a flight beyond the pitch of those,
Whose worthles Pamphlets are not sence in Prose.
Let learnëd *Iohnson* sing a Dirge for thee,
And fill our Orbe with mournefull harmony:
But we neede no Remembrancer, thy Fame
Shall still accompany thy honoured Name,
To all posterity; and make us be,

* Eupheme, Fama Bona—'Celestiall goddesse euer-liuing fame,/
Mineruaes daughter by faire *Maias* sonne' (Charles Fitzgeffrey, *Drake* 1596)
—inherited her father's power over Fate or the Fates; and at the Tuileries
garden—crowning the entrance-pillars—we see Coysevox's *Mercury and
Fame* mounted on winged steeds.

† Chambers unaccountably omits both this Elegy and the lines of
I.M.S. printed in the Second Folio.

Sensible of what we lost in losing thee:
Being the Ages wonder whose smooth Rhimes
Did more reforme than lash the looser Times.
Nature her selfe did her owne selfe admire,
As oft as thou wert pleasëd to attire
Her in her native lusture, and confesse,   [*lustre*
Thy dressing was her chiefest comlinesse.
How can we then forget thee, when the age
Her chiefest Tutor, and the widdowed Stage
Her onely favorite in thee hath lost,
And Natures selfe what she did bragge of most.
Sleepe then riche soule of numbers, whilst poore we,
Enjoy the profits of thy Legacie;
And thinke it happinesse enough we have,
So much of thee redeemëd from the grave,
As may suffice to enlighten future times,
With the bright lustre of thy matchlesse Rhimes.

Repr. *The Sh. Allusion-Book*,
re-ed. J. Munro 1909, 1.422–423

Instead of the editors' preposterous '*About* 1637', this Elegy by
its contents dates itself with Basse's and Holland's, 'Shortly
after April 1616'.

With C. M. Ingleby, we are here most struck by the lines

Nature her selfe did her owne selfe admire,
As oft as thou wert pleasëd to attire
Her in her native lusture, and confesse,   [*lustre*
Thy dressing was her chiefest comlinesse.

And especially, because Ben Jonson (for the Folio seven years
later), immediately after seeing Shakespeare now as an Apollo,
now as a Mercury—

... *like* Apollo *he came forth to warme*
Our eares, or like a Mercury *to charme*!

—continues in the very vein of the unknown Elegist:

Nature her selfe was proud of his designes,
And ioy'd to weare the dressing of his lines!
Which were so richly spun, and wouen so fit,
As, since, she will vouchsafe no other Wit. [deign to accept

The question whether or not Jonson borrowed this *topos* from the Elegist is immaterial. The important point is that it struck them both as *significant and apt for Shakespeare*. And here, as we now realize, both of them are seeing and presenting Shakespeare exclusively *as Mercury*.

For with the Elizabethans the ingenious Mercury was famed not only for perfection of taste and choiceness in his dress, but also as the original inventor, designer, or weaver of *the first garment* (auctor primae vestis: Tertullian, *De Pallio* III. 5). Accordingly, in *Lady Alimony* 1.2 a playwright's brain is seen as *Mercury the ingenious weaver*: 'Come, sir, what brave dramatic piece has your running *Mercury* now upon the loom? The title of your play, sir?' And in astrology, along with 'Poets, Orators, . . . Embassadours' etc., Mercury signifies 'Taylors'. (William Lilly, *Christian Astrology*, 1647, 78.)

Both Elegist and Jonson drew their picture of the *couturier* Mercury–Shakespeare fashioning rich dresses designed to fit a goddess from memory of a familiar classical tale about the ever waxing and waning Moon:

> Greek poets feigned that Jove, when he saw Diana (the Moon) walking naked, and considering that this would look not at all seemly for a virgin, bade Mercury make her a dress. And yet, when Mercury had made many for her, he could however get none of them to fit; for while he was preparing one to her measure, she was daily changing shape, so that afterwards she could not put it on.
>
> Tr. from Curione's additions to Valeriano, lib. 1. c. 42

This is a striking variant of Aesop's *The Moon and her Mother***** and its reflection shows in I. M.'s *Newe Metamorphosis* 1.2.78, where Mercury aptly puts the mutable spruce gallant, ever changing his fashions, into the inconstant Moon.

We find further illustration in passages where Mercury brings rich dress, or at least the means of making it. Thus we have him bringing *mulberry seeds* as Jove's reward to Venus — seeds grow mulberry trees whose leaves feed worms which spin silk, silk makes fine raiment:

---

* Cf. Gabriel Harvey, *op. cit.*, D4ᵛ, and Samuel Rid, *Art of Jugling*, 1612, ed. 1614, 'To the . . . Reader'.

By *Maiae's* sonne (before it grew to night)
He sent a Napkin ful of little seeds,
Tane from the tree where *Thisbes* soule did light,
To make her selfe and boy farre brauer weeds   *[Cupid*
   Than *Pallas* had, or any of the seu'n,
   Yea, then proud *Iuno* ware the Queene of heau'n.
                    Moffett, *op. cit.*, B4

And in *Lingua* 1.11 Mercury brings a 'gorgeous Robe' as the
prize for the best of the Five Senses.

Mercury from birth manifested a keen interest in apparel.
So keen, that according to Eratosthenes he stole both his
mother's and his aunts' clothes. Again, the Homeric Hymn
pictures him, yet scarce unswaddled, outlining to his mother
his plan to burglarize Apollo's house at Delphi of riches 'and
much apparel'. And 'during the Hermes-Festival in Samos
stealing was permitted; Plutarch specially mentions that *clothes*
could be stolen' with impunity. (Schrader, *op. cit.*, 123.)

For Mercury's own dress, Ovid (*Met.* 2) makes a feature of
the god's sharp attention in sprucing himself to woo Princess
Herse, the fairest virgin. As Golding gives it,

So great a trust and confidence his beautie to him gave:
Which though it seemëd of it selfe sufficient force to have:
Yet was he curious for to make himselfe more fine and brave.
He kembd his head, and strokt his beard, and pried on every
   side,
To see that in his furniture no wrinkle might be spide.
And forbicause his Cloke was fringde and garded brode
   with golde,
He cast it on his shoulder up most seemely to beholde.
He takes in hand his charmëd rod that bringeth things
   asleepe,
And wakes them when he list againe. And lastly taketh keepe
That on his faire welformëd feete his golden shooes sit
   cleene,
And that all other things thereto well correspondent beene.

We have already seen Mercury in the Schifanoia fresco
'dressed in rich stylish costume'; and now we find our old

friend William Baldwin (he of the 'Love and Live' Delphic caduceus) making a striking literary use of Mercury's famously beautiful dress. In his elegy on King Edward VI he represents God as despatching his messenger Death to the young King at Greenwich, but ordering him to appear 'in comely shape', and out-Mercury Mercury.

> Whan doulful Death had heard this hard devise, [*command*
> He trymd him selfe in his most comly guyse,
> Like Mercury in euery kind of grace,
> Save that he had a much more lovely face.
>
> *The funeralles of King Edward the Sixt*, 1560, B3

When Du Bartas—in Sylvester's translation—describes the dancing-dress of Apollo and of Mercury for the royal wedding-ball, he devotes far more attention to Mercury's than to Apollo's, making his description of the 'medly Mantle' worn by the 'eloquent and quick interpreter' a rich feast of curious fancy in embroidering Nature's variety:

> How strange a suit! His medly Mantle seems
> Scarlet, Wave-lacëd with Quick-silver streams;
> And th'end of every Lace, for tuft, hath on
> A precious Porphyre, or an Agate stone;
> A crie of Hounds have here a Deer in Chase;
> There a false Fox, here a swift Kid they trace:
> There Larks and Linots, and sweet Nightingals
> (Fain'd upon fainëd Trees) with wings and tails
> Loose hanging, seem to swell their little throats,
> And with their warbling, shame the Cornets' notes.
> Light Fumitory, Parsly, Burnet's blade,
> And winding leafe his crispy Locks beshade . . .
>
> *The Magnificence, Second Book of Fourth Day of Second Week*. Sylvester, *Works*, ed. Grosart, 1.234

We have noted the Mercury-'dressing' passage in Jonson's extended praise of Shakespeare for the First Folio. Now when *I.M.S.* comes to write his own lengthy eulogy of the poet for the Second Folio, it is clear that he aims to vie with Jonson's. And when he takes up the Mercury-'dressing' topic for expansion, it looks very much as though he drew inspiration for his picture of Nature's various beauties worked by the Muses into *Shakespeare's robe* from this very Du Bartas–Sylvester passage about *Mercury's mantle* just quoted:

> *These joyntly woo'd him, envying one another*   [the Muses
> *(Obey'd by all as Spouse, but lov'd as brother)*
> *And wrought a curious robe of sable grave*
> *Fresh greene, and pleasant yellow, red most brave,*
> *And constant blew, rich purple, guiltlesse white*
> *The lowly Russet, and the Scarlet bright;*
> *Branch't and embroydred like the painted Spring*
> *Each leafe match't with a flower, and each string*
> *Of golden wire, each line of silke; there run*
> Italian *workes whose thred the Sisters spun;*   [nun's thread
> *And there did sing, or seeme to sing, the choyce*
> *Birdes of a forraine note and various voyce.*
> *Here hangs a mossey rocke; there playes a faire*
> *But chiding fountaine purled: Not the ayre,*
> *Nor cloudes nor thunder, but were living drawne,*
> *Not out of common Tiffany or Lawne,*
> *But fine materialls, which the Muses know*
> *And onely know the countries where they grow.*
> . . . . .
> *So with this robe they cloath him, bid him weare it*
> *For time shall never staine, nor envy teare it.*

But whether or not Sylvester's Du Bartas directly inspired *I.M.S.* to elaborate Mercury's 'medly Mantle' into Shakespeare's 'curious robe' made for him by his loving sisters the Muses, that rich robe for the eloquent poet strongly suggests that here too his mental image is again 'Mercury–Shakespeare'.

Finally, there is the epigram of Samuel Sheppard* (1651) '*In Memory of our Famous Shakespeare*'. A glance through it is enough to show that the title conveys '*our Famous Mercury*'. For Sheppard sees Mercury–Shakespeare with his invention, the lyre, charming Apollo:

> Sacred Spirit, whiles thy *Lyre*
> Ecchoed o're the Arcadian Plaines,
> Even *Apollo* did admire,
> *Orpheus* wondered at thy Straines.

* Repr. *Shakspere Allusion-Book*, 1909, 2.11.

Further, his 'Divine wit and skill' make him—like Mercury—
the 'chosen darling' of the Muses. And here Sheppard returns
to Mercury–Shakespeare's supreme sartorial skill in fashioning,
for their glory, eternal 'garments gay':

> Thou wert truely Priest Elect,
> Chosen darling to the Nine,
> Such a Trophey to erect
> (By thy wit and skill Divine)
>
> That were all their other Glories
> (Thine excepted) torn away,
> By thy admirable Stories,
> Their garments ever shall be gay.

From this topic of dress let us turn to another aspect of the
versatile Mercury in the court of Jove. Chaucer in the *House of
Fame* mentions

> Ganymede,
> That was y-bore up, as men rede,
> To hevene with dan Jupiter,
> And maad the goddes boteler.

A *butler*, says the *OED*, was formerly 'one who hands round
wine, a cup-bearer', citing John Stow: 'These Citizens did
minister wine, as Bottelers'. And the heraldic charge on the
Boteler arms was the butler's cup.

Before that upstart Ganymede's arrival, this office of Butler
had always been one of the many onerous duties of Mercury,
humorously described by Lucian. In Heywood's translation,
Mercury detailing his grievances complains,

> ... When the whole day
> I have toild, not having time to wipe away
> The dust and sweat, new labor I begin;
> Supper comes on, and I must then serve in
> Ambrosia: e're the Phrygian had to doo   [*Ganymede*
> With *Ioves* crownd Cup, I filld him Nectar too.

Or, as Jonson gives it in *Cynthia's Revels* 1.1, 'wait mannerly at
a table with a trencher ... fill out *nectar*, when *Ganimed's* away'.

Holding *Mercury the Butler* in mind, we turn to the report of a curious little English book entitled *A Hermeticall Banquet, drest by a Spagiricall Cook*. It was published 1652, but

> written before 1632, as it is dedicated to Sir Isaac Wake, who died in that year. The author is describing the court of the Princess Phantasia: '*Ovid* she makes Major-domo. *Homer*, because a merry Greek, Master of the Wine-cellars. . . . *Shack-Spear*, Butler . . .'
>
> C. B. Carew, *Notes and Queries* 3.1.266a

What reason, we ask, could the author have had for selecting Shakespeare for *Mercury's* place except that he thought of him as Mercury—as we have seen that Freeman, Brooke, Holland, the Elegist, Jonson, *I.M.S.*, and Sheppard all did?

Of more fundamental importance than any of the foregoing was Mercury as *Teacher* of mankind. 'Hermes, teach us all the story, kindest of the heavenly Powers.'* And not teacher only, but giver both of the ability to learn and of the love of learning. 'We ask the boon of learning easily,' writes Callimachus, 'the gift of Hermes.' In Ficino's words, 'It is Mercury who draws us to inquire after learning.' And as Edgar Wind points out, the painting by Correggio in the National Gallery, London, 'in which Amor is taught by Mercury how to read, is . . . a very popular subject in the Renaissance because it represents the love of learning'.† Sir Walter Ralegh notes in his *History of the World* that the second age of man is compared 'to Mercury, wherein we are taught and instructed'; and Tomaso Garzoni, another contemporary of Shakespeare's, after quoting both Philo and Cicero on Voluptuousness as the enemy of litera-ture and learning, illustrates Mercury the Teacher with a vivid Anacreontic parable:

> As did that Poetical Corybant in Anacreon, who, drinking of Pleasure's poisonous cup before Jupiter's door, could never more find the chamber of Mercury, his master and teacher. *Sinagoga de gl'Ignoranti*, 1589, ed. 1605, 51

* Aristophanes, *Peace* 602, tr. B. B. Rogers. Mercury taught Amphion his miraculous skill: Horace, *Od.* 3.11.1–2. 'Mercurius . . . Didasculus, Scholarcha, docens Aoniam pubem . . . imbuens rudes ingenua arte mentes'. Giordano Bruno, *De Imaginum . . . Compositione*, 135.

† *Op. cit.*, 77. And see Mercury as Teacher, carved in a capital of the Doge's Palace, Venice. Seznec, *op. cit.*, Fig. 21 and p. 72.

Marino similarly, in his Canto X of *The Marvels*, presents Mercury delivering a long informing lecture on the Moon's wonders, 'in the role of the irrepressible pedagogue with a captive audience'. (H. M. Priest in his translation of *Adone*, 1967, 181.) Mercury, fabled in I. M.'s *Newe Metamorphosis* as an outcast from Olympus, wandering the world penniless, applies for employment: '*Hermes* my name . . . can children teach, or any office doe.'

In 1614 Thomas Freeman, addressing '*Shakespeare*, that nimble *Mercury* . . .' extols him as instructor: 'Who loues chaste life, there's *Lucrece* for a Teacher.' And the anonymous Elegist in 1616, after showing Shakespeare as Mercury dressing Nature in her 'native lustre', goes on to bewail him as Mercury the Tutor:

> How can we then forget thee, when the age
> Her chiefest Tutor . . . in thee hath lost.

Mercury had long been identified with the Ibis-headed Egyptian god Thoth or Hermes Trismegistus. Citing Cicero and Lactantius, William Baldwin writes: 'this is he whiche slewe Argus, & was the ruler of the Egipcians, and gaue them lawes, & instructed them in learning, & deuised markes & shapes of letters after the forme of beastes, & trees.* He was called Trismegistus, because he was the chefest Philosopher, the chefest prest, & the chefest kynge.' (*A treatise of Morall Phylosophie*, 1547, B3; also eds. 1564 & 1567.)

Thus Mercury the Teacher became also Sacred, King, Lawgiver; as Chapman has it, *Hear royal Hermes sing th'Egyptian laws.* And it is evidently because these Egyptian Hermes-attributes are fused in Dryden's mind with Mercury's *teaching of wit and art*, and his *magic* rod, that he writes

---

*   *To Mercury the Elder.*

Rest, Maja's *sonne* . . .
Take not such pains as thou hast done of old,
To teach men Hieroglyphicks, *and to unfold*
Egyptian *hidden Characters* . . .

Sir Francis Kynaston, verses to [John Wilkins's] *Mercury,
or the Secret and Swift Messenger* . . . , 1641, A5.

Shakespear, who (taught by none) did first impart
To *Fletcher* wit,* to labouring *Johnson* Art.
He, Monarch-like, gave those his Subjects Law,
And is that Nature which they paint and draw.

But *Shakespear*'s Magick could not copy'd be,
Within that Circle none durst walk but he.

But *Shakespear*'s pow'r is Sacred as a King's.
1676. Qu. Sh. Allusion-Book, 2.139

Again Shakespeare is Mercury; and for Dryden, *thrice-greatest*:
master of what Sidney called 'that delightful teaching, which
must be the right describing note to know a Poet by'.

Monumental Hermes, his four-square guiding pillar erected
upon a heap of stones—to which every passer-by religiously
added another—was thus identified not only with that
Egyptian King of Language Hermes Trismegistus (Thoth) but
also with the Egyptian royal memorials: both obelisks (*pillars*)
and pyramids (*stone-heaps*).

As William Baldwin observes in 1547, 'For Jamblichus &
diuers other, wryte much of Mercurius Pyllers. And Mercurius
was of suche fame among ye Egyptians, that they put forth all
theyr workes vnder his name.' (*Op. cit.*, B2.) Iamblichus'
recent translator corroborates: 'The sacred books of the
Egyptians were called the "books of Thoth", a god identical
with Hermes and like him prince of eloquence.' (Édouard des
Places, S.J., *Jamblique des Mystères d'Égypte*, 1966, 38*n*.)

Bearing in mind this *Egyptian pyramid-pillar* and *sacred book*
association with Hermes of the stone-heap, so familiar to the
age of John Milton, let us now turn to Milton's lines dated
1630, printed in the Second Folio 1632 as '*An Epitaph on the
admirable Dramaticke Poet*, w. SHAKESPEARE':†

What neede my *Shakespear* for his honour'd Bones, [*or* needs
The labour of an age in pilëd Stones,
Or that his hallow'd reliques should be hid

---

* We have seen Mercury identified as *Wit*; and here is Dryden's
definition of it: 'wit, which is no other than the faculty of imagination'.

† Also in Benson's 1640 *Poems . . . Shake-speare*, and Milton's, 1645.

Under a Star-ypointing *Pyramid*?
Dear son of memory, great heir of Fame,
What need'st thou such weak witnes of thy name?

Here Milton twice gives us his poet as Mercury. For it was great *Hermes* whom the Greeks invoked as the happy or gifted '*son*' of *Memory*.* 'In his song praising the gods, Hermes honoured Mnemosyne . . . first, for at his birth Fate had given Maia's son over to her.' (*Homeric Hymn to Hermes* 429–430.)

Again, naturally no one in 1630 was planning to honour Shakespeare with a pyramidal stone-heap which would take twenty years of ant-like toil in the piling, or engineering the erection of a huge Egyptian obelisk over his bones. Milton brings in these monstrous memorials sacred to *the great Egyptian Mercury* obviously only to scorn them as needless for witness to the name of *our greater English Mercury*, Shakespeare:

> Thou in our wonder and astonishment
> Hast built thy self a live-long Monument.
> For whilst toth' shame of slow-endeavouring art,
> Thy easie numbers flow, and that each heart
> Hath from the leaves of thy unvalu'd Book,
> Those Delphick lines with deep impression took,
> Then thou our fancy of it self bereaving,
> Dost make us Marble with too much conceaving;
> And so Sepulcher'd in such pomp dost lie,
> That Kings for such a Tomb would wish to die.

With *thy unvalu'd Book* Milton here presents his Prince of Eloquence also as the English 'Thrice-greatest Hermes of the priceless Book' to match Ben Jonson's picture in the First Folio of Shakespeare as 'monumental Hermes':

> *Thou art a Moniment, without a tombe,*
> *And art aliue still, while thy Booke doth liue . . .*

Everyone recognizes a more evident ground of the identification: Shakespeare the playwright-and-actor with his genial quick wit, his matchless 'smooth Comicke vaine', delighting

---

* μάκαρ Μνήμης τελεσίφρονος υἱὲ μέγιστε. Liddell and Scott, *Greek–English Lexicon*, 1940, 1770b.

the company as the Mercury of the Court. For on Olympus, Hermes was always summoned as 'our usual manager of mirth'.

Iupiter sends downe *Mercurie* to make them pleasant.

such court guise

As Mercury did first devise . . .

Mercury, be quick, with mirth furnish the heavens . . .*

As Stubbes remarked, the ancients particularly dedicated 'the action and pronuntiation' of their plays 'to *Mercurie*'; the device of Jonson's Euphantaste ('a well conceited Wittinesse . . . honouring the court with the riches of her pure inuention') is 'upon a *Petasus*, or *Mercuriall* hat, a Crescent'; Sir George Buc, blazoning the arms of 'the Art of Revels', gives 'a *Mercuries Petasus Argent*'; and Shakespeare's fellow poet-playwright Drayton for his armorial crest chose Apollo and Mercury: *On a sun in glory or, a cap of Mercury* . . .† To them all, Mercury's Hat meant *Invention in Dramatic Poetry*.

To 'do service to *Mercurie*', says Plutarch (tr. Holland, 692) men 'attend . . . plaies, daunces, weddings, Masques'; and Du Bartas (tr. Sylvester) says that to celebrate Solomon's wedding, 'Here many a Hermes findes out new delights.' In reporting the royal marriage of Frederick and Elizabeth (1613), John Taylor the Water Poet draws a more vivid picture:

> [*Mercury*] as a Seruant on this Wedding waits . . .
> His rare inuentions and his quaint conceits . . .
> He in imaginary showes affords
> In shape, forme, method, and applausefull words.
> *Works*, 1630, 3.122

In precisely the same way, Mercury–Shakespeare waited on the Court wedding of 26 January 1595 with his invention that most enchanting of marriage-plays, *A Midsummer-Night's Dream*; at the Court's crowning festival with his mad-merry

* *Bacchus Bountie*, 1593, C3ᵛ; Milton, *Comus* 962–963; John Tatham's verses on Ford's *The Sun's Darling*.

† *Anat. of Abuses*, L7; *Cynth. Rev.* 5.7; *The Third Universitie* . . . 1615, Ch. 47; B. H. Newdigate, *M. Drayton and his circle* 1941, 150.

leap- or women's-year 'topical', *Twelfth Night*, 1600/1; at the Court's preparatory school Gray's Inn 1588/9 with the leap-year Christmas merriment of his *Love's Labour's Lost*, and later with his *Comedy of Errors*.

With our new light, further instances of the identification now become obvious. 'But Lord! what a gentleman, after all, was Shakespeare! . . . a born prince,' exclaimed Leigh Hunt. From the first, men recognized the yeoman of Stratford's lovable nature as *native gentle*, like that of the great gentleman of Olympus. Even his rival, the jealous Ben Jonson, confesses 'I lov'd the man, and doe honour his memory (on this side Idolatry) as much as any.'

Hermes–Mercury deserved the universal love he inspired. His actions proved him not only generous and faithful, but also 'kindest of the heavenly Powers' (Aristophanes, *Peace* 602). Ausonius calls him *facilis*—'gentle, good-natured, kind, courteous'. Hermes Hegemon is the one 'who gently shows the way to him who has missed it'. For Bishop John Hooper in 1548, Mercury is 'a gentle . . . god', and in Jonson's *Cynthia's Revels*, Echo affectionately calls him 'kind *Mercurie*'.

> Then from above (O bountie most admired!)
> Saint *Hermes* shin'd: whose gentle light presageth
> That the anger of the Heav'ns asswageth.
> Sylvester, Works, ed. Grosart, 2.37

Apart from gentle Apollo—'the fairest are ever the gentlest' —Mercury the Poet is the only major god consistently called *gentle*. And with the Elizabethans the only poet consistently called *gentle* is Shakespeare. As I noted in *Shakespeare's Motley*, the praise of contemporaries sounds no similar chorus of 'gentle Marlowe', 'gentle Daniel', or 'gentle Drayton'. In his Sonnets, Mercury–Shakespeare tells his *King*, his *Sun*, his *God*, (81.9) *Your monument shall be my gentle verse*, and (100.6) urges his Muse, *straight redeeme In gentle numbers time so idely spent*.

Shortly after the completion of the Sonnets, Spenser, prince of poets, is the first (as Dryden perceived) to hail the new poetic Spirit. In *The Teares of the Muses* written before March 1590, under *Thalia*-Comedy Spenser first laments the stage's loss of 'Our pleasant *Willy*' who 'is dead of late'—the famous mimic, Tarlton (died 1588), who imitated Truth 'under Mimick shade': players were called *shadows*. He mourns a theatre now given over to the 'Scurrilitie' and the 'Contempt' of the Marprelate wrangle; and he praises *one* writer (but only one) for preferring to be silent, neglected, rather than sell his pen to so base a use.

Spenser hails him as

> *that same gentle Spirit, from whose pen*
> *Large streames of honnie and sweet Nectar flowe* ...

This is the actor-playwright Shakespeare *as poet of the Sonnets*; and the allusion to him as their 'Mercury' shows not only in *gentle* but also in *honnie*, as will appear below.

As Malone realized, in *Colin Clout* (published 1595), we have Spenser's even more generous second tribute to the gentle, heroically sounding *Shakespeare* of the Sonnets:

> *And there though last not least is* Aetion,
> *A gentler shepheard may no where be found:*
> *Whose* Muse *full of high thoughts inuention*
> *Doth like himselfe Heroically sound.*

To the mental link with *gentle* Mercury, Spenser here adds Mercury, god of *Invention*;* and he obviously knows that this Mercury–poet's divine and royal Muse (Son. 78.1; 38.9) is King Phoebus–Hatcliffe, *full of high thoughts inuention*; for as Sidney writes, '*Phœbus* ... the high conceits thy heav'nly wisedomes breed.' And like 'Shake-speare' himself, these praises of his King *Heroically sound*. Spenser similarly had 'Heroicall argument, in the person of our most gratious soueraign', Elizabeth. (*Shep. Cal.*, gloss to *October* 43.) And Servius notes at the beginning of *Aeneid* 1. that 'a poem is heroic which is made up of divine and human persons, containing truths with fictions'.

'By their *gentle* or noble verse the Sonnets of Shakespeare reveal him as *Aëtion* the true-born noble *Eaglet*, proved by his

---

* 'INVENTION. LXXXIV. ... par une Image de Mercure ... les Anciens ont figuré ... l'Invention.' C. Ripa, *Iconologie* (ed. J. Baudoin), 1644. 'And thou ... *Cyllenian Mercury* ... Now thriue inuention in this glorious court.' Jonson, *Cynthia's Revels* 5.5. 'Hermes ... Of quicke Inuention.' John Taylor, *Works*, 1630, 2.126*b*.

fixing his eyes upon the excellent beauty of his Sun' (*Mr. W. H.*, 196). For not only does the Eagle represent *High Thought*, but in Chapter 9 that royal bird will also reveal its unsuspected presence in the poet's biography.

In the Folio, remembering how Shakespeare came forth 'like a *Mercury* to charme', Ben Jonson calls him 'My gentle *Shakespeare*'; and of the engraving says 'It was for gentle Shakespeare cut'. In his *Timber* he praises the 'brave notions and gentle expressions' of 'our Shakespeare'. To Heminges and Condell, their fellow was 'a most gentle expresser' of Nature. Suckling writes of 'gentle Shakespear's eas'er strain', and for John Benson the Sonnets are 'gentle straines'.

Sir John Denham in 1647 cites 'SHAKESPEARE'S gentler Muse', and in 1658 Sir Aston Cokaine follows with

> Now *Stratford* upon *Avon*, we would choose
> Thy gentle and ingenuous *Shakespeare* Muse . . .*

So much for *gentle* Mercury; now for Mercury *the Friend*. Ever since

> *Hermes gaue Phœbus an eternall state*
> *In his affection*

and

> . . . *King Apollo honor'd Maia's Sonne*
> *With all the rights of friendship: all whose loue*
> *Had Imposition from the Will of Ioue*

the two had stood, the divine exemplars of friendship: Apollo the far god, Hermes the near. To Aristophanes (*Peace* 394), Hermes is 'the friendliest of the gods to men, and the most generous giver'; and the Orphic hymn addresses 'Hermes . . . O friend of man.'

Ben Jonson's Cynthia—by whom he meant Queen Elizabeth —describes him as

> *Mercury*, thy true propitious friend
> (A *deitie*, next IOVE, belou'd of vs) . . .
> *Cynthia's Revels* 5.11

---

* 'Ingenuous', meaning *noble, generous*, brings back both John Davies of Hereford on Shakespeare's character, 'generous yee are in *minde* and *moode*', and Sir Henry Salisbury on his plays—'thease noble straynes'.

And Sir William Cornwallis identifies Friendship with the Peace-bringer Mercury—Ovid's *Cyllenius pacifer*: 'Friendship, which name commonly to our vnderstandings is *the messenger of Peace.*' (*Essayes, ed. cit.,* 22, with italics added.)

Likening the Planet Mercury to Prudence and Friendship, Natale Conti (*op. cit.,* lib. 5. c. 5) says, 'In every vicissitude of Fortune, Friendship does the self-same.' And the fourth-century Julius Firmicus Maternus is quoted describing men born under Mercury as *faithful friends.**

Mercury was typically the Friend; and so was Shakespeare of the Sonnets, the Friend matchless in devotion. He appears in 1594 as *W. S.* 'the old player' in *Willobie his Avisa,* the poem by young Henry Willoughby, friend and connection by marriage of Shakespeare's Thomas Russell. (See my *I, William Shakespeare,* 1937, 53–62.) To the lovesick Willobie, *W. S.* is 'my faithful friend'. And *W. S.,* describing himself as 'a frend whose faith is tryde', assures him 'Ile helpe to mende what is amisse'—like friendly Hermes Eriounios, the Helper in love-affairs.

We find no other author styled *friendly.* But for readers in 1604 the poet is 'Friendly Shakespeare'. Anthony Scoloker in his Epistle to the Reader writes hopefully of his *Diaphantus,* 'It should be ... like *Friendly Shakespeare's Tragedies* ... it should please all, like Prince *Hamlet.*'

Heminges and Condell in the First Folio call Shakespeare 'so worthy a Friend'; and to the anonymous eulogist (whom I take to be Sir John Suckling) the engraving of Shakespeare in the Second Folio is '*the Effigies of my worthy Friend*'. And to find Suckling in a letter of 1639 claiming the poet as 'my Friend Mr. *William Shakespear*' gains importance when we reflect that at the poet's death Suckling was a child of seven. Like Milton with his 'my *Shakespear*', he might as justly have claimed him as 'my Poet'; for to his world Mercury–Shakespeare was both Poet and Friend in the works which survived him, as well as in his lifetime.

And also *Companion;* for Hermes is 'the Companion ever

* 'De i costumi che dà Mercurio. Dal Materno. ... Significa amici fedeli...' G.-B. della Porta, *Della Celeste Fisionomia,* lib. 2. c. 39, ed. 1622, 50.

and for ever' in Giordano Bruno's words —*Comes seculi seculor-um*. The Homeric Hymn declares, 'Hermes accompanies all men and gods.' Zeus sends him (*Il.* 24.334) to guide Priam safe into the enemy's camp: 'Hermes, since what you love best of all is to be man's companion . . .'

To other men and gods he comes as a companion to guide or to help at need. Far otherwise with his great Friend, King Phoebus Apollo the Sun. For here he is the planet Mercury, 'Phoebus' companion' as Claudian calls him, inseparable from the sun (*soli individuus*), and his closest attendant (*proximusque comes*). '*Mercurie* departeth not from the Sun . . .' (Meres, *Palladis Tamia*, 1598, 116ᵛ, citing Pliny lib. 2. c. 17.)

Similarly with Shakespeare of the Sonnets and his Sun, God, and King: a *companion* so close that he repeatedly *identifies* himself with his Friend. As I pointed out in *Mr. W. H.*, John Davys envies him next after Spenser and Daniel:

> O could I sweet Companion, sing like you,
> Which of a shadow, under a shadow sing . . .
> > *Orchestra* (entered 25 June 1594), 1596, stanza 129

—Shakespeare, hymning his *shadow*-king Will Hatcliffe, who *paces forth* (Son. 55) in glory as 'King Apollo' *under a shadow*, a royal *canopy*. Since (as we shall see) the epithet *sweet* means *eloquent*, when added to *Companion* it makes evident Davys's and his readers' identification of Shakespeare with Mercury.

In 1611 (ent. S.R. 1610, a year after the Sonnets of 1588–89 had appeared in print) the famous friendship of the Unequals, of King and Companion, of gentleman and plebeian player, was familiarly recalled to the poet by his friend Davies of Hereford:

> To our English Terence, Mr. Will.
> Shake-speare.

> Some say (good *Will*) which I, in sport, do sing,
> Had'st thou not plaid some Kingly parts in sport,*

---

* *in sport* (or *in jest*) merely means *in stage plays*. See *Caes.* 3.1.114; *Ric. II* 4.1.290; *3 Hen. VI* 2.3.28; *Ham.* 3.2.244. No suggestion whatever of giving offence by 'making sport of'. Staunton's mistake is followed by Dr. Simpson, *Ben Jonson*, 9.191, 262–263.

Thou hadst bin a companion for a *King*:
And, beene a King among the meaner sort.*

And finally we have John Milton, again seeing Shakespeare as Mercury. Not this time either as adoptive *son of Memory* or as the English thrice-greatest Hermes of the priceless Book, but as *Companion* of an unhappy King. Often presented in poetry as Apollo, this King was the poet's admirer Charles I, who—already fifteen and a half when Shakespeare died—had known him both as player and as poet. Writing in *Eikonoklastes* (1649) of the King's solaces in prison, Milton names 'one whom we well know was the Closet Companion of these his Solitudes, *William Shakespeare*'.

Gentle, kind, courteous, the Friend, the Companion. But beyond all this Hermes–Mercury was *mighty, powerful*: Homer's *sōkos Hermes, kratos Argeiphontes*, the god stronger than Fate—who alone could cross the thresholds of Heaven and Hell, and bring back the dead to life. Also the *power* who *comes down with learned hat and rod*, the Power of the mind, of the word, of speech (Potens mentis . . . vocis et sermonis potentem. Macrobius, *Saturn.* 1.19.9, 1.12.20); the divine Might of wit, of eloquence, of learning (Per Mercurium . . . intelligitur vis ingenii, eloquentiæ ac doctrinæ. J. Camerarius, *Symbolorum . . . Centuria*, 1590, 2); 'the powerfull tongue of facund Mercury'; 'in his tongue consists his cheefest might'; 'Mercury, whose . . . invincible & omnipotent Eloquence.'†

In Renaissance literature as in Shakespeare, the Man of Eloquence is Mark Antony. As the story goes—from North's Plutarch, *Life of Marius*—so great was the force of his 'sugred and sweet perswasions' that he turned the furious rage of two cruel captains sent by Marius to kill him into 'lenitie and mercie'. (Lodowick Lloid, *The Pilgrimage of Princes*, 1586, 25ᵛ.) Small wonder that when Shakespeare's Cleopatra is striving to

* 'A Servant of a King is a King.' Tilley S239; 'The servant of a king may be a king.' T. Middleton, *Wisd. of Solomon Paraphrased* 1597, 5.16.1. 'Among the meaner sort'—yeomen, plebeians—shows Davies recalling the early friendship, *before* the 1596 grant of arms which raised Shakespeare from plebeian to *gentleman*.

† Gascoigne, *Princely Pleasures at Kenelworth*; Richard Davies, *Chester's Triumph*, 1610; G. Harvey, *Pierces Supererogation*, 1593, Aa 2ᵛ-3.

haul up her dying Antony into the Monument she longs for the help of his 'father', the mighty Giver of Eloquence: 'The strong-wing'd Mercury should fetch thee vp.' And when admirers speak of Shakespeare's *might*, what they are praising is his Mercury-power of Eloquence: '*when* ... Mighty Shakespear *wrote*' (Robert Veel, 1672); '*Shakespear*'s pow'r' (Dryden, 1676).*

Adding to his power, the wingèd god was also swift as thought, quick, nimble—like his planet, swiftest of all. 'As a swift thought darts through the heart of a man, ... so glorious Hermes planned both thought and deed at once.' (*Homeric Hymn to Hermes*, tr. Evelyn-White, Loeb 1936, 367.) '*Mercury* himselfe, the most-nimble, and supereloquent God' ... '*Mercury* the nimble Post of Heaven' ... '*The nimble* Mercury'.†

To the slow 'elaborate Ben', naturally, Freeman's '*Shakespeare*, that nimble *Mercury*' was *too* quick: 'He needed the trigger in his wheel.' For as Owen Feltham wrote of Tom Randolph, such was Shakespeare's genius that 'like the eyes quick wink, Hee could write sooner then another think'. As his intimates Heminges and Condell testify, 'His mind and hand went together.' This Mercury-quickness of Shakespeare's was repeatedly remarked upon. Thomas Fuller contrasted 'the quickness of his Wit and Invention' with Jonson's slowness, and Samuel Butler later did the same: 'of more quick and ready parts' than Jonson. In a play of Robert Wild's written about 1646 we find

Shakespear.

His Quill as quick as Feather from the Bow!

And about 1680 William Fulman's note reads 'Will: Shakespear: of great quickness and invention.'‡

The only god characterized as both *mighty* and *nimble* is Hermes: both *sōkos* and *elaphros*. As Shakespeare's contemporary John Marston has it,

With Cáducéus *nimble Hermes* fights ...
O be propitious *powerfull* God of Arts ...
Scourge of Villanie, 1599, E3ᵛ; italics added

* Qu. *Shakspere Allusion-Book*, 1909, 2.181, 139.

† Gabriel Harvey, *op. cit.*, X3; William Basse, *Tom a Bedlam*; John Taylor, *Works*, 1630, 2.60.

‡ Qu. *Shak. All.-Bk*: Fuller, 1.484; Butler, 2.234; Wild, 1.502. Fulman, Bodl. MS. Tanner 403 f. 41ᵛ.

Thus in the Hon. Edward Howard's phrase of 1673 the Mercury–Shakespeare identification is again unmistakable: 'mighty Shakespear's nimble vein'. (Qu. G. Thorn-Drury, *Some 17th Century Allusions to Shakespeare*, 1920, 66.)

Let us turn now to consider the personal epithets *honey-tongued, mellifluous, sweet*; and the adjective *sugared*—as sugared mouth, sugared pen, sugared vein, sugared words, sugared sonnets. Modern understanding of them is commonly very far from the precise meaning they conveyed. And when even Shakespearean scholars are found imagining that *sugared sonnets* means 'sonnets of conceits' or alternatively 'sweet versification', and that *honey-tongued* means a poet 'of passion', it is time to go beyond Lorenz Morsbach's excellent article of 1912, cited by H. E. Rollins, *The Sonnets* (Varior. Shak.), 2.54, and the *OED* itself, to seek the derivation which both unifies and illuminates them. That source we readily find: it is Hermes Logios, Mercury, God of Eloquence. (See Erasmus, *Adagia s.v.* Facundia: Mercurii typus.) And Poetry, says Ben Jonson, 'indeed . . . is the most prevailing Eloquence, and of the most exalted *Charact* [carat]'. (*Discoveries. Works*, ed. Simpson, 8.633, and cf. 9.371.) Thus Benson, epitomizing Shakespeare's Sonnets in 1640 as *perfect eloquence*, is calling their author a 'Mercury'.

'Speech, whose symbol in general is Mercury' (Valeriano 34.26). Speech—Thought uttered by the Mouth and the Tongue, 'conceit's expositor'. As Marino's Mercury himself informs Adonis,

> The mouth, 'tis true, is the first messenger
> of speech, the unique office of mankind.
> Reason cannot expound a single thought   [or *unfold*
> not first discovered and expressed through it.
> Divine interpreter, through whom is shown
> whate'er the intellect of him who speaks
> would print within the breasts of other men,
> the voice subserving as the go-between.
>
> *Adone*, 1623, 7.125, tr. H. M. Priest

Man's mouth and tongue were thus under the special care of *Mercury the Soul*—cf. Shakespeare's *tounges (the voice of soules)*—

and 'the tongue moreover was sacred to Mercury . . . the protector of speech'. (Valeriano, 33.40; and compare Conti, 1.10, end.) 'And as the heathen have consecrated their . . . tongue to *Mercurie* . . .' (Adam Hill, *op. cit.*, 7).

The organ of speech is also the organ of taste; moreover—as everyone knows from the Bible—the savour of Truth or Wisdom is 'sweeter than honey'. To Mercury, god of wisdom or truth both inward and uttered, were consecrated both honey and sweet figs; and as Plutarch relates,

> celebrating a feast unto *Mercurie* the nineteenth day of the first month, they eat hony and figges, saying withall this mot, *Sweet is the trueth*.*

The thought is still current today, in the Hebridean folksong *The Cockle Strand*:

> *Truth be on my lips, and sense in all I say,*
> *Sweet taste of honey in my mouth, when I come back this way.*

The Elizabethans knew that honey was Mercury's: 'as the heathen dedicated . . . honie to *Mercurie*'; '*Joviall Mercury* . . . To you corruptles *Hunny* . . .' (Adam Hill, *loc. cit.*; Marston, *Sophonisba* 3.1.)

Here is the *honey of gentle Mercury*, recalled by Spenser before March 1590 in hailing the *eloquent truth* of gentle Mercury–Shakespeare's sonnets: 'that same gentle Spirit, from whose pen Large streames of honnie and sweet Nectar flowe'. The immortalizing 'nectar of the gods', as scholarship finds, was *honey*; and *Poetry* (says Nashe) *is the hunny of all flowers*.

As a result, what *honey-tongued, honeyed, mellifluous, sugared, sweet* brought to mind, when applied to poets and poems or to speakers and speech, was *Mercury*: either the Poet or the divine Interpreter or Speaker for the gods, great Giver of Wisdom's Eloquence—true, choice, pleasing, powerful, all-persuading. The honey-god's reflection shows in the poets: 'Mellifluous,

---

* *Plutarchs Morals*, tr. Holland 1603, 1313; cf. Valeriano, 53.41. Bishop John Hooper in 1548 depreciates the heathen's Mercury: 'a gentle, swete, and fyggie god, that . . . will not see thabhomination'. Qu. *OED*, *s.v.* Figgy.

sweete . . . elloquence' (Rowlands); 'mellifluous, pleasing
Epithetts . . . in my sweet Rhetoricke' (Drayton); 'conserv'd
in such a sugred phrase That Eloquence itself envíes your
praise' (Sidney); 'Eloquence, that is but wisdom speaking
well' (Fulke Greville); 'I praise hir honny-sweeter eloquence
Which from the fountaine of true wisedome floweth' (Lodge).
And they agree in describing him:

> And nexte in ordre is Mercuryous
> That in spechë hath most excellence
> Of rethorik and sugrid elloquence . . .

> Witty Mercury, with his doulce & sugred eloquency

> Cyllene, in sugred speech, gaue her a grace*

Mentioned especially, of course, is the organ of Mercury's
sweet eloquence:

> The heauens Herrald may not make compare
>   of working words which so abound in thee,
> Thy hony-dewëd tongue exceedes his far,
>   in sweete discourse, and tunefull mellodie . . .

> mellilinguis Te canat Maiâ genitus

> Mercurie the next, a god sweet tong'd we know†

> sweete toung'd Mercury

> mellifluous Mercurie

> there was wit, there was a sweet tongue: . . . *Mercury*
> wou'd have been glad to have had such a tongue in his
> mouth I warrant him.‡

Spenser's Mercury-identification of 'that gentle Spirit, from

* John Lydgate, *Troy Book* 2.5604–5606; *Womans book*, pr. T. Reynold,
1545, B8, qu. *OED*; Nicholas Grimald, Tottel's *Miscellany*, poem 141,
ed. Arber, 105.

† R. L[inche], *Diella*, 1596, 27.1–4; T. R.'s verses to John Davies of
Hereford's *Microcosmos*, 1603; Giles Fletcher, *Licia, ca.* 1593, 25.7.

‡ Marston, *Entertainment . . . at Ashby*, 1607; Weever, *Mirror of Martyrs*,
1601, repr. 1873, 231; Dryden, *Troil. & Cress.* 1.2.

whose pen Large streames of honnie and sweete Nectar flowe'
is echoed repeatedly:

And *Shakespeare* thou, whose honey-flowing Vaine

mellifluous & hony-tongued *Shakespeare*

Honie-tong'd *Shakespeare*

Melicert . . . his honied muse*

And should anyone still hesitate to accept this evidence of
their mental identification of Shakespeare with Mercury, his
fellow-dramatist Heywood puts it beyond question:

Mellifluous *Shake-speare*, whose inchanting Quill
Commanded Mirth or Passion, was but *Will*.
The Hierarchie of the blessed Angells, 1635, 206

Because of this connotation, perhaps the most characteristic
Elizabethan epithet for Mercury is accordingly *sweet*:

O *Maiaes* sonne, *Cyllenius* sweete

Fortune. Sweet Mercury, I give thee my consent

Œnone. Sweete Mercurie†

sweete Mercurie delights thee moste

Hee that charm'd *Argus* eyes, sweet *Mercury*

And thy ripe wit, lend me sweet *Mercury*‡

Clearly, the particular praise of '*sweet* Shakespeare' for the
choice eloquence both of his *sugared sonnets* and of his other

---

* Richard Barnfield, *Poems in Divers humors*, 1598, E2ᵛ; Francis Meres,
Palladis Tamia, 1598, 281; John Weever, *Epigrammes*, 1599, E6; Henry
Chettle, *Englandes Mourning Garment*, 1603, D3.

† Melbancke, *op. cit.*, 210; *Rare Triumphs of Love and Fortune*, Hazl. Dods.
6.230; Peele, *Arraignment of Paris*, 1584, 3.1.114. And Mercury's identification with the Celtic god Hercules–Ogmios the Eloquent explains
Armado's 'Most sweet Hercules!'

‡ Thomas Lodge, *A Fig for Momus*, 1595, D2ᵛ; Donne, *Anatomie . . .
Second Anniversary*; John Raynolds, *Dolarnys Primerose*, 1606.

poetry draws its contemporary force from the praisers' mental picture, 'Mercury–Shakespeare':

sweet Companion   John Davys, 1594

Lucrecia Sweet Shakespeare   William Covell, 1595

Sweete Mr Shakespeare! ... O sweete Mr Shakespeare! I'le haue his picture in my study ... I'le worshipp sweet Mr Shakespeare   *1 Return from Parnassus*, 1601

Sweet Swan of Auon   Ben Jonson, First Folio

Sweetest Shakespear facies childe
                                              Milton, *L'Allegro*, 1632

Shakespear deserves the Name of *sweetest*, which *Milton* gave him   *The Athenian Mercury*, 1694

*   *   *

Here we have freshly recalled the thoughts of Mercury's rare qualities held by the Tudor–Stuart age. These now reveal the pointed significance of the tributes offered to Shakespeare in his familiar poetic shape—for, as Keats alone in modern times perceived, he led *a life . . . figurative*—as Mercury.

To the Renaissance mind, the Ever-living Poet is no one but *Immortal Mercury*. And to the Sonnets' readers in 1609, what Englishman can be OVR.EVER-LIVING.POET but *our Mercury*, Shakespeare?

8

Tiger's Heart and Words of Mercury

THE numerous chorus of poets and critics we have quoted celebrates Shakespeare in many and various voices—both in his twenties as the new poet of the Sonnets, later at the height of his triumphs, and throughout the decades beginning at his death. But in one thing they are unanimous: in seeing him as Mercury. The multiplied examples of this common view of theirs give their unequivocal Yes to the question we asked them.

Two early ones unnoticed in well-known passages remain —one *before* Spenser praised the young Sonnets-poet as 'Mercury' prior to March 1590, the other after. Since the later passage is more familiar, let us take it first.

It comes late in 1592, when the attack by the dying dramatist Robert Greene, M.A.—'scholar and gentleman', who had died destitute 3 September—was published. We realize that Greene attacked him as an 'upstart Crow' because—while still a well-paid actor, a plebeian crow beautified only by the elegant lines which gentlemen-playwrights from the University lend him to speak*—he had developed into a dangerous rival for their rewards: *as a playwright*, whose wares the actors were now buying. (The once-supposed charge of 'plagiarism' is imaginary. Every informed student of Shakespeare at present is aware that Greene makes no such charge.)

But since upon one point modern experts differ sharply about what Greene is here saying of Shakespeare, we should look again at this familiar passage. In it, Greene warns three gentlemen-playwrights 'his Quondam acquaintance'—whom we

---

* Compare Nashe (preface to Greene's *Menaphon* 1589) of the university writers: 'sweete gentlemen ... that haue ... tricked vp a company of taffata fooles with their feathers'. And Greene himself (*Francescoes fortunes* 1590, 132), quoting Cicero to the actor Roscius: 'Why ... art thou proud with *Esops* Crow, being pranct with the glorie of others feathers?'

recognize as Marlowe, Nashe, and probably Peele—against 'these painted monsters' the players. For these (in Chambers's paraphrase) 'have been beholden to him for the lines they have spoken, and have now deserted him. They will desert his friends likewise, since they have now a writer of their own', a player like themselves:

> Yes trust them not: for there is an vpstart Crow, beautified with our feathers, that with his *Tygers hart wrapt in a Players hyde*, supposes he is as well able to bombast out a blanke verse as the best of you: and beeing an absolute *Iohannes fac totum*, is in his owne conceit the onely Shakescene in a countrey.

Now here is the moot point: What exactly was it that Greene conveyed to his readers *by picking out this particular line* of Shakespeare's—Oh Tygres Heart, wrapt in a Womans Hide (*3 Hen. VI* 1.4.137)—and pointedly altering it to read 'with his *Tygers hart wrapt in a Players hyde*'?

Interpreters disagree. John Semple Smart, followed in our day by Peter Alexander, takes it for nothing more than venomous ridicule of *the player Shakespeare* and *his contemptible style*: 'his' means 'abominable fustian such as his line *Tygers hart, wrapt . . .*' pointed up by the spiteful change of *a Womans* to *a Players*. But Smart's examples, to illustrate such use of 'his', are all modern ones. If he could have adduced a single Elizabethan specimen he might have had some hope of persuading.

J. Dover Wilson, still believing that Greene here charges Shakespeare with plagiarism, sees in this line some added indictment of the upstart Crow. And he makes the incontestable point: 'if . . . the *player's hide* is Shakespeare's, the *tiger's heart* must be his as well'.

Before tackling the puzzle of what Greene conveyed by accusing Shakespeare of having a tiger's heart concealed in his bosom, we notice that all critics ponder this curious passage by itself, neglecting Thomas Bastard's counsel (*Chrestoleros* 1598): ''Tis hard to learn without a precedent.'

I find an instructive precedent, five years before Greene's *Groatsworth*, in William Rankins's *Mirrour of Monsters*, 1587, p. 17. For here similarly we have a gentleman-playwright—

Rankins—bitterly attacking those monsters the ingrate players for their treachery to him, *to whom they are all most bound.* Consummate hypocrites, with their pretence of kind-hearted scruple they even *deceive themselves, more unnatural than the cruel Tiger*:

> Such is the nature of those Plaiers, whether grounded by nature, or insinuated by some preposterous education I know not, but when the cheefe of their mischeefe is put in practise, [they protest that] they hate harmes, when in effect they deceive themselves, more unnaturall then the cruell Tygre, yet [as they pretend] hate they harmes, and [say that] loth are they to doo good to one man, to whome they are all most bound, least they should hurte another, therunto enjoined by their vertue of hating harme.

Rankins chooses the *tiger* to expose the *doubleness* of the ingrate players, just as Greene—in striking at a particular player, Shakespeare—singles out his *tiger* line, and puts 'Players' into it. This is the pointer.

Having missed it, critics have mistaken Greene's *tiger* quotation for 'a charge of cruelty': an error which leads straight to a mare's-nest. For Chettle, in defending Shakespeare against Greene's imputation, refutes no charge of 'cruelty'. What he *does* refute is a charge of *double-dealing*, of dishonesty. Against it he brings the testimony of 'divers of worship'—that is, of *several gentlemen**—to Shakespeare's 'vprightnes of dealing, which argues his honesty': in a word, his square dealing has shown the plebeian to be a *gentleman* by nature—'gentle Shakespeare'.

Thus Greene's charge, like Rankins's, is obviously not the tiger's hackneyed *cruelty*, but another notorious *unnatural* viciousness of his, *just like the deceptive feigning of actors*—whom

---

* Not *noblemen*; those were termed 'of honour'. See *OED s.v.* Worship *sb.* 4. '1598 Stow *Surv.* 265 In the cloyster were buried many persons, some of worship and others of honour. 1592 Greene *Upst. Courtier* F2 The other two ... seemed meaner then himselfe, but yet Gentlemen of good worship.' And we may add: 'A Gentleman ... the highest title of a gentleman is worshippfull. ... Esquire ... his title is Right Wo[rshi]pp-ful.' *A Treaty of dignities, and degrees.* British Library MS. Addl. 25257.

Stubbes (1583) calls 'doble dealing ambodexters' and 'dissembling *Hipocrites*'. On hunting the tiger we find it at once.

In Chaucer's *Squire's Tale*, the tercelet 'That semed welle of alle gentillesse, Al were he ful of treson and falsnesse' is unmasked as 'this tygre, ful of doublenesse', 'this ypocryte'. And in Capaccio's treatise on Devices, the archetype of Hypocrisy and Dissimulation is the Tiger. (*Delle Imprese*, 1592, 84.) Francis Meres, as his first instance under the heading *Hypocrisie*, gives the Tiger:

Hypocrites

   As the Tyger when he hunteth for his prey, doeth hide his clawes: so hypocrites for their commodity speake faire, when they meane ill.   *Palladis Tamia*, 1598, 318

It is a commonplace. Lodge has this same dissembling tiger in his *Rosalynde*; Greene gives it three times at least—in *Mamillia*, in *Alcida*, in *Greenes Never Too Late*; and in the anonymous play *Wily Beguiled* it is

   Well, trust him not: the tiger hides his claws
   When oft he doth pretend the greatest guiles   [*intend*

—which recalls Greene on the players: *Yes trust them not.*

So much for the Elizabethans' *tiger as hypocrite.* But there is more. They also present *that excellent actor* (ὑποκρῐτής) *Mercury as the Hypocrite par excellence.* With rancorous *odium academicum*, Dr. Gabriel Harvey holds up his rival, the supple and eloquent Dr. Andrew Perne—'Old Andrew Turncoat'—as a 'Doctour of Hypocrisie', 'an hypocrite . . . as convertible as Mercury':

   No man could . . . lullaby the circumspectest Argus more sweetly: or transforme himselfe into all shapes more deftly; or play any part more kindly [*i.e.*, naturally].*

To sum up: Harvey cites *the excellent player Mercury* as the Hypocrite; Rankins illustrates hypocrite *players* with the dissembling *tiger*; and Greene puts the *tiger's* heart into that

---

* *Op. cit.*, Bb2ᵛ, Bb3ᵛ. 'O Mercurie, . . . Dooblenesse is thy furtherer.' Lodge, *Catharos*, 1591, B1ᵛ. 'Dissembling Mercury!' Beaumont, *Masque*.

'double-dealing' *player Shakespeare*, whom Chettle rates as *excellent* in the quality of playing.

Now is there ground enough here for the indicated conclusion, that Greene and his readers in 1592 thought of Shakespeare as Mercury? To warrant taking that step, all we need is to have *Greene showing double-dealing Mercury with a tiger in his bosom*. And on looking back we find him giving that very picture in his *Planetomachia* (1585), in great Jupiter's address to his son, the planet Mercury in evil or retrograde aspect:

> And you *Mercurie* [breed in mens mindes] pollicies, sleightes, faire promises & small performance, causing men by your variable impression to flatter friend or foe, to sweare in mouth, and forsweare in hart, to beare two faces vnder a hood, *to carry a Lamb in his shield, and a Tygre in his bosome*: with the one hand to present spice, and wyth the other hemblocke . . .

The italics are mine. Mercury carrying the innocent lamb is Hermes Kriophoros, later identified with the Good Shepherd. It is of course Mercury the planet *only in evil aspect* who also carries the tiger in his bosom. Robert Burton's sketch of the *hypocrite* recalls both Harvey and Greene: 'to act twenty parts & persons at once for his advantage, to temporize and vary like *Mercury* . . . as meek as a lamb, & yet again grin like a tiger . . .' *Anat. Mel.*, 'Democritus Junior to the Reader' (ed. Shilleto 1923, 1.70).

There it is. And to leave no doubt that it is '*Mercury*'– Shakespeare whom he is attacking, Greene adds the clincher, identifying that 'Shake-scene' as *being an absolute Johannes Factotum*. This is conclusive; for whether you choose to take *Johannes Factotum* as 'Johnny Do-all', or as 'Jack of all trades', or as 'universal genius', you unavoidably still have *Mercury*, since Mercury *is each of these*.

As Kasmilos or Kadmilos, the never-resting do-all servant on Olympus up to his ears in business, the number and variety of his manifold duties are too well known. Again, Mercury is Grand Master of all the arts and crafts. Gabriel Harvey speaks of 'every Mercuriall occupationer, that is, every Master of his craft'; and in the first scene of Dryden's *Amphitryon* Mercury says, 'you know I am a kind of Jack of all Trades'. Finally, as 'universal genius', the Inventor of Letters and of Eloquence, the Poet, the Inventor of stringed Music, of the Dance, of Wrestling, of Dress, of Astronomy, Numbering, and Geometry, the Teacher, the Law-giver, the Founder of Religious Sacrifices, &c., is Mercury—'*of the Gods whole session The most ingenious Genius*'. (*Homeric Hymn to Hermes*, tr. George Chapman.)

We have gone below surface-appearances back to the connotations of the Elizabethans. And now we may well ask, Could any reader of Greene's venomous attack in 1592 miss that *player-and-poet Mercury*—that multi-faced hypocrite the protean Mercury with his tiger's* heart wrapt in a player's hide, that absolute Johannes Factotum—in this *player-and-scribbler Shake-scene*, this double-dealing tiger, this perfect Johnny Do-all?

Just as with all the others we have quoted, Shakespeare is unmistakably 'Mercury' also to Greene and to his readers here in 1592, as he already was in 1590 to the prince of poets, Edmund Spenser.

*   *   *

The words of Mercury

Now if recovered knowledge can cast light in 1592, we may not neglect to test what it might be able to do earlier still: at the very date of our miniature, 1588/9.

In *Mr. W. H.* (230–237) I detailed the reasons for seeing *Love's Labour's Lost* as written and presented for Gray's Inn's Christmas saturnalia 1588/9, before Prince Will Hatcliffe. But since then we have added a capital fact to our knowledge of that Prince. We have now recognized him as *ex officio* the publicly royalized and glorified *Apollo* of the Delphic and proudly oracular Gray's Inn, whose coat of arms still today is Apollo's immemorial symbol, the golden Griffin, *Knowledge*. This prime feature, never before realized, provides as we shall find the missing key to the most enigmatic line in *Love's Labour's Lost*.

* '*Countries subiect to Mercury . . . Hircania*'—the land of tigers, south of the Caspian Sea. J. Maplet, *op. cit.*, 18ᵛ.

Many readers must share Richard David's feeling, expressed in his New Arden edition, that 'of all Shakespeare's plays this is the most personal'—and not only because of its wealth of echoes from the Sonnets. The more one lives with the play, the stronger grows one's sense of our poet's full sympathy with the moment and very mood of this guest-thronged gala of young Grayans 'flowing and swelling o'er with arts and exercise'. More, one feels that as their *gracioso* he knows they like him. He therefore warms to his work, expands, writes *con amore*. For although it is not a lyric but a play, and one cannot put a finger on every precise *how*, the man himself irresistibly comes through. Dr. Johnson knew no play 'that has more evident marks of the hand of *Shakespeare*'.

To turn now to the text, printed a decade after its first performance. For Shakespeare's contemporary readers, the year 1598 is a notable one. It marks the first appearance of any book with his name printed on the title-page. In 1598 *four* such appeared: the second edition in Quarto of *Richard III*, the second and third Quartos of *Richard II*, and the first Quarto of *Love's Labour's Lost*; this last being the first play which *came out as Shakespeare's*. And of these four Quartos first printed with his name, *Love's Labour's Lost* is the only one advertised as 'Newly corrected and augmented *By W. Shakespere*'—claiming revision of an earlier publication of this comedy. For if *corrected* be taken merely to promise unusual accuracy in printing, the text does not bear it out.

The printed play's detail most peculiar and arresting is its end, its final sentence. And beyond the *content* or meaning of this sentence (which is striking in itself), the compositor was sent to another fount to get for it *a larger size of type*, to catch every reader's eye. Who could have sent him, one asks, but the author-and-corrector? And why insist upon procuring this *conspicuous type*, *never used in his other books*, except that he, Shakespeare, had a pregnant and important *message* in this final sentence?—

The wordes of Mercurie, are harsh after the
 songes of Apollo.

We note that here is no speech-heading to indicate who it is that delivers this parting line. And since (as Chambers observes) 'Mercury has nothing to do with what precedes'—for except in one simile neither Mercury nor Apollo appears in the play— small wonder that criticism is nonplussed, its few guesses random and diffident.

A pleafant conceited Comedie.

Then nightly finges the ftaring Owle
Tu-whit to-who.
  A merrie note,
    While greafie Ione doth keele the pot.

When all aloude the winde doth blow,
And coffing drownes the Parfons faw;
And Birdes fit brooding in the Snow,
And Marrians nofe lookes red and raw:
When roafted Crabbs hiffe in the bowle,
Then nightly finges the ftaring Owle,
Tu-whit to-who,
  A merrie note,
    While greafie Ione doth keele the pot.

The vvordes of Mercurie, are harsh after the fonges of Apollo.

FINIS.

In my view it is Chambers who comes close to the truth when he says 'it looks like the beginning of an epilogue'. For I see it as *an epilogue*. An epilogue not merely beginning, but complete. Further (although the briefest), an epilogue as graceful, as courtly, and as pithily eloquent as any he ever wrote. And finally, a *personal* epilogue, *spoken by Shakespeare of himself as the Poet Mercury, the author*. Coleridge, describing this play, saw young Shakespeare as 'this youthful god of poetry'.

As by magic, the line brings the very place and the very moment before us. We are in the Delphic temple, 'Oracle of the *Graii*', the brightly lit Hall of Gray's Inn. Outside the walls it is cold Winter: but here within, the eternal Spring of the Golden Age is come again.

Surrounded by the gay Christmas throng of young Purpoole gallants and their lady-guests, Shakespeare and his
fellows are winding up the bantering saturnalian wit and
mirth of his 'domestical merriment' of Love Unrequited before
Purpoole's Prince of True Love, 'Apollo': presiding in his
festive character as the god of dance and of song.

In propitiation, and to extol their royal Apollo Cantor
whom they have chaffed with 'Pompey the Big', 'Pompey the
Huge', Shakespeare closes with music: songs of Spring and of
Winter, those opposites which are here with us at once. But
he has a more obvious reason for this duet of *Hiems*-Winter
and *Ver* the Spring, and for giving *Ver* the lead.

From Ferne's *Blazon of Gentrie* (1586) we learned (*Mr. W. H.*,
201) what the gold colour of the Topaz signifies: in Planets,
the Sunne—Phoebus Apollo; in Virtues, *Faith & Constancy*; in
Ages of Man, *Yong age of adolescentia*; in Seasons of the Year,
Springtime. As Shakespeare sings to his Phoebus, *only herauld
to the gaudy spring, 'the spring . . . doth shaddow of your beautie show'.*
Here is *Ver* for *the faithful* young Apollo of the Sonnets—
fair, kind, and true—, of Hilliard's *Dat pœnas*, and of Gray's
Inn.

Now before turning to Ferne's revealing list for Mercury's
colour, we remind ourselves again of that god's astonishing
duality. On the one hand, Hermes is familiar as a babe or a
handsome youth; and on the other—in the bearded and
ithyphallic herms—he is an experienced old man, type of
Prudence and the efficient power of Eloquence. Thus *Mercurius Biformis* appears twofold in a double statue as Hermer-
cules: the *puer senex, paedogeron*, or 'hoary youth'. (Cf. E. Wind,
op. cit., 99–100, 200, 202*n.*, and E. Panofsky, *Stud. in Iconology*,
1939, fig. 68.)

This realization prepares us for what we now find in Ferne's
list under Mercury's colour, Purple. For it signifies in Planets,
Mercury; in Precious Stones, *Amethyst*; in Virtues, *Temperance
& Prudence*; in Ages of Man, *Cana Senectus* (*Hoary Old Age*);
and in Seasons of the year, *Winter*. (Mercury therefore figures
prominently in Caron's painting *Le Triomphe de l'Hiver*. J.
Ehrmann, *Antoine Caron*, 1955, Pl. II.) Here is *Hiems*-Winter
for the eloquent Mercury–Shakespeare: the 'Nestor' of the

Sonnets, *beated and chopt with tand antiquitie*, in reply to the stripling Apollo of Purpoole's *Ver*.*

Then to end with a final grace (since epilogues should close with a prayer for the sovereign, as in 2 *Hen. IV*), the humble player-and-poet—who no doubt played his mercurial Berowne,† bewitched by Lady Rosaline's black eyes—steps out in an Epilogue as Mercury–Shakespeare: to bow low to the company, to apologize for his play, and to honour his listening sovereign, his Friend, True Loving Apollo. And because 'Apollo himselfe loveth brevitie'—witness his *Nothing in excess* and his *Know thyself*—as Mercury the Soul of Wit he achieves all this in the brevity of a single line:

> *The words of Mercury are harsh after the songs of Apollo.*

Here, like the close of a royal proclamation—*Vivat Rex*—, King *Apollo* bears the emphasis, the crown. And for the print of 1598, the large type compels attention: as though the herald Mercury–Shakespeare were sounding again the *oyez!* of his Sonnet 104: *hear this*.

Consider what his brief pronouncement implies. It shows again what we already know, that at Gray's Inn 1588/9 Will Hatcliffe, the Sovereign of Purpoole, was familiar to the whole audience as their King *Apollo*, as he presents himself in his contemporary Hilliard portrait-Device, the wry-legg'd Loxias with his 'fine secret' label, W H. More than that, it now reveals that *Will Shakespeare* was also familiar to them as *their Apollo's poet-friend, his Mercury*. Finally, it shows that Shakespeare *repeated and underlined this identification* for his readers ten years later. Crowning Dr. Johnson's perception, here in the text now stands conspicuous *the most* 'evident mark of the hand of *Shakespeare*'.

To sum it up, in his personal epilogue to *Love's Labour's Lost* spoken 1588/9, we hear the blond young poet Shakespeare

---

* In 1613/4, when Gray's Inn had another Phoebus-Sol, their Masque of Flowers recalled this *Love's Labour's Lost* feature of Winter and Spring: *Invierno and Primavera . . . received their despatch from the Sunne, by Gallus* [the Cock], *the Sunne's Messenger*. Repr. Nichols, *Progr. of James I*, 2.736.

† See Walter Pater, *Appreciations*, 1889. And cf. Anon., 'Berowne as Shakespeare', *TLS*, 16 Nov. 1946.

with unmistakable words identifying himself as the Poet Mercury, Friend of Apollo. At that same time, in the poetical portrait-Device of 1588, Hilliard's CLASPING A HAND, we see a blond young MAN with unmistakable signs identifying himself as the Poet Mercury, Friend of Apollo.

Now is or is not this sitter the blond young poet whom (as we have seen) his contemporaries—friends and enemies both—universally saw as 'the poet Mercury': *William Shakespeare*, drawn to the life?

In a question so momentous as this, we should welcome some clear evidence for or against from an independent quarter; and we look to the next chapter.

9

Lord Strange's Man

HAVING looked with the eyes of 1588, and surmised in these *Athenians for love* (the humble Poet 'Mercury' declaring True Friendship with his beloved 'King Apollo') those Unequal Friends of 1588 the plebeian Sonnets-poet Mercury–Shakespeare and his *Sun, God,* and *Sovereign* Prince Will Hatcliffe, *ex officio* the Apollo of the Delphic Gray's Inn, we have been making ourselves look *with the eyes of the educated Elizabethan.*

Can we possibly have failed to catch some feature of it far more obvious to the man in the street than any of those we have noticed? A feature which any 'letterless companion', any illiterate loiterer of the time, would recognize on sight? The bare suggestion is annoying enough to make us think again.

Now what sort of feature would that be? A distinguishing mark or sign, doubtless, of a kind common in that age and unusual in ours. And the obvious common Elizabethan sign which comes first to mind is the household *badge* or *cognizance*: a king's, a peer's, a knight's, or a gentleman's distinctive device or emblem which identified his retainers, his servants. Made of silver, lead, dyed cloth, or embroidery, the badge might be worn(as sometimes by gentlemen-retainers) on the hat; but the ubiquitous and thronging blue-coated serving-men normally wore it high on the left sleeve, where the soldier's shoulder flash is still worn today.

Those badge-marked followers made so prominent a figure in the Elizabethan scene as to strike the foreign observer. Paul Hentzner, for example, the German tourist of 1598, remarks that 'the English magnates, both at home and out of doors, draw after them great troops of household retainers'. As

William Basse says, 'attended and well mand With serving resolutes'. And a dialogue of 1579 runs:

> But what bee these tall fellowes of whom you speake?
> They bee our servingmen, that attend upon our Table, and follow us in the streetes, when wee bee at *London* . . . and furnish our Halles at home . . . Were it for the worship of a Gentleman, having good lande and revenues, to keepe no more servauntes then . . . those that for their necessary uses they must needes imploy? If wee Gentlemen should so doo, how should wee furnish our Halles? how should wee be ready for quarrellers?
> I thought I had knowen all the retinue of a Noble mans, or a Gent[lemans] house. But now I finde I do not, for it semeth a whole Army or Camp.
>
> *Cyuile and vncyuile life*, 1579, E3, F2;
> with *u, v*, modernized

As for 'quarrellers', in the feud between the families of Juliet and Romeo it is by their enemy's badge that the armed Capulet serving-men recognize that 'Here comes [two] of the house of Montagues.' And when the inevitably resulting fight has to be broken up by club-swinging citizens, these can tell by those badges which heads to hit—'*Down with the Capulets! down with the Montagues!*'

Although Edward IV and Richard Crookback had been gone now for a hundred years, Shakespeare could rely on the common playgoers to know their badges—the *sun in splendour* and the *white boar*: 'Made glorious summer by this sun of York' and 'this most bloody boar'. But a few extracts will serve to demonstrate how far we modern readers are from knowing what the humblest Elizabethan Cockney knew about those everyday sights, the familiar badges.

We draw first from a popular chapbook *ca.* 1595: a collection of *Jests*—many of them traditional and common, but a few possibly authentic—of the late famous clown, Dick *Tarlton*:

> [At an expensive *ordinary* or *table d'hôte* eating-house, Tarlton] being set amongst the gentlemen and gallants, they enquired of him why melancholy had got the upper

hand of his mirth. To which he said little, but, with a squint eye . . . looked for a jest to make them merry. At last he espied one that sate on his left side, which had a very red face, he being a very great gentleman, which was all one to Tarlton, hee presently in great haste called his host, Whoe doe I serve, my host, quoth Tarlton. The Queenes Majestie, replied the good man of the house. [*Tarlton, an Ordinary Groom of Her Majesty's Chamber, was by far the most notable member of her company of players.*] How happens it then, quoth Tarlton, that to her Majesties disgrace, you dare make me a companion with servingmen, clapping my Lord Shandoyes cullisance [badge] upon my [left] sleeve, looking at the gentleman [at his left] with the red face. . . . The gentlemans salamanders face burned like Etna for anger. The rest laughed heartily.

The point of this crude and impudent joke—quite dark to us until we look it up—is that Lord Chandos's heraldic crest was *an old man's head*. And nothing could be clearer here than that the chapbook-reader, the man in the street, knew it as his badge: *a head scarlet or flame-coloured*, displayed in cloth on the blue sleeves of his men—'the Shandoyses'.

Our next extract vividly exposes the fugacity of some of these items of common knowledge. Question: Why did Queen Elizabeth, writing in 1597 to console Lady Norris of Rycote (afflicted by the death of her son, England's great soldier Sir John Norris), call her '*Myne owne Crowe*'? Thomas Fuller—who was eight years old when Shakespeare died—already found himself no less stumped by this question than our modern historians do. Lady Norris, he hazarded, 'being (as it seemeth) *black* in complexion'.

Turning to the Queen's visit of 1592 to her loving Norrises at Rycote, we find—among the speeches (written most probably by Lyly) memorized to greet the great guest with—Lord Norris addressing her in the character of 'an olde gentleman'. And after mentioning 'the Crowe my wife' he goes on to assure his Queen that

> although nothing be more vnfit to lodge your Maiestye, then a crowes neste, yet shall it be most happy to vs, that

it is by your highnesse made a Phœnix neste. *Qui color ater erat, nunc est contrarius atro.**

'Whereby the colour which was black, is now the contrary to black.' And later, when the rich gifts have been offered, he adds

> For my selfe, my crowe, and all our birds, this I promise, that they are all as faithfull in their feathers [*i.e., black* for *constancy*] as they were in their shels.

Bond, Lyly, 1.485, 489

The simple explanation of all this—already forgotten in Fuller's time—appears in an old list of 'Crests & Badges':†

> *Norreys Crest   a crow sable langued gules.*

Wearing it as their master's badge, those familiar flocking servants of Lord and Lady Norris, whose motto was *Feythfull serve*, made a colony of faithful *crows*: 'the Norrises'—like 'the Capulets' and 'the Montagues' of the theatre.

Not less illuminating, finally, and more important for understanding Shakespeare, is the example following.‡ Critics have discussed the rhapsodical rhetoric of Hotspur's famous speech

> By heauen, me thinkes it were an easie leap,
> To plucke bright Honor from the pale-fac'd Moone

without ever thinking to ask *why*—unless he is lunatic—it is especially in *the moon* that Harry Percy sees bright honour, for him to pluck and 'wear without corrival'. But on the ground in Shakespeare's playhouse, each penny 'understander' understood the *wherefore*.

The identifying badge which every Percy wears is his family's

---

* Adapting Ovid's familiar *Qui color albus erat, nunc est contrarius albo*— *Met.* 2.541, on Apollo's raven or 'crow'.

† MS. Harl. 2076 f. 52. Shortly before the year 1500, William and Margaret Berneweysued Sir Henry Merney(married to the widow of John Norreys, esquire) for payment for '80 bages of ravens hedys browderd' made for the said John Norreys.—*P.R.O. Early Chancery Proceedings*, III, 1906, 368.

‡ Corrected and enlarged from my 'Taking Shakespeare at his word', Univ. of Cincinnati, *Shakespeare Studies* I, 1965, 137–141.

silver crescent moon, displayed both in the popular ballad *The Rising of the North Countrie*—

> Erle Percy there his ancyent spred,   [*ensign*
> The Halfe-Moone shining all soe faire

—and in Drayton's *The Barons' Wars* 2.24:

> The Noble Percy . . .
> With a bright Cressant in his Guidehome came.* [*guidon,
> pennant*]

Similarly,

> Northumber . . . his *Crescent* fils
> Chapman, verses on *Sejanus*, line 142

and—addressing Algernon Lord Percy—

> my Pen . . . shal runne
> Beyond the Moone, to make thy Moone a Sunne.
> John Davies of Hereford, prefixed
> to *Humours Heau'n* . . .

Again before Shrewsbury fight Shakespeare presents the renowned Percy Moon—equally unseen by the modern eye—in the King's stern demand of Thomas Percy Lord Worcester (who, as Westmoreland had warned him, was a planet 'Maleuolent to you in all Aspects'):

> Will you
> . . . moue in that obedient Orbe againe,
> Where you did giue a faire and naturall light . . . ?

---

* '[Anagram] For the Earl of Northumberland:

> *Henricus Percius*. Hic pure sincerus.

Upon which, with relation to the Crescent or silver Moon his Cognisance, was framed this:

> "Percius 'hic pure sincerus,' Percia Luna
> Candida tota micat, pallet at illa polo." '
> W. Camden, *Remains* . . ., ed. 1870, 188–189.

And once more at the climax, when armed Rebellion confronts Rule: Harry Percy meets Harry Monmouth.

> I am the Prince of Wales, and thinke not *Percy*,
> To share with me in glory any more:
> Two Starres keepe not their motion in one Sphere,
> Nor can one England brooke a double reigne,
> Of *Harry Percy*, and the Prince of Wales.

The two great *stars* which cannot move in one planetary sphere are Shakespeare's *moist star* or *wat'ry star*—the Moon, or Harry Percy, and his majestic rising *day-star*—the coming Sun or King, Henry, 'This Starre of England'.

Moon, planet, and star—which we took to be three far bodies in space—are in fact all one: the Percy Moon, symbolizing its mighty wearers. By its light we now instantly realize with Shakespeare's audience that Percy's honour-seeking leap presents no moonstruck fancy, but rebellion; that the astrological metaphor of the other passages is likewise focused by Westmoreland, King, and Prince upon that malevolent mutinous Moon whose exorbitant pull makes the tension of this political drama.

Further, that Percy Crescent also casts light upon an earlier passage of the play. When the rebel lords are dividing England up (before having conquered it), Harry Percy utterly rejects the winding Trent-boundary of his share:

> See, how this Riuer comes me cranking in
> And cuts me from the best of all my Land,
> A huge halfe Moone, a monstrous Cantle out.

Since on the map it resembles a half-moon, the veriest child will recognize that monstrous cantle to be *Percy* property. Percy demands it as obviously his own. And his own he will have, even if he must shift England's greatest Midland river to get it.*

---

* While we are on the moon, I may recall my reply to the specious but shallow objection ('the crescent moon cannot be eclipsed') raised to my identification of *The mortall Moone* (Son. 107) as *the deadly* Spanish Armada in *crescent formation*. For surely the moon can be eclipsed in any phase— 'cloudes Gan to eclips Lucinas siluer face' (Greene & Lodge)—just as

Some of the leading peers did not limit themselves to a single badge. The Somersets, Earls of Worcester, used several, as did the Radcliffes, Earls of Sussex. The Stanleys, Earls of Derby, were known both by the Eagle and Child and by the Eagle's (Hawk's, Griffin's) Foot; and Queen Elizabeth herself, not only by the Tudor Rose but also (among others) by the sceptred Falcon on a stock, the Phoenix, the Pomegranate, the Pelican, and the True-love Knot.

In *Mr. W. H.* (pp. 165–170) I pointed out Purpoole's obvious purpose of pleasing the Queen by choosing for their prince Will Hatcliffe, his arms *three quatrefoil-primroses or True-loves*. Yet at the same time I failed to fathom their equal cunning seven years later in the election of Will's supplanter, Henry Helmes. But now if I am asked what they found in that young gentleman's arms—*three helmets*, giving the Principality of Purpoole its Heroical Order of the Helmet—to flatter that helmeted Pallas Elizabeth Tudor with, I can call in Michael Drayton to supply the answer in a line of his *Englands Heroicall Epistles*—

    . . . the Helme (the TUDORS ancient Crest)

—with his added note, '*The Armes of* Tudor, *was three Helmets*'.

Already in Dick Tarlton, known by her Majesty's cognizance as a 'Queen's man', we have touched on the companies of players who wore their lord's badge as their protection and their pride. In Shakespeare's youth, as most readers well know, Lord Leicester's players, wearing his *white ragged staff*, cut a leading figure enhanced by the great wealth and power of their renowned master. On the very day of Leicester's death,

---

the sun can: 'the Sun eclipst with steaming smoke' (Weever, *Mirr. of Martyrs*). And as for enemy crescents enduring eclipses by shattering defeats at sea, 'The silver crescents in the tops they [the Turks] carried . . . from his fury suffer'd sad eclipses.' (Fletcher, *A Wife for a Month*.) Exhilarating, to find Dover Wilson (ed. *Sonnets* 1967), after spurning my interpretation of *The mortall Moone* with 'the moon is only eclipsed when full' (lxxxviii), silently *adopting* (217–218, to refute Chambers) my identical explanation (*Shakespeare's Sonnets Dated*, 1949, 10) of 'our Terrene Moone Is now Eclipst' as *the crescent* of Antony's and Cleopatra's *Mediterranean Fleet*.

and long before that news reached them, his players obtained
the jailing of a cobbler in Norwich for nothing more heinous
than 'lewd woordes uttered against the ragged staff'. And even
four years later Tom Nashe sounds a warning: 'The ragged
cognizance on the sleeue . . . carried meate in the mouth when
time was: doe not dispraise it yet, for it hath many high par-
takers.'

Returning to Shakespeare, everyone knows that as a player
he served successively two Lords Chamberlain, favourite
cousins of the Queen's: Henry Carey first Lord Hunsdon, and
his son George Carey second Lord Hunsdon.*

If therefore Shakespeare was known by the Hunsdon crest,
wearing that badge for nine of the best years of his life, 1594–
1603, one might have expected to find it mentioned in one
of the countless works devoted to him. But I think (always
under correction) that it first appeared in my *First Night of
'Twelfth Night'*, 1954:

> bearing . . . their noble master's cognizance, *a silver swan*†
> *flying*: the badge which, as well as being 'the proper
> ensigne of Poetrie . . . the swanne', gave their great poet
> his nickname, the sweet *Swan of Avon*. For these are the
> Servants of the Right Honourable the Baron Hunsdon,
> Lord Chamberlain of Her Majesty's Household, the finest
> company of actors in Christendom.

Describing Robert Carey, Henry Lord Hunsdon's youngest
son in his *Polyhymnia*, Peele calls the noble father *our silver
Swan*:

> By this the Trumpe cal'd Carey to the Tilt,
> Faire bird, fair Cignet of our silver Swanne . . .

---

* In Plate VI of Chambers's *William Shakespeare* (1.64), the lower
portrait, labelled *Henry* by mistake for *George* and painted 1581, evidently
cannot represent George Lord Hunsdon. For Hunsdon, born 1547, at this
date was but *34 years old*, and the miniature gives this man's age in 1581
as *53*—a man old enough to have been Hunsdon's father.

† The Careys had a royal example for their choice: 'K[ing] H[enry] 4:
Crest a swan silver, wings displayed.' MS. Harl. 2076 f. 44. When
Shakespeare wrote *The History of Henrie the Fourth* he was wearing his royal
hero's crest.

Hilliard's superb portrait at Berkeley Castle of George Lord Hunsdon shows his *Swan* badge. In the colour-enlargement illustrating my article 'Queen Elizabeth's Master Painter' (*Sunday Times Magazine*, 22 March 1970, 47) we see on his left shoulder a small white jewel: *a Swan arg., wings endorsed* (lifted & backed).* The Hunsdon *Swan* is described in the armorials as *rising, volant, flying*. In Jonson's praise in the First Folio we can now understand that he is recalling not only the charm of Shakespeare's poetry, but also his Hunsdon badge, the *flying Swan*:

> *Sweet Swan of* Auon, *what a sight it were*
> *To see thee in our waters yet appeare,*
> *And make those flights vpon the bankes of* Thames,
> *That so did take* Eliza, *and our* Iames!

Any eyes now recognizing that *the Swan* instantly connoted the Lords Chamberlain Hunsdon will at once turn to the sumptuous playhouse across the Thames in Paris Garden—whose flag displayed The Swan. The traveller Johannes de Witt describes it about 1596, the year after it was completed and opened:

> But of all the [four] theatres, the finest and most spacious is the one whose sign is the Swan . . . inasmuch as it may receive three thousand persons in its galleries.

Situated in Surrey beyond the control of the City authorities, the Manor of Paris Garden had been granted in 1578 by the Crown to *nominees of Henry Lord Hunsdon*. These conveyed it to the Cure family, one of whom in 1589 sold it to Francis Langley. Five years later, when the plague had abated in 1594, Langley set about building London's finest theatre there. Whereupon the Lord Mayor, urged by the City's inveterate hostility to

---

* 'Out of the name of the late Lord Hunsdon, Lord Chamberlain, and his Creast the white Swan, was this Anagram and Distich thereon composed:

> *Georgius Carius Hunesdonius.*
> Hujus in suos candor egregius.
> "Hunsdonii egregius resplendet pectore candor,
> Hujus ut in cygno nil nisi candor inest." '
>
> Camden (*ed. cit.*), 190.

playhouses, tried to get Lord Burghley to forbid the project—but in vain.

This rebuff to the Lord Mayor suggests 'interest' at Court and in the Privy Council on Langley's behalf. And the fact that the Queen's cousin Lord Hunsdon not only maintained a company of players but a few years before had had the disposal of Paris Garden points to the Lord Chamberlain as the likeliest source of that 'interest'. But however it was, Langley in the face of the City Fathers' hostility clearly needed all the backing from the Lord Chamberlain he could get.

And so when it came to choosing a sign for his new theatre, we may be very sure that his choice was not suggested (as J. Q. Adams fancied) 'by the large numbers of swans which beautified the Thames', but by a reason as hard-headed and prudential as Drake's for renaming his ship *The Golden Hind*, badge of his backer, Lord Chancellor Hatton. (E. St. J. Brooks, *Sir Christopher Hatton*, 1946, Ch. XVIII.) Langley sought a palladium, a protection. For if the City's attack pressed his playhouse hard, he could hope that no Hunsdon would suffer *The Swan* 'upon the bankes of Thames' to come to grief.

Unfortunately for both Langley and the players, however, in the year after the Swan was opened Henry Lord Hunsdon died, 22 July 1596. And though his heir George of course maintained the Hunsdon patronage of Shakespeare's company, the dead Hunsdon's all-important office of Lord Chamberlain passed to William Brooke Lord Cobham, who did not like stage-players. He would not protect them against the enmity of London's rulers and their determined efforts to drive them out of both City and suburbs. As Tom Nashe wrote to a friend in the late summer, 'now the players ar piteously persecuted by the L. Maior & the aldermen, & howeuer in there old Lords tyme they thought there state setled, it is now so vncertayne they cannot build vpon it'.

It is at this low point in the fortunes of the Hunsdon company that my discovery of a document about Shakespeare threw significant light. Since I detailed its reaching implications in *Shakespeare versus Shallow* (1931), it is enough here to recall only that it reveals Shakespeare, having moved from Bishopsgate south to Bankside (near the new Swan Playhouse), joined with Francis Langley in a quarrel with the rascally local justice of the peace William Gardiner and his stepson-and-tool William Wayte. My obvious conclusion is that the new Lord Hunsdon's Swan-wearing Servants had for a time settled to act in Langley's Swan: less exposed to persecution there than in Shoreditch. During their stay, the earlier *Hamlet* of their repertory at the Theatre must have been a drawing card, as the line in Dekker's *Satiromastix* reveals: 'My names Hamlet revenge: thou hast been at Parris garden hast not?'

After but seven months, luckily, their 'vncertayne state' ended with the death (5 March 1597) of Lord Cobham and the appointment some ten days later of their master, George Lord Hunsdon, as Lord Chamberlain. And shortly before this welcome event the company had left the Swan.

So much, then, for Shakespeare's badge as a 'Hunsdon's man', the *Swan* which identified him to all eyes in the period 1594–1603. But here we are focused upon him much earlier: in 1588, most probably New Year's 1588/9, the date of CLASP-ING A HAND. Our precise question is, Whose man was the player Shakespeare *then*? In his twenty-fifth year whose badge did he wear?

The late leading authorities J. T. Murray, Percy Simpson, and Sir Edmund Chambers—afterwards also joined by T. W. Baldwin—were all convinced that Shakespeare (at least after Leicester's death in September 1588) was one of *Ferdinando Lord Strange's* players. Baldwin makes it 1588 *or earlier*. One strong piece of evidence for the conviction is familiar: Shakespeare's *Titus Andronicus*, by a specific statement in Jonson's *Bartholomew Fair*, is dated as having first been acted between 1584 and 1589; and the title-page of that play (entered 6 February 1594, before Ferdinando's death) gives the Earl of Derby's Men (who in the late 1580s were Lord Strange's) first in the list of owners of the play.

Recent study of other early works of Shakespeare's concurs in this conclusion for the period before 1592: 'the evidence ... especially as regards 2 and *3 Henry VI*, is in favour of Strange's as Shakespeare's company'.*

* A. S. Cairncross, ed. *3 Henry VI* (Arden 1964), xlv. And see E. A. J. Honigmann, ed. *King John* (Arden 1954), liii.

Further, one would naturally expect a player *who was also a poet* to find service with Lord Strange, later described as

> The most honourable and worthy Prince Ferdinand
> Earle of Darbie, Viscount Kenton, Baron Stanley of
> Latham, Strange of Knocking, Mohun of Dunster, Lacy,
> Woodville, Bassett, &c., King of the Isle of Man, and
> [Great-]Great Grandchild to King Henry the Seaventh.

For that young scion of Tudor royalty, in Chapman's view 'most ingenious', and styled *Amyntas* as a Virgilian shepherd, not only wrote poetry himself, as Sidney says (unnoticed by modern critics) in *Astrophil and Stella* 6—

> Another humbler wit to shepheard's pipe retires,
> Yet hiding royall bloud full oft in rurall vaine

—but as Spenser adds, by lines substituted in *Colin Clout* just after *Amyntas* had died, the lamented poet-earl with his great wealth also *supported poets*:

> *Amyntas* floure of shepheards pride forlorne:
> He whilest he liuëd was the noblest swaine,
> That euer pipëd in an oaten quill:
> Both did he other, which could pipe, maintaine,
> And eke could pipe himselfe with passing skill.* [*exceeding*

And William Covell (*Polimanteia*, 1595), deeply mourning the Muses' great loss in Ferdinando's death, expects the poets to 'honour him . . . who liuing honoured you'. If Tom Nashe, dedicating his *Pierce Penilesse* (1592) to Lord Strange as *Amyntas*, is warmly grateful for 'benefits receiued', is it credible that the noble 'maintainer of poets' had not extended his kindness also to his servant Shakespeare of the Sonnets?

Now since Shakespeareans have not been aware of the cognizances of Chandos, Norris, Percy, and Hunsdon, it is no surprise to find Lord Strange's badge similarly unknown to

---

* Two short poems by Ferdinando–*Amyntas*, together with the one already known, have recently been printed with valuable comment by their discoverer, Dr. Steven H. May (*Modern Philology* 70, 1972, 49–52), except for his forgetting that '*passing* skill' means *exceeding, transcendent*; not 'passable or tolerable skill'.

them. The only attempt in that direction which I have seen is Sir Edmund Chambers's, as follows: 'Strange's men would naturally have worn the Stanley badge,' he wrote, illustrating that badge with a report dated 1592 about a disguised priest who 'uses to travel in a blue coat with the eagle and child on his sleeve'. (*Op. cit.*, 1.45.)

To the casual eye, this assumption of Chambers's looks plausible enough. In my *I, William Shakespeare* (1937) I accepted it myself. (And at page 145, in noting Shakespeare's connection with the Bushells of Broad Marston, I pointed out the strong probability that in 1591 Edward Bushell and Shakespeare were fellow-servants in the household of Ferdinando Lord Strange.) For the Stanley badge was the Eagle and Child, and Lord Strange was a Stanley. But when one considers Henry Stanley fourth Earl of Derby and his heir Ferdinando Stanley Lord Strange a little more closely, its impossibility in practice is only too obvious.

In 1572, at the age of twelve, Ferdinando had become 'Baron Strange' on the death of his grandfather Edward and the succession of his father Henry Lord Strange as Earl of Derby. Ferdinando was married in 1579 to Alice Spencer, youngest daughter of the wealthiest commoner in England—with whose family Edmund Spenser claimed he was allied—and had set up his own household. By 1588 he was the father of three daughters. His was a household both large and princely, as befitted such a peer: 'of descent from Royall lynage' by his mother, and heir of the richest noble in the realm. The servants of the Earl his father would of course wear the Stanley badge, the Eagle and Child. His own throng of servants, however, would wear *his* household cognizance: the hereditary Strange badge; *not* the Eagle and Child. The question faces us: *What was that badge?*

We turn to James Fairbairn's *Book of Crests* (ed. 1905, 1.532*b*, 340*a*), and under the name *Strange* find the three following:

Strange of London, *two hands clasped* . . .
Strange of Gloucs. & Wilts., . . . *two hands clasped* . . .
Lestrange, Le Strange, Norf., *two hands* . . . *conjoined* . . .

In a flash we are back to the central gesture which our MAN displays. But with a marked difference. In our portrait-Device, the *joined hands* are placed vertically, *in pale*. In all these three, by contrast, they are placed horizontally, *in fesse*; and none of them is assigned to Lord Strange.

But for me, those horizontally joined hands for other Stranges, and the necessity for Lord Strange's badge to show a distinctive difference, were enough to stir a strong suspicion, namely: that his hereditary badge would turn out to be *joined hands placed vertically or upright*. And after a brief search I ran it down, in J. G. Nichols's *Collectanea Topographica et Heraldica* III (1836), 75, 'Badges temp. Hen. VIII':

> STRANGE   Two hands conjoined in pale, the upper one
> Or, the other Gules*

with the motto *Sans changer ma vérité*; and adding that 'the motto now used by the house of Stanley [*i.e.*, *Sans changer*] is a portion of the motto of Strange'. We shall be returning to this motto of Strange.

Here is revelation. Now at last we can look at the portrait as any non-playgoing Cockney in 1588—ignorant both of the player Shakespeare and of any literary Mercury–Apollo symbolism—would look at it in Hilliard's shop-window.

To our eyes, what are those *joined hands upright* but the very image of the great Lord Strange's familiar, exclusive, and time-

---

* From MS. Harl. 4632 f. 246ᵛ, whence the Rev. Thomas Willement (Folger MS. M. b. 58, f. 437) sketched it, mentioning another, with motto, in MS. Harl. 1410. It was copied from Nichols without acknowledgment in Fanny B. Palliser's *Historic Devices*, 1870, 310. I find the *joined hands placed upright* as a watermark in a fifteenth-century paper made at Fabriano, Italy: C. M. Briquet, *Les Filigranes*, 1907, no. 11616.
Where did Henry Lord Strange get the name Ferdinando (Ital.; Sp. Fernando) for his infant heir in 1559? We recall that the Holy Roman Emperor Ferdinand I crowned at Frankfort 1558 was the Hapsburg Fernando, born in Spain. (Cf. Ferdinando Gorges and Ferdinando Heyborne, similarly named for him.) Another attraction for Lord Strange-of-the-Joined-Hands was Ferdinando's marriage-emblem, famous since 1521: *Joined Hands*, with the lemma *Thus for ever*. Puttenham (*Arte* Y2, Kk2ᵛ) reports 'the Emperor *Ferdinando*, a most noble minded man' and 'of pleasant discourse', but lacking the princely comeliness of walking slowly 'and with a certain granditie' . . . 'I haue seene him runne vp a paire of staires so swift and nimble a pace, as almost had not become a very meane man . . .'

honoured badge? None but a servant of his who had a right
to it could or would venture to display the peer's personal
sign in his picture. *The portrait of this handsome, choicely dressed
sitter tells the common man in the street nothing more than 'I am Lord
Strange's man.'*

Yet it has taken the most common Elizabethan Cockney to
make us see the first obvious feature of this pictured poet—
'Mercury', declaring True Friendship with London's royal
'Apollo' of 1588, namely: that with his *Ecce signum** he identifies
himself proudly to all as *Lord Strange's man.*

Had we acted from the start on David Piper's acute advice—
that Elizabethan portraiture 'is perhaps easiest read if considered almost as heraldry'—we might have saved time.

If our method of investigation was sound, and the resulting
surmise correct, it should not lack support. That confirmation
is now before us. Earlier, we recognized our young MAN of
1588 as the Poet 'Mercury', declaring True Friendship with his
King, his Sun, his God, 'Apollo'. This is precisely the peculiar
thing which the young Poet 'Mercury'-Shakespeare does
with his beloved 'Apollo', Will Hatcliffe, in the Sonnets of
his pupil pen, 1588–1589.

Again as 'Mercury' in his epilogue to *Love's Labour's Lost* at
Gray's Inn 1588/9 he compliments his listening King 'Apollo'.

Now we recognize our blond young MAN, the Poet 'Mercury' of 1588, as *Servant of Lord Strange.* And so also is Lord
Strange's blond young player, the Poet William Shakespeare.

Convincing. For would even the devil's advocate venture to
contend that it was not 'Mercury'–Shakespeare of the Sonnets
to Gray's Inn's young 'Apollo', but some other golden-haired
poet-and-servant of Lord Strange's who in 1588 sat to Nicholas
Hilliard as 'Poet Mercury' clasping 'King Apollo's' hand?

---

* *Boy.*   Marry, sir, I hear you pertain to signor *Ferando*
       [Another Italian form of *Ferdinando*].
   Sander. Ay, an thou beest not blind thou mayest see—*Ecce signum*,
       here. [*Shows badge.*]

The Taming of a Shrew (ca. 1589), 1594, B4. Spelling modernized. The
attention called to the *Ferando–Ferdinando* badge corroborates Chambers's
suggestion (*El. Stage* 4.48) that the play originally belonged to Lord
Strange's men.

No longer is this identification a surmise. It is a conclusion imposed by converging facts: facts which interlock Shakespeare's life, his public character, and his sonnets, with this miniature *impresa*-portrait.

*   *   *

Who could rest here? Hunsdon's *Swan* came much later; and our finding Strange's badge and motto opens an avenue to the poet's years about 1588, which ignorance has called 'lost'. Our one way to find out whether or not it will lead us to further discovery and light is to follow it. With the symbol of Lord Strange's badge we are on the familiar ground covered in Chapter 4. His *Joined Hands* declare Faith, Truth, True Friendship, True Love: its integrity emphasized by his 'word' SANS CHANGER MA VÉRITÉ: *Unchanging, my truth.*

Beyond the Elizabethans' habit of referring to a magnate by his heraldic sign crest, or badge—such as *Swan* for Lord Hunsdon, *Bandog* for the Earl of Lincoln, *Reindeer* for the Earl of Essex, *Crow* for Lady Norris, *Moon* for Percy, &c.—we recall their trick of including such allusions in their writings, 'inserted conceitedly into the matter'. So, for example, Roger Cocks, dedicating his sacred verses *Hebdomada Sacra* in 1630 'To the Right Honourable James, Lord Strange' with

> Poetry, noble Lord, . . .
> If hand in hand with Piety she goe

makes delicate but obvious allusion to his *Joined Hands*.

Returning to Shakespeare's master, Ferdinando, called 'the good Lord Strange', we find him taking his motto of *true faith* with the seriousness it demands. In 1593 he writes to Sir Robert Cecil, trusting 'her Majesty may see I have said nothing but truth . . . I . . . will pray that all men may ever carry like faith as myself, to her'.

Among the Latin elegies on the death of his father Henry Earl of Derby, Matthew Gwynne in anagrammatizing FER-DINA(N)DUS S. produces FIDES DURANS—*unchanging truth* or faith; and Henry Price salutes him as *verè GNESIA proles*—'heir *in truth* of *the true or right kind of Eagle*'. (Matthew Gwynne, *Epicedium* . . ., 1593, A3ᵛ, B4ᵛ.) About the same time, Anthony

Munday addresses him as 'true heire and succeeder, in your fathers noblenesse and vertues'. (*The Defence of Contraries*, 1593, Dedication.) In the year after Ferdinando's own untimely death as the Earl of Derby, William Covell bewails him as the 'trulie Hon[ourable] . . . a true worthie object of everlasting mourning for the sacred Muses'—their dear dead shepherd *Amyntas*. (*Polimanteia*, 1595, Q2.) This common harping on *truth* and *true* unmistakably echoes the *truth* or *faith* of his motto.

But it is particularly in the late 1580s that we look for Lord Strange and his *Joined Hands*, depicting that True Friendship which Chapman calls 'the cement of two minds': the Hands showing Friends *loving, conjoined, chained, glued, unchanged*. (Poole, *English Parnassus*, 1657, 99.) In 1589 we find Thomas Newton addressing 'the Lord most illustrious and of highest hope, Ferdinando Stanley Lord Strange':

> If, Ferdinand, thou long'st to bind to thee
> Thy Britons with unfeignëd love's cement . . .*

More interesting still are the homely old-fashioned rimes in the young lord's praise written about 1587 by Richard Robinson of Alton (Alveton, Staffordshire), included in his *A Golden Mirrour*, 1589, C3ᵛ–D1ᵛ. There are thirteen ten-line stanzas, out of which 130 lines I quote the 22 following. *Fame* finds the author asleep:

> Arise (quoth she) write after me
> My sentence do not change,
> Here shalt thou view a creature true,
> Who may be callëd Strange.

> And if thou learnëd be quoth shee
> Behold the noble Wight:
> Whose modest minde apeares to be
> A wise and virtuous Knight:
> Descent of noble Parentage
> And rarest creature of his age:

---

*   Deuincere tuos tibi Ferdinande Britannos
             Si cupis, infictæ glutine amicitiæ . . .
                         Newton's additions to John Leland,
                              Principum Encomia, 1589, 114.

A man so fixt and firme of fayth,
    That never yet did change,
And stands to trueth for life or death,
    This man is very Strange.

His lowly minde men ever finde
    Still fixëd not to change;
Which winnes mens harts in every parts,
    And that must needes be strange.

No favor, feare, no frend, nor foe,
    Can cause his mynde to chaunge . . .
Thus have I pen'd, and also end
    My Dreame of Noble Straunge.

Writing his Sonnets with his *pupill pen* in 1588 and 1589, young Shakespeare was proud to be a servant of the noble *Amyntas*, maintainer of poets, summoned to Parliament as Baron Strange. And now, with our new knowledge of his master's motto, and of its echo in Robinson's lines of 1587 —

My sentence do not change,
Here shalt thou view a creature true,
    Who may be callëd Strange

—let us reread Sonnets 123 and 93, written soon after:

123

1   *No! Time, thou shalt not bost that I doe change,*
2   *Thy pyramids buylt vp with newer might*
3   *To me are nothing nouell, nothing strange . . .*
14   *I will be true dispight thy syeth and thee.*   [scythe

93

1   *So shall I liue, supposing thou art true . . .*
5   *For their can liue no hatred in thine eye,*   [there
6   *Therefore in that I cannot know thy change,*
7   *In manies lookes, the falce hearts history*
8   *Is writ in moods and frounes and wrinckles strange . . .*

At the poetic pole opposite to Robinson's singsong, here twice repeated, and in like emphatic place, is that same unmis-

takable trio, the *strange, change,* and *true* of the young poet's
master: STRANGE. *Sans changer ma vérité.*

A modern reader, to whom Lord Strange is only a name,
and his motto unknown, might let the Sonnets' repetition of
this feature pass as insignificant. But the Elizabethans—for
numbers of whom Lord Strange was still Tudor heir pre-
sumptive, likely to succeed Queen Elizabeth on the throne of
England—reading the poems of his poet Shakespeare, would
certainly both mark and approve; as the poet's noble master
would—that shepherd *Amyntas* of royal blood—the poetical
Lord Strange himself. Indeed they could no more miss it than
readers of 1630 could miss the *Joined Hands* in Cocks's lines to
James Lord Strange:

> Poetry, noble Lord, . . .
> If hand in hand with Piety she goe . . .

Shakespeare's display in his portrait-Device dated 1588 of
Strange's exclusive *Joined Hands upright,* and his echo in Sonnets
123 and 93 of the peer's personal motto, present him in 1588/9
as a servant of Ferdinando Lord Strange. And there is no evidence that he served any other master until after Ferdinando's
death in 1594 he became—with other 'Strange's–Derby's
players'—Lord Hunsdon's man. We now recognize this as a
most natural move, since the two families were intimately
linked. Hunsdon's heir George and Ferdinando had married
the Spencer sisters, Elizabeth and Alice.*

In 1590 Peele's *Polyhymnia* applauds the ship-device of
Shakespeare's Lord and his feat in the tilt on Accession Day:

> The Earle of Darbies valiant sonne and heire,
> Brave Ferdinande Lord Straunge, straunglie embarkt,
> Under Joves kinglie byrd, the golden Eagle,
> Stanleyes olde Crest and honourable badge . . .

---

* Speculation about Shakespeare's possible employment shortly before
the year 1594 has been various. But it should be remembered that when
one finds an early play of his reported as acted by X's company, it is far
from safe to assume that therefore Shakespeare had left the service of
Lord Strange and become a member of X's. For (a) his own company may
have sold or leased it to X's, or (b) his company may have temporarily
disbanded, and he have sold it to X's.

And in *Pierce Penilesse* (1592, I4), to bring Ferdinando before us with his Eagle ('Stanley *high thought*'), Nashe calls him '*Ioues Eagle-borne Ganimed*, thrice noble *Amyntas*'. The Stanley legend of the Eagle and Child here follows Xenophon's sublime spiritual view (*Symposium* 8.30, adopted by Alciati and Conti), as against the sensual, pathic-catamite version of the myth. As Abraham Fraunce presents it,

> *by the rauishing of* Ganymede *by* Iupiter, *vnderstand the lifting vp of mans minde* ... *to heauenly conceipts: that* Ganymedes *may be deriued of* γάνυμι, *to ioy and reioyce, and* μήδεα, *signifying aduice & counsaile, as though mans soule thus rauished by* Ioue, *might wel be sayd to enioy his heauenly comfort and counsaile.**

Francis Thynne's 45th Emblem (1600) holds that *Ganymede*

> a prudent mann doth signifie,
> who doth his minde to Heavenlie things addresse,
> and flies to Heaven by livinge vertuouslie ...†

At his father Henry's death on 25 September 1593 Ferdinando succeeded to the earldom as the richest subject in the realm of England, to be hailed by Henry Price as the '*heir in truth of the Eagle*'. From that day his servants were no longer marked by the *Joined Hands*. Now distinguished as 'Derby's Men', they proudly wore Stanley's old crest, the golden *Eagle*. And by that *Eagle* they were publicly known for close on seven months: until their master's tragic death—the leading physicians pronounced him murdered by poison and witchcraft—on 16 April 1594.

---

* *3 Countesse of Pembrokes Yuychurch*, 1592, I3; cf. G. Sandys's Ovid, with his Commentary on *Met.* 10, *s.v. Ganymedes*.

† And George Wither's Emblem similarly (1635, Bk. 3, no. 22):

> By *Ganymed*, the *Soule* is understood,
> That's washëd in the *Purifying flood* ...
> The *Ægle*, meanes the Heav'nly *Contemplation* ...

Alexander Ross (*Mystagogus Poeticus*, 1647, Ch. VII) devotes twelve paragraphs to the ideal and Christian interpretation of *Ganymede*. Cf. 'Emblems' (British Library MS. Addl. 27335 f. 93): *Ecstasis, seu Mentis raptus. Ecstasis symbolus est Ganymedes* ...

In his last agony Ferdinando–Ganymede turned for comfort to the high thought of his *Eagle*: '*knowing for a certaintie that I must now die*, . . . *I am resolued presentlie to take away with mee onely one part of my armes, I meane the Eagles wings; so will I flie swiftly into the bosome of Christ my onely Sauiour* . . .' (Stow-Howes, *Annales*, 1615, 767*b*.)

Bearing the poetical Ferdinando and his *Eagle* in mind, let us revert once more to Spenser's *Colin Clout's Come Home Again*, written on a visit to England in 1591 and published 1595. Near the close of his citation and appraisal of the chief poets, which ended with the 'noblest' *Amyntas* and the 'gentle shepherd', Spenser substitutes a correction and lament obviously written shortly after 16 April 1594 on the loss of Ferdinando–*Amyntas*:

432   There also is (ah no, he is not now)
      But since I said he is, he quite is gone,
      Amyntas quite is gone and lies full low,
      Hauing his *Amaryllis* left to mone.   [*his Countess, Alice*
      Helpe, O ye shepheards helpe ye all in this,
      Helpe *Amaryllis* this her losse to mourne:
      Her losse is yours, your losse *Amyntas* is,
      Amyntas floure of shepheards pride forlorne:
      He whilest he liu̐d was the noblest swaine,
      That euer pip̐d in an oaten quill:
      Both did he other, which could pipe, maintaine,
      And eke could pipe himselfe with passing skill. (*exceeding*
      And there though last not least is *Aetion*,   [=Eaglet
      A gentler shepheard may no where be found:
      Whose *Muse* full of high thoughts inuention,
      Doth like himselfe Heroically sound.

This heroically sounding shepherd *Aëtion*, though last not least, following next to *Amyntas*, and distinguished as most *gentle*, is evidently—to Malone it is *unquestionably*—the *heroically sounding gentle Shakespeare*. And Spenser can be praising the new poet *only for his Sonnets* of 1588–89; properly called *heroical* because (*a*) their theme is *Friendship*—which 'eclipses *love* . . . and is the *heroical affection*, sung by the poets'—and (*b*) their subject (as we noted in Chapter 6) is a *King-God*. (L. Dugas,

L'Amitié Antique, 1914, 1; Puttenham, Bk. I, ch. XL.) And since to Spenser he is *Eaglet* [High Thought] *of the only kind of Eagle which can gaze at the Sun* (Mr. *W. H.* 195), this *Sun* is Mercury–Shakespeare's *Muse*, King Phoebus Apollo: both the inspirer and the theme of his high-thoughted Sonnets.

But now in this *Eaglet* Spenser's second enrichment of identifying allusion springs into view. At Ferdinando's death, Shakespeare had for half a year been publicly known by his master's *Eagle*. By Ben Jonson's later London Shakespeare will be recognized as a *Swan*. But by Spenser's London of 1594 he is known as an *Eaglet*. And Spenser's praise of him in *Colin Clout* immediately follows his praise of the lamented 'Eagleborne' Stanley whom *Aëtion* the gentle Eaglet has followed for more than five years.

10

Love's Labour's Lost, 1588/9

Of all Shakespeare's plays this is the most personal; a solution of the puzzle he has set here (and I had better say at once that I cannot provide it), would not only satisfy the most rabid detective ardour, but illuminate Shakespeare's own early life and the conditions that shaped his career and his first plays—an essential background of which at present absolutely nothing is known.

RICHARD DAVID, ed. *Love's Labour's Lost*, New Arden, 1956, xvii

I think that this play is more likely than any other to suggest the avenues of investigation if there is ever to be a 'breakthrough' in our knowledge of Shakespeare's theatrical beginnings.

ALFRED HARBAGE, *Philological Quarterly* 41, 1962

The disclosures already made reveal *Love's Labour's Lost* in an aspect both fresh and seasonable, since we now realize that this play—like *Twelfth Night* 1600/1—was a *leap-year* piece,* in which by 'ladies' law' *the women rule*: when, as the Princess says (4.1.39–40), *praise we may afford To any Lady that subdues a Lord.*†

---

* Leap Year 1588—see above, page 109 *note*—ran until 28 February 1588/9. And cf. '*Twelfth Night* for Leap Year', *Times Literary Supplement*, 17 Nov. 1961, p. 823.

† 'What, 'tis womens yeere! *Dian* doth rule, and you [daughter] must domineer.' *Jacke Drums Entertainement* (acted 1600/1), 1.1.166–167; *Maid's Metamorphosis* 4.1.157, and *Patient Grissell* 157, both of 1600; Chapman, *Bussy D'Ambois* 1.2.82, qu. Chambers, *Eliz. Stage*, 2.253; Heywood's *How to Learn of a Woman to Woo*, at Court 30 December 1604, and *The Wit of a Woman*, also of 1604, lines 340 and 76: 'let me looke to the yeare' and Erinta to Isabella, 'let vs gouerne men'. In Ben Jonson's leap-year play *The New Inn*, acted 19 Jan. 1628/9, his Prudence 'The Chambermaid is elected *Soueraigne* of the *Sports*' and—like Shakespeare's leap-year gentlewoman Maria, Sir Toby's conqueror—'gouernes all, com-

For it had its first night during the Christmas saturnalia of 1588/9, most probably on Twelfth Night, in the Hall of the Delphic Gray's Inn before Purpoole's boy-King Apollo, Prince True-love. Pages 230–235 of *Mr. W. H.* uncovered topicalities in it, chiefly jests chaffing the 'Pompey' Prince, Will Hatcliffe. And Chapter 8 above has added the epilogue which Mercury–Shakespeare spoke to his Apollo-Prince Will—*The words of Mercury* . . .—casting powerful personal light on that genial performance by Lord Strange's Men.

But our recovery of Lord Strange's badge and his motto has enriched the background further; and as Chapman says, 'New light gives new directions.' On a rereading of *Love's Labour's Lost,* unnoticed parts of it now stand out fresh with revealing topicality. And what they show us is the reason why in composing his play Shakespeare inserted them, like the references to Don Virginio Orsino later in his *Twelfth Night.*

It was because his great master Lord Strange and his lady were to be Prince Will's guests of honour at the Purpoole feast and this hilarious 'women's year' comedy presented by Lord Strange's Men which followed it.

Purpoole boasted noble Stanleys as old members of Gray's Inn. A quarter-century before, both Ferdinando's grandfather Edward Earl of Derby and his father Henry Lord Strange had been admitted to the society. And prominent among the chief arms shining in painted glass in the Hall's windows stood the ancient-noble Stanley escutcheon, *Argent, on a bend azure three bucks' heads cabossed or.* (See Ferdinando's portrait, in E. K. Chambers, *William Shakespeare,* 1930, 1, Pl. IV.)

Thornton Wilder suggested to me that for the gala, to honour the heir to the rich earldom of their member, Gray's Inn doubtless adorned their Hall with great painted cloths, featuring a grand achievement of the ancient Stanley arms. It is most probable. But at all events, we shall certainly find Shakespeare including in his play fine artful allusion to the famous arms of his master, the Principality of Purpoole's great guest of honour.

---

mands, and so orders, as the *Lord Latimer* is exceedingly taken with her, and takes her to his wife . . .'

For his King of Navarre, whose short-sighted scheme of study *excluding women* inevitably subjects his Court to the poetic justice meted out by rigorous leap-year ladies, Shakespeare significantly chose the name *Ferdinand*. Scholarship has already noticed that no historical ruler of French Navarre had borne that name, and has also connected it with the ostentatious repetitions of *strange* in Act 5.*

But another identifying feature has passed unremarked. At 2.1.5–7 Boyet describes King Ferdinand as

> the sole inheritour
> Of all perfections that a man may owe,
> Matchlesse *Nauarre* . . .

Does not this recognizably describe Lord Strange? In *Pierce Penilesse* (1592, I4), Nashe gives his readers Shakespeare's master, Ferdinando–*Amyntas* (future King of the Isle of Man), as 'the matchlesse image of Honor . . . a singular man of perfection'—repeating both those extreme terms. And in all Shakespeare there is but one other occurrence of *matchless*: to describe his young hero-Prince *firm of word*, the *true* Troilus; the feature which recalls his own young Lord Strange, *unchanging, true*.

All the listening members of the collegiate Gray's Inn on their admission to the society had sworn to keep its rules and statutes. But the acted Ferdinand and his courtiers, on founding their 'little Academe', had—with a folly criminal in leap year

---

* Dr. W. Schrickx (*Shakespeare's Early Contemporaries*, 1956, 248–251) pointed out that since no King of Navarre ever bore the name *Ferdinand*, Shakespeare was herein probably complimenting Ferdinando Lord Strange. Also with the playing on *strange* in 5.2. For 5.2.174, the Quarto gives

> What would these stranges?   [Fol. strangers?

Dr. Schrickx suggests *Strange's players*, understood. He remarks further that the *change–strange* in King Ferdinand's speech (lines 209–210) is repeated in the lines immediately following; and also quotes Rosaline's

> 218 Since you are strangers, and come here by chance,
> 219 Weele not be nice, take handes, we will not daunce.

If Dr. Schrickx had known Lord Strange's badge and his motto, he would of course have perceived much more in these passages.

—sworn to a novel, provocative rule *excluding women from their sight* for three years' space.

At once the leap-year ladies sweep in upon these miscreant flouters, to subdue and torment—as Rosaline will *o'ersway* and *torture* Berowne. Magistrates inexorable, at the close they condemn the culprits to twelve months' hard.

The feature emphasized is Ferdinand's stubborn *faith* or *truth* in keeping that unpardonable oath: like Ferdinando's *truth* in *Sans changer ma vérité.* Only when *compelled by all-powerful Love* can he be forced to break it. But for his perjury, his truth-changing, his punishment is fixed: he must endure a painful year of probation.

> *Princess.* No, no my Lord, your Grace is periur'd much,
> Full of deare guiltinesse, and therefore this:
> If for my Loue (as there is no such cause)
> You will do ought, this shall you do for me.
> Your oth I will not trust: but go with speed
> To some forlorne and naked Hermitage,
> Remote from all the pleasures of the world:
> There stay, vntill the twelue Celestiall Signes
> Haue brought about their annuall reckoning.
> If this austere insociable life,
> Change not your offer made in heate of blood . . .   [*Sans*
> Then at the expiration of the yeare,   *changer*
> Come challenge me . . .   5.2.799–814

And to crown it, we now see Shakespeare making the Strange's boy who plays his character Maria pointedly *display Lord Strange's Joined Hands:* just as he himself does in his contemporary Device executed by Nicholas Hilliard. When Katherine asks her — about the chain of pearl and the long letter which Longaville has sent her —

> Dost thou not wish in heart
> The Chaine were longer, and the Letter short?   5.2.55

Maria, *joining her hands*, holds them up with the asseveration

> I, or I would these hands might neuer part   [*Ay,*

—that is, '*stay glued in truth till death*'. The singularity of this action-and-wish of Maria's has naturally puzzled observant critics, as it would baffle every reader ignorant of Lord Strange's famous cognizance.

Again in the same scene (218–220) the *Strange Joined Hands* are played up to King Ferdinand:

> *Ros.* Since you are strangers, and come here by chance,
> Weele not be nice, take handes, we will not daunce.
> *King.* Why take we hands then? *Ros.* Onlie to part friends.

And lastly (815–816, 820–821), once more with Ferdinand:

> *Prin.* And by this Virgin palme, now kissing thine,
> I will be thine: . . .
>
> If this thou do denie, let our hands part,
> Neither intitled in the others hart.

As for the marked appearance, especially in Act 5, of *strange* and *change*, we need only list the occurrences to note their conspicuous frequency:

4.2.134	one of the strange Queenes Lords
143	a sequent of the stranger Queenes
3.377	We will with some strange pastime solace them
5.1. 6	strange without heresie
2.134	And change you Fauour too
137	But in this changing, What is your intent
174	What would these stranges? [Fol. strangers?
King. 209	Then in our measure, do but vouchsafe one change
210	Thou bidst me begge, this begging is not strange
Ros. 212	Not yet no dance: thus change I like the Moone
King. 213	Will you not daunce? How come you thus estranged
Ros. 214	You tooke the moone at ful: but now shee's changed
218	Since you are strangers
238	Will you vouchsafe with me to change a word
292	Therefore change Fauours
468	The Ladies did change Fauours
542	These foure will change habites

772 Full of strange shapes   [Q, Ff straying
809 Change not your offer
842 Ile change my blacke Gowne for a faithfull friend*

Further, Shakespeare introduces (4.1) an extended episode
on the Princess's taking a stand by invitation in Ferdinand's
park armed with crossbow 'to kill horns'—to shoot driven
deer. And he follows it (4.2) with a dispute between the School-
master Holofernes, Sir Nathaniel the Curate, and Constable
Dull upon the age of the buck (shown by its head) which the
Princess shot. If there is more here than mere haphazard choice
of some occasion for feeble wit-cracking, we should be glad to
learn Shakespeare's reason for lugging in such apparently
extraneous matter.

Only when we here connect *the renowned armorial bearings of
his listening master Lord Strange* do we see at last what his audience saw. For that episode cunningly leads up to Master
Holofernes' 'extemporall Epytaph on the death of the Deare'.
And the hornëd subjects of his jingle, known by their *heads*,
are *three*—Pricket (2nd yr.), Sorel (3rd yr.), and Sore (4th yr.):
three bucks' heads for *Stanley*.

> The *prayfull Princesse pearst and prickt* [rich in prey
>   *a prettie pleasing Pricket,*
> *Some say a Sore, but not a sore,*
>   *till now made sore with shooting.*
> *The Dogges did yell, put ell to Sore,*
>   *then Sorell iumps from thicket:*
> *Or Pricket-sore, or else Sorell,*   [Pricket, Sore,
>   *the people fall a hooting.*
> *If Sore be sore, then ell to Sore,*   [L
>   *makes fiftie sores O sorell:*   [Sores one SoreL
> *Of one sore I an hundred make*
>   *by adding but one more L.*

* The play *Fair Em* of Strange's Men presents the same allusions:
change, strange, 1.1.17, 1.3.44, 1.4.62, 4.3.15, 5.1.94; and *joined hands*, 1.4.70,
2.1.19 & 26, 3.2.40. Shakespeareans will note them also in *1 & 3 Hen. VI*
and especially in *Two Gentlemen of Verona*. And in both *Fair Em* and *TGV*
the emphasis on *true, truth,* and *faith* is strikingly marked.

Clear so far; and perhaps we may now see one or two more passing allusions. The *Eagle*, 'Stanley's old crest' (the Eagle Tower dominated their seat, Latham House, and the Earl's officer of arms is Eagle Pursuivant), is brought in twice:

4.3.226–28   What peremptory Eagle-sighted eye
                  Dares looke vpon the heauen of her brow,
                  That is not blinded by her maiestie?

334   A Louers eyes will gaze an Eagle blinde

In 1607 Marston similarly twice brings it into his *Entertainement of the Countesse Dowager of Darby* to honour Ferdinando's relict Alice: '*on wch an Eagle pearcheth*' and '*in a fayre Oake satt a goulden Eagle*'. (*The Poems of John Marston*, ed. A. Davenport 1961, 201, 202.)

Moreover, the *Eagle's* or *Hawk's Foot* stood familiar to all as a famous Stanley cognizance. And when the Earls of Derby borrowed the Strange *Joined Hands* badge, they put *a columbine flower* over it for difference. Here one suspects canting heraldry; for *Hawksfoot* was the old English name for the Columbine, a flower which is not forgotten in *Love's Labour's Lost*. When the lofty Armado—presenting Hector, that Flower of Men—proclaims 'I am that Flower', the interrupting Longaville specifies 'That Cullambine.'

Again, Ferdinando's baroness Alice—in 1593 Barnabe Barnes's 'virtuous and most beautiful Lady, Pride of our English Court', to whom her cousin Edmund Spenser dedicated his *Teares* (written before March 1590) which praised her husband's servant the gentle Mercury–Shakespeare—was the youngest daughter of the fabulously rich Sir John Spencer of Althorpe, with the Spencer motto *God defend the right*. This high thought is also familiar to all as the prayer publicly offered before *a judicial combat*, a wager of battle.

When Costard (in Constable Dull's custody) is questioned about Armado's charge against him of consorting with Jaquenetta, he makes—in clownish vein of mock-heroic—high-flown allusion to the listening great lady's family with his coda (1.1.210): 'As it shall follow in my correction, and God defend the right.'

And last, a curious word in that First Quarto here strikes even the casual eye. Its oddity recalls the scientific investigator's counsel, *Watch out especially for anything odd.*

It is in line 88 of Act 2 that it confronts us. The Princess of France has arrived on business of state before King Ferdinand's palace. But apprised of his newly sworn oath to let no woman through his 'forbidden gates', she sends Lord Boyet in to sound him on the point. After a short parley he comes out.

> *Prin.* Now, What admittance Lord?
> *Boyet. Nauar* had notice of your faire approch,
> And he and his compettitours in oth,
> Were all addrest to meete you gentle Lady
> Before I came: Marrie thus much I haue learnt,
> He rather meanes to lodge you in the feelde,
> Like one that comes heere to besiedge his Court,
> Then seeke a dispensation for his oth:
> To let you enter his vnpeeled house.

Here the significant *odd*—the word *unpeelĕd* describing a house—is not only odd. It is *unique*. For it appears nowhere else in known English writing; and no one in the centuries since Shakespeare has been able to tell what it means.*

On reflecting, we assemble three tentative queries:

1. Have scholars considered *all* of the *OED*'s examples of *peel*?

2. What of a possible clue in Boyet's words? *He rather means to lodge you in the field   Like one that comes here to besiege his Court Than seek a dispensation for his oath   To let you enter his unpeelĕd house.* For we mark the military phrases *besiege* and *enter*. Can

---

* A quarter-century after Q1 (1598), the epithet baffled the editors of the First Folio and of Q2. They substituted *unpeopled*. And although Furness properly rejected Schmidt's guess for *unpeeled*, 'stripped, desolate' (since *peeled* means 'stripped' and *unpeeled* '*not* stripped'), he gave up any attempt to explain the term and printed the 'emendation' *unpeopled*.

With Craig (1904) I follow the judgment of the Cambridge editors (1863, 1891) W. G. Clark and W. A. Wright: 'We have retained in this passage the reading of the first Quarto, "unpeeled," in preference to the "unpeopled" of the second Quarto [1631] and the Folios [1623, 1632], which is evidently only a conjectural emendation, and does not furnish a better sense than many other words which might be proposed.'

unpeelëd—with them—perhaps have something to do with *siege warfare*?

3. To this we now join Purpoole's guest of honour, Shakespeare's master Ferdinando Stanley Lord Strange, of Lancashire, Cheshire, and the Isle of Man, openly adumbrated in his 'Ferdinand, King of Navarre'. And we ask, might not 'his unpeelëd house' embody an allusion to one of his Stanley houses in the north country?

Pursuing these three we find, first, in the *OED s.v.* Peel *sb.*[1]:

1. [Peel] †2. A palisade or fence formed of stakes; a stockade; a stockaded or palisadoed (and moated) enclosure, either as the outer court of a castle, or as an independent fort or defensible position. *Obs.*

†3. A castle; esp. a small castle or tower. *Obs.* [Quotations, from Chaucer, 'castel . . . pel'; Churchyard, 'piel'.]

4. The general name . . . for the . . . fortified dwellings built in the 16th c. in the Border counties of England and Scotland for defence against . . . forays. Probably orig. short for *peel-house*.

5. Hence the proper name [Peel] of a place in the Isle of Man. (Cf. Castletown in the same island.)

2. With *unpeelëd house* we now compare 'vamures *unpallisado'd'* (*OED*), and Shakespeare's *forted* residence; *pales* and *forts* of reason; weakly *fortress'd*; *unfenced* desolation.*

3. And from history, Shakespeare, and Manx authority as follows:

'In 1406 Henry IV granted to Sir John Stanley the island, castle, peel, and lordship of Man.' This recalls Shakespeare's marked repetition in *2 Henry VI*: *With Sir John Stanley, in the Isle of Man* (2.3.13); *Stanley is . . . To take her with him to the Isle of Man* (2.4.78); [Sir John Stanley:] *Why, madam, that is to the Isle of Man* (2.4.94). For Lord Strange's Men, an emphasis both natural and proud.

'*Peeley*, "a fortress, tower"'—as in PEEL. . . . the ancient round tower . . . in . . . the little island off PEEL-*town* . . . afterwards applied to the . . . extensive fortifications . . .

* *Meas. for Meas.* 5.1.12; *Ham.* 1.4.28; *Lucr.* 28; *K. John* 2.2.386.

probably erected there by the Stanleys. These were repaired by Ferdinando, Earl of Derby, and an old engraving, dated 1593, represents them in perfect condition.'
A. W. Moore, *The Surnames & Place-names of the Isle of Man*, 1890, 137.

Cleared (like that baffling *perttaunt*) of its centuries-long 'murk of unknowing', the poet's unique *unpeelëd*—meaning *unforted, unfortress'd*—now again stands deft and apt to the listening noble Stanley his master, an allusion savoured by all.

And do not Pompey–Costard's burlesque 'arms' and 'legs' —*lay my Armes before the legs of this sweet Lasse of France*—call up the Stanley *arms* quartering as Kings of Man the Manx triskele: *legs*? (See I. Moncreiffe & D. Pottinger, *Simple Heraldry*, 1953, 30.)

*　　　*　　　*

Who can doubt that more allusions remain in the text still unseen? But those now obvious, noticed both here and in *Mr. W. H.*, have already given us evidence enough to establish the date, place, and occasion—*the mood, the quality of persons, and the time*—of the First Night of *Love's Labour's Lost*. It was at *the Sonnets-time: leap year 1588/9*. Its author was not 30, as most scholars currently assume.* He was *a youth of 24*. And its date 1588/9 excludes any fancied allusion to the later group of 'atheists' supposedly called 'The School of Night'.

Shakespeare obviously wrote his 'Strange change' and his 'joined hands' allusions before September 1593, when his master's name changed from Strange to Derby, and his badge from Joined Hands to Golden Eagle. And the fact that both the 'Navarre' feature and the 1588/9 personal allusions to Hatcliffe and Lord Strange are retained in the 1598 Quarto makes any material revision by Shakespeare of the original most unlikely.

And now we can see why it was that to please Robert Cecil Lord Cranborne's great guests Queen Anne and her brother Ulric Duke of Holstein, along with most of the Court, in the

---

* Exceptions in the past are Coleridge, Gervinus, R. G. White, Fleay, and Furnivall, who all dated it extremely early. Also in our day T. W. Baldwin, who places it between Aug. 1588 and Aug. 1589, and A. B. Harbage, who points out (*Philological Quarterly* 41) that the 'Navarre' feature unquestionably shows its date to be prior to August 1589.

January of 1604/5 Shakespeare and Burbage revived the 16-year-old *Love's Labour's Lost*. Supremely suitable, since it was a courtly comedy specially written for a leap (women's) year; 1604/5 was the first *leap year* of the new reign, and a royal *Woman* was the guest of honour.

As her own celebration of this 'women's year', the Queen presented on Twelfth Night (6 Jan.) an *all-ladies'* masque, written to her order by Ben Jonson: *The Masque of Blackness*. And Candlemas Night of the next leap year (2 Feb. 1608/9) found her presenting another *all-ladies'* masque by Jonson, *The Masque of Queens*.

A further piece of internal evidence which places the production of this comedy in or about 1588/9 has passed unnoticed. After detecting Ferdinand and his two courtiers not only forsworn for love but 'sonnetting' too, Berowne throws their recent tenets at them mercilessly. His mocking lines

> You'll not be periur'd, 'tis a hatefull thing:
> Tush, none but Minstrels like of Sonnetting . . .

voice two current beliefs: (a) *to be perjured is hateful* and (b) *cultivated people dislike sonnets*. Clearly, if this play dated from the mid-1590s, *during the flood of sonnet-publication produced by the reading public's novel and strong interest in sonnets*, Berowne's 'cultivated people dislike sonnets' would be no stinging taunt. It would be nonsense.

But as I have pointed out (*Mr. W. H.* 69), *in and about 1588* the reading public *did* dislike sonnets. For James Aske complains in his *Elizabetha Triumphans* of 1588,

> But if any man write loving Songs, and amiable Sonnets, they, as foolish toyes nothing profitable, are of every one misliked.

From this it is again evident that the play belongs not in the sonnets-reading vogue of 1593/4 or 1594/5 (and *neither* of these was a leap year), but in 1588/9; that just like *it is hateful to be perjured* 'Tush, none but Minstrels like of Sonnetting' voices the common opinion at this First Night of *Love's Labour's Lost*.

And in the presence on that night of the poet-Mercury's

royal Friend the Apollo-Prince and of his Prince's great guest the poetizing *Amyntas* Lord Strange, the player-poet's master and patron, we now see manifest reason why 'this youthful god of poetry' out-Mercury'd himself in devising his gay, courtly, wit-cracking domestical mirth—for the year when 'the Shees have th'upper hand'—why he wrote this 'the most personal of all his plays' *con amore*, a Labour of Love. For *Labour is light, where Love doth pay.*

II

Through Humility, Genius

BY way of introduction let us take this surmise: that no possible soil could have produced wisdom such as Shakespeare's but a ground of *humility*. His friend John Davies of Hereford, noting that 'Humility is the surest foundation of highest glory' and 'doth best become the highest knowledge', prescribes it for 'the Poet of skill divine':

> *Humility*, that can advance thy *name*
> To highest height of *immortalitie.*
> > Microcosmos. *Works*, ed. Grosart, 1.81*a*

And in our day the insight of Sir Walter Raleigh (*Shakespeare*, 1907) finds *ingrained humility* as Shakespeare's great gift, 'his native endowment'.

If so, and (as Cicero puts it) 'that best becomes a man which is most really his own', must not the Mercury-colours chosen by Shakespeare for his 'Sonnets' portrait-Device 1588 both perfectly become him and present him as he is—*in the humility of steadfast love for his Friend*?

Let us see. First, for his White and Black, the two *native* or *true* colours. 'If the colour white shall be joined with the black ... they signify a person of lifelong humility.' (Coronato Accolti, *Del significato de' colori*, 1568, 38ᵛ–39.)

> *In siluer and sable to declare*
> *The stedfast loue he alwaies meant.*
> > Lord Vaux (Tottel's *Miscellany* 1557 no. 211),
> > qu. Puttenham, Dd 3

Next, for the Violet (Purple, Murrey) of his hat and his amethyst brooch: 'By the [flower] Violet is signified a most excellent virtue called Humility.'* Further, 'It may seeme

---

* Henry Goldingham, *The Garden Plot*, a poem (with commentary on

strange that such a poore violet virtue [*sc.* Humility] should ever [*i.e.* always] dwell with Honour.'*

White and Black, Violet: humble Mercury's colours. These three stand strikingly together, marked as his choice both for painted *impresa* and for poetic image. In Sonnet 12, leading with the white and black of *day* sunk in *night*, he goes on—

> 12 3 *When I behold the violet past prime,*
> *And sable curls or siluer'd ore with white* . . . [all siluer'd

And his *Murrey* drives home the *steadfast love* of his White and Black: 'The *Murrey* reveals steadfast will in love. . . . *Murrey.* Steadfastness of soul in loving, and contempt of life for [the sake of] the beloved.'†

The three chosen by Shakespeare to declare the personal *high thought* or *resolution* of his portrait-Device executed by Nicholas Hilliard are the identical three first named by that master-painter in his *Arte of Limning.* Enumerating the seven basic colours, he lists *white, black, murrey, red, blue, green, yellow.* And he adds that these colours (after white and black, both in the diamond) are represented in 'the five principal precious stones bearing colour', beginning with 'ammatist orient for murrey'. (Sir John Pope-Hennessy, *A Lecture on Nicholas Hilliard,* 1949, 21.)

Pursuing the Amethyst farther, we find Francis Meres (*Palladis Tamia* 85ᵛ) quoting the 14th-century Joannes Gorus on the Christian virtues shown by the colours of the stone:

> As that Amethist is good which is beautified with the mixture of two colours, purple and violet, so is that temperance profitable, that is adorned with two vertues, with charitie, and humility.
>
> *I. a S. Geminiano lib. 2. de metallis & lapid. cap. 36*

---

its symbolism) dedicated to Queen Elizabeth. Pr. from MS. Harl. 6902 with spelling modernized by the Rev. F. Wrangham, 1825, 70.

* Owen Feltham, *Resolves,* 1628, 2.6.12, qu. *OED*; and compare Nicholas Breton, '*Oh that same minde of true humilitie . . . Doth show the honour that will euer hold.*' *Pasquils Mistresse,* 1600, C2.

† 'Salda voglia il *Morello* apre in amore. . . . *Morello.* Fermezza d'animo in amare, & dispregio di vita per la cosa amata.' *Il Mostruosissimo Mostro di Giovanni De' Rinaldi . . . del Significato de' Colori,* 1584, A3, A3ᵛ.

As well in painting as in poetry, the amethyst's colours always identify Christ Jesus the Saviour. 'Violet, the Word Made Flesh'; 'Cloathed with Christs Purpur-Mantle'; and (Donne) 'So, in his purple wrapp'd receive mee Lord.'

Humility is the root of Christian strength. Thus the Regalia declare the source whence Britain's monarchy draws its sanction: at the tip of the King's Sceptre stands a cross on an *amethyst*; and on the top of the Mound, again an *amethyst*. 'Thy Sum of Duty let Two Words contain . . . Be Humble, and be Just.' (Prior, after Micah.)

Since the Amethyst signifies both Humility—'the love divine'—and Mercury, Roger Bacon found it rational to conclude that the Christian religion is under the planet Mercury. (Lynn Thorndike, *History of Magic and Experimental Science*, 2.672.) And for Neckam, Mercury corresponded to *Pietas*, gift of the Holy Spirit. Many astrologers held that his good influence 'makes *Ecclesiasticall* Men; yea oft . . . Bishops and Prelats'—'such as with painful wit Have dived for knowledge in the Sacred Writ'. Lodge writes, 'O *Mercurie*, . . . in former ages Deuotion was thy father.'* In the second century of our era, San Mercuriale was the first Bishop of Forlì, where his church stands today. And Pope John II—A.D. 532–535 under Justinian—was also named *Mercurius*.

The Middle Ages readily presented Mercury in picture as a Bishop, turning his chlamys of violet, his hat, and his staff of power into robe of episcopal violet, mitre, and pastoral crosier. (Cf. E. Panofsky, *Meaning in the Visual Arts*, 1955, Pl. 14.) Further, they could point to classical authority for their image of Mercurius Episcopus—*ton episcopon Herman* (*Anthologia Graeca*, ed. F. Jacobs 1813–17, 1.190.1)—the overseer, the superintendent. For Plutarch describes men at bedtime pouring their last libation to Mercury, 'the wisest God of all others, as if he were there present with them, and their superintendent to oversee them'. (*Morals* tr. Holland 1603, 762.)

So much, then, for the essential *humility* of Mercury, 'of the Gods whole session The most ingenious Genius'.

*   *   *

* Seznec, 90*n.*; Sadler, 25; John Day, *Parliament of Bees*, Character 2, under *Wednesdays*, Mercury's day; *Catharos*, 1591 B1ᵛ.

Genius—Shakespeare's genius perhaps more than any other's, because it out-tops knowledge—eludes definition. Only by seeing what it creates do we know it is there. But we long to ask, how does a man enable his genius to convert its latent power into active working energy? Or what mode of conducting the mind or spirit will free his genius to exert its inscrutable force?

In the light of the testimony of John Keats, who—as J. Middleton Murry holds—'probably had more knowledge of what it felt like to be Shakespeare than any man who has lived', I should attempt a conjecture as follows:

To *experience*—and only thus come to *understand**—both Nature and Human Nature: it is possible only by unique *empathy*; by somehow *joining, identifying with them* in all their forms.† For *only this course* will effectually turn on the full power of creative imagination, produce something of what we find supremely in Shakespeare.

But in the process to import or impose *one's self*—whether in opinion, preference, or judgment, as almost everyone cannot help doing—is at once to pull the switch, cut the mysterious current off. The *genius* vanishes; the man remains. *Self* or *identity* makes him no more than 'poetical'. In Keats's words, 'A Poet is the most unpoetical of any thing in existence, because he has no Identity—he is continually in for, [?informing] and filling some other Body.' Again, 'I must say one thing that has pressed upon me lately, and increased my humility and capability of submission—and that is this truth—Men of Genius are great . . . but they have not any individuality, any determined Character.'

To cast off essential Self, and thus lightened to travel throughout Nature and Human Nature, taking on their heterogeneous characters: this is Shakespeare's unparalleled

* Cf. Keats: 'nothing ever becomes real till it is experienced'.

† Compare Pico della Mirandola's idea [*De dignitate hominis*] 'of man as a Protean being who has no nature of his own but can freely become all natures'. (Eugene F. Rice, *The Renaissance Idea of Wisdom*, 1958, 107, with his quotation from Pomponazzi on the human soul's power to *become all*: 'cum omne quod est, aut sit sensibile aut intelligibile, humana anima cum utrunque comprehendat, . . . ipsa erit omnia'.) And see Wind 191 and note.

voyage of discovery; for his works are the log, the record kept by genius. And as for that great Denial, the Negation which releases that multiple Capability—call it submission, humility, abnegation, self-effacement, selflessness, or whatever else—, its strange rewards have long been recognized; from the worldly Horace's 'the more a man denies himself, the more he will obtain from the Gods' to Jesus Christ's 'he that humbleth himself shall be exalted'.

In Keats's sense, the Poet's having no Identity, no Character, means that thereby he is capable of many Characters: the *multiformity* of Shakespeare perceived by Coleridge. And this, as we shall find, was the mysterious capacity distinguishing that eloquent god, the Poet Mercury. Paul the Apostle— the eloquent wonder-worker who was firmly believed by the people of Lystra (*Acts* 14) (until he vehemently denied it) *to be Mercury come down to earth*—recounts (1 *Cor.* 9) how, protean in his travel as ambassador for Christ, *he took on characters* the most diverse: '*I am made all things to all men.*' As Gabriel Harvey noted, 'S. Paule ... became all vnto all, and as it were a Christian Mercury, to winne some.' (*Pierces Supererogation*, 1593, L2.)

'*Mercury* ... is called the God of indifferency, who is for al companies, for with the good, he is good, and with the bad, he is as bad.' (John Maplet, *op. cit.*, A4ᵛ.) This is the Mercury 'for all' whom Thomas Freeman sees present in the living Shakespeare of 1614:

> So fit for all thou fashionest thy vaine ...
> Who loues chaste life, there's *Lucrece* for a Teacher:
> Who list read lust there's *Venus* and *Adonis*,
> True modell of a most lasciuious leatcher.

And Heywood, who (p. 140 above) likewise recognized his fellow-playwright Shakespeare living a life of allegory as Mercury, gives the astrologer's view of the planet. Do we not find in it our self-effaced Poet's capability of taking on characters by joining and identifying with them?

> For to what Star or Planet whatsoe're
> He doth apply himselfe, their strength, their state,

Their force, he doth so liuely imitate,
As if he alter'd nature, to the end
That his owne influence might on theirs depend.
Therefore the Poets did on him confer
The name of *Hermes*, or Interpreter
Vnto the gods.*

To keep our thinking clear we must remember the contrast between two Elizabethan senses of *indifferent*: usually, *neutral*; neither good nor bad. But of Mercury, not *neutral*, but *either* good *or* bad. The coolness of unconcern which A. W. von Schlegel supposed in Shakespeare the dramatist—'a certain cool indifference, but still the indifference of a superior mind, which has run through the whole sphere of human existence and survived feeling' (*On Dramatic Art and Literature*, tr. J. Black and A. J. W. Morrison, 1846, 369)—, this is not the Elizabethans' multiform God of Indifferency. Their unneutral Mercury–Shakespeare is not only 'for all' but by his unique power of *identifying* seems to *be all*, *solus instar omnium*, one as it were all: *living* all. Hazlitt said it:

> He was like the genius of humanity, changing places with all of us at pleasure . . . His genius shone equally on the evil and on the good . . . He had only to think of any thing to become that thing.

Coleridge too: 'Shakespeare becomes all things, yet forever remaining himself.' And Margaret Marchioness of Newcastle earlier:

> Who would not think he had been such a man as his Sir *John Falstaff*? and who would not think he had been *Harry* the Fifth? . . . nay, one would think that he had been metamorphosed from a man to a woman, for who could describe *Cleopatra* better than he hath done, and many other females . . . too many to relate?

---

* *The Hierarchie of the blessed Angells*, 1635, 280. And compare (Thomas) *Blundeville his Exercises*, 1594, 224ᵛ–225: 'The nature of euery one of the Planets. . . . *Mercurie* is . . . plyant to the nature, bee it good or bad, of euerie other Planet or fixed Starre whereto it is ioyned.'

Of Shakespeare we know what the ancients knew of Mercury: *He is a Proteus who is ever the same, although he changes face.** Further, as we learned in Ripa, 'By an image of Mercury the ancients figured Invention': that is, *Imagination*. Shakespeare's inimitable shape as a poet similarly is like *the imagination* in George Puttenham's definition—'in his much multiformitie *vniforme*, that is well proportioned'. (*The Arte of English Poesie*, 1589, D3ᵛ.)

In the Mercury-persona he assumes in the Sonnets to accompany the Apollo-figure of his Friend, however, we do not find the Genius capable of all characters. Here is the Man himself (feigned as a god) *telling his own tale* of pain and bliss, as Dover Wilson sums in brief what Keats and C. S. Lewis have shown: 'As a dramatic poet, Shakespeare has no identity; as a man and a lover he is as selfless and humble as the clod in Blake's poem "trodden with the cattle's feet".' Yes. And we remember that 'dramatic poet' includes not only the plays but *Lucrece* too.

For when *as the self-effaced Poet* the myriad-minded Genius like Mercury or Imagination *joins with the bad*—e.g., with the lust-breathëd Tarquin—he does it without personal peril. But he has a life apart from imagination; and when *as a man* he joins himself with that lascivious Venus Black Luce Morgan, he is *seized, enslaved* by Lust, and suffers in his own person its exquisite anguish, its madness, its despair: never more poignantly painted than here in his self-report.

> *And that deepe torture may be cal'd a Hell,*
> *When more is felt then one hath power to tell.*

Throughout he seems to say *I versify the truth; not poetize.*

* '*Le Mercure de l'Antiquité* ... Il est un Prothée, qui est toujours le même, quoi qu'il change de face ...' Salmon, *Dictionaire Hermétique*, 1695, 116.

Shakespeare & Hilliard Present
Shakespeare as the Poet Mercury, 1588

Hilliard, I consider, has been equalled by none of his compatriots, except possibly Gainsborough, in the power of making a likeness into a thing of beauty. . . . I do not know of any portraits more delicately poetic. . . . His wide-eyed man grasping a hand could be Shakespeare himself.   RAYMOND MORTIMER, 1961

Shakespeare at 24 devised this peerless *impresa*-portrait as his 'return-love'—'a small token of no small friendship'. And in this richly speaking dress and pose he sat to England's greatest painter, Nicholas Hilliard: the Poet 'for native and sweet invention', the Painter 'for lively illustration of what the former should devise';

> And not alone in habit and device,
> Exterior form, outward accoutrement,
> But from the inward motion to deliver

his heart's heroic thought to the seeing eye. It has survived *unpriz'd precious* in two authentic examples by Hilliard's hand.

Now after centuries in the obscurity of unrecognition—the *Howard* was labelled 'Earl of Essex' before 1700—it springs to light as the world's only known likeness of the living Shakespeare.

. . . it is an oval on a blue ground, surrounded by letters of gold. The head is done with so much skill, force, and delicacy, that in my opinion it leaves far behind it all of this kind which I have seen. I say truly that methinks Limning could not go farther; and that here the art reached perfection. The Master who did it was an Englishman. But there is no note of his name: a name that for this alone should be ever-living.

This is Francisco Pacheco—painter, critic, and both teacher and father-in-law of the great Velázquez—in his *Arte de la Pintura* 1649 appraising the only Hilliard miniature he had ever seen. Had it been this one, he would have said the same.

Infinite riches in a little room. Here for the first time is Shakespeare, *alive and young*: here his unknown *work of autobiography*, a document which authenticates itself; here the image of his finest sonnet *Love alters not*: all presented at once by Hilliard's brush. Like his Queen in her own autobiographical portrait-Device, the young poet here acts out the testimony of his heart's truth in picture-and-word for the understanding eyes of his friends.

Thus at the time of *Love's Labour's Lost*, with Donne's mystic language of the hand *identifying* both himself—Coleridge's 'youthful god of poetry'—and his beloved 'divine' Friend above him, he here puts into our grasp what we have so long, so vainly sought: *the one master-key which opens the thought at the heart of his Sonnets of 1588–89*, those poems born of a high devotion that have baffled the generations for whom—as Dr. Johnson wrote—'the tradition of his friendships ... has perished'.

*   *   *

'A Device'—as quoted in Henri Estienne's *L'Art de faire les Devises* 1645, and translated 1646 by Thomas Blount—'is a mysticall medley of picture and words, representing in a narrow roome, to all those whose fancies are not altogether blunted with want of knowledge, some secret meaning, in favour of one or more persons'.

In his *Etymologicon* (1671), Stephen Skinner's Latin definition of *Device* is briefer: '*Symbolum, Emblema*'—'some fine and ingenious Comment (*Commentum*), Invention, or Figure Hieroglyphic, attended by an acute thought, intent, or Saying.' Here the meaning of *comment* needs to be determined.

To look up the Latin *commentum* is to find it comes from *comminiscor*, 'devise, invent, imagine'; and its primary meaning is '*A device or invention*'—as in Jonson's *Epicoene* 5.4.53: 'Tut, a device ... A mere comment.' Only secondary is our familiar but very different sense, 'also a Comment or Exposition upon an Author'. Burton (*Anat. Mel.* 3.2.2.2.) similarly employs *comment* in its primary sense: '*Plato* calls beauty ... nature's master-piece, a dumb comment'—that is, *a silent invention* of imaging genius, such as a triumph of the painter's art.

As for Shakespeare, has any critic realized that when he called Marlowe's rival verses to young Will Hatcliffe *comments of your praise*, what he conveyed to the reader was *not* 'expositions' or 'expository treatises', but *poetical inventions of your praise?*—precisely as in Sonnet 79, *what of thee thy Poet doth inuent* or (83) *in praise deuise*:

> 85 1 *My toung-tide Muse in manners holds her still,*
> *While comments of your praise richly compil'd,*
> *Reserue their Character with goulden quill,*
> *And precious phrase by all the Muses fil'd.*

Brathwait, too (*A Strappado*, 1615), of the sonneteer Phantasto's 'farre fetcht straines inuented': 'Now of her Beauty wouldst thou Comment make.' Leone Ebreo (*Dialogues of Love*) describes such imaginings: 'Poets' comments are wont to fold in and contain more intentions and allegorical senses.' (Leo Hebraeus, *De Amor. Dial.* 2.) And Shelley employs it in his *Ginevra*, lines 5 and 8:

> Fancying strange comments in her dizzy brain ...
> Strange as a dreamer's mad imaginings

—like Shakespeare's *idle Comments* (*K. John* 5.7.4), repeated (line 18) as *strange fantasies*, delirious imaginings.

'*Shakespeare led a life of Allegory: his works are the comments on it.*' By this rarest of insights, John Keats the poet outstrips all the critics in seeing *what is there*. Yet it is evident that Keats has here been as universally misunderstood as Shakespeare has.

Despite its use by Wordsworth (*Prel.* 10.89, *Sky-prosp.* 12), we today know *comments* only in its secondary sense—'expositions', 'explanations'. But Shakespeare's works are not expositions or explanations, and Keats did not mean to say that they are. They are his *inventions*: a *poet's comments* which 'fold in and contain more intentions and allegorical senses'.

In his Sonnets Shakespeare relives the outward vicissitudes and inward motions of his friendship with Gray's Inn's boy-'Apollo' in aptest allegory. On Poetry's high scene his beloved

Will pacing forth under his royal canopy is King Apollo, and himself the golden god's humble Friend, the Poet Mercury.

Moreover in these *poet's comments* on that life of friendship—his true imaginings which give it immortality—the youthful poet's persona as 'Mercury' neither conceals nor alters his actually lived intensities of high thought and deepest feeling; just as in his Device as 'Mercury' young Shakespeare's symbolic garments, ornaments, and colours neither conceal nor alter his true features. The allegorical world of his 'life figurative' is *mundus alter et idem*: another world, and yet the same. For—just as Dr. Johnson says of his plays—both in his Sonnets and here in his poetical *impresa* '*Shakespeare* approximates [brings close] the remote, and familiarizes the wonderful.'

What then is this personal Device of the poet's—his *ancient things made novelty*—executed by the great Hilliard? Like Nature's masterpiece, Beauty, it is his painted *dumb comment*, his *silent invention* on that rare Friendship of Unequals: *Picta Poesis*, the Sonnets Pictured.

23 9 *O let my looks be then the eloquence,* [Q *books*
And domb presagers of my speaking brest.

For to poems, 'where oftentimes feeling and effectual words do passe the Reader without due consideration, pictures are such helps that they make wordes as it were deedes . . .' 'The use of the picture . . . is that (having read over the booke) you may reade it (as it were againe) in the very picture.'

In these Joined Hands you may read again both 116—True Love—and 87–91, Mercury–Shakespeare's apprehended loss of his Golden* Friend—his Sun, King, and God—as gold leaves mercury: *thou maist take All this away*. For it is a hand *given* from the 'region cloud' *above him* which as Mercury he clasps. A *given* hand, which may be withdrawn.

To acquaint your eyes with my mind. Plutarch asks, 'They also who without word uttered at all, signifie the conceptions of theire minde by certaine symbolicall devises . . . are they not . . . commended and admired exceedingly?' And we ask, here

---

* The essential *gold* of the Sun God's dress appears on the bit of sleeve above the ruff-cuff in the *V&A*, and more markedly in the *Howard*.

in his Device what is the mind which our exceedingly admired poet signifies by symbol?

His thoughts are *four*:

1. By displaying *Two hands conjoined in pale*, the hereditary and exclusive badge of the great Lord Strange, future fifth Earl of Derby, Shakespeare the Player proudly identifies himself to all eyes as *Lord Strange's man*. Here in 1588 he is one of Lord Strange's Players.

2. By following the prescribed *deification* of the human figure and presenting himself and his superior, the Owner of the Hand, feigned as the ideal perfect Friends *Mercury* and *Apollo* with white hands joined as those *Athenians for love, Attici amoris ergo*, Shakespeare the Poet utters his high-hearted thought, *Godlike Friendship*; and again with his FOUR clasping fingers: his *Index* (Apollo)—*2 Joined Middles—Little Finger* (Mercury) say APOLLO—FRIENDSHIP—MERCURY. Here in 1588 with the fingers of one hand—royal Apollo above, Mercury his humble friend below—without a word he declares in full *the essential subject of his Sonnets*.

3. By manifold unmistakable attributes and signs of the divine Poet Mercury shown in objects, forms, letters, and colours of costume and ornaments, and by his Mercury-art of speaking gesture, 'An Art that showes th'Idea of his minde', Shakespeare here unfolds the secret of his portrait-Device in which 'the garments and ensignes deliver the nature of the person'. 'These your vnvsuall weeds, to each part of you Do's giue a life.' To the seeing eye he says, *Find Mercury and you find me*. Like Mercury of the Homeric Hymn—'*I reuerence, with my soule, the* Sunne'—here as in his Sonnets of 1588 he is *divinus amator*, Lover of the everlasting Light: the Poet Mercury reverencing his *louely Boy* Will as his *Sun*, his *Sovereign*, his *God*, his young King Phoebus Apollo, Beauty, Love, and Truth: *Faire, kinde, and true*.

4. By clasping the left, the *heart* hand of this Apollo above him, Mercury–Shakespeare identifies *Will*, his *constant heart*, his Apollo. For the one and only Apollo of London in 1588 is the sovereign Apollo of the Delphic Gray's Inn elected the year before, aged 19: Prince Will Hatcliffe, presented as that faithful god of True Love—*fides*—in his own companion-

Device *ca.* 1588 also executed by Nicholas Hilliard, that master-piece *Young 'Apollo W H' Leaning against a Tree*: *my loues picture* of Sonnet 47—

> *With my loues picture then my eye doth feast,*
> *And to the painted banquet bids my heart.*

FOUR is the number of Mercury, and Friendship's number is FOUR. On the stage of Elizabeth's England, as Ben Jonson recalls, Shakespeare came forth *like a Mercury* to charm. In 1588 *like a Mercury* he spoke to Apollo his play's brief Epilogue. And here in his Device *like a Mercury* joined to his Friend Apollo, limned to the life by the Queen's master-painter for the same Wonderful Year of victory over the Invincible Armada, 1588—when, as our Olympian Herald of Peace proclaims with *Vivat Regina—O live!*

> *Incertenties now crowne them-selues assur'de,*
> *And peace proclaimes Oliues of endlesse age*

—these *four* are the four authentic tidings of himself and of his Friend brought in silent eloquence by Jove's heavenly Harbinger, man's Guide and kind Friend, that true *four-square* Mercury, *norm of mankind*: the wise, humorous, gentle Player-Poet, our Companion ever and for ever. 'Honoured and admired as a man framed according to the true Standard of the Human Nature', he alone *by the genius of humility*—as John Keats the poet first perceived—can enter and explore both its Heaven and its Hell.

For us, intent upon this portrait—by which as *Autangelist*, Messenger of Himself, he tells us more than we dreamt any picture could tell—, it is this knowledge that conjures up those haunting lines of his, with but the pronouns altered:

> *Th'idea of his life shall sweetly creep*
> *Into our study of imagination:*
> *And every lovely organ of his life*
> *Shall come apparell'd in more precious habit,*
> *More moving-delicate, and full of life,*
> *Into the eye and prospect of our soul*
> *Than when he liv'd indeed.*

Assuredly none but Shakespeare and his fellows can lend us lines fit to stand with his unique living likeness: the young Sonnets-poet presenting himself in Humility's Violet, Humility's Black and White, as Coleridge's youthful god of poetry in *godlike friendship*, the jewel of humanity. *Hermes gave Phœbus an eternall state In his affection.* And here in steadfast love's humility he ever holds the hand of his faithful Apollo, as his fellow-poet Nicholas Breton declares: 'loues Humilitie . . . euer holds the hand of Faithfulnes'.

> *But here it is. Prepare*
> *To see the life as lively mock'd as ever*
> *Still sleep mock'd death. Behold, and say 'tis well.*

> *. . . this remains the same*
> *As it was drawn; . . . here will still be seen*
> *Blood on the cheek, and down upon the chin.*
> *Here the smooth brow will stay, the lively eye,*
> *The ruddy lip, and hair of youthful dye.*

> *But that which my admiring spirit doth view,*
> *In thought whereof it would for ever dwell,*
> *Eye never saw, the pencil never drew,*
> *Pen never could describe, tongue never tell:*
> *It is the invisible beauty of your mind,*
> *Your clear imagination, lively wit,*
> *So tuned, so tempered, of such heavenly kind*
> *As all men's spirits are charmed and rapt with it.*

13

In Retrospect

You have read my report of finding, from evidence contained within two miniature paintings, young Shakespeare and his Fair Friend—*my louely Boy* of the Sonnets—both portrayed by Queen Elizabeth's master-painter, Nicholas Hilliard. The story is the product of a sustained effort to offer you the steps of that absorbing pursuit both clearly and in their order. But it will be realized that this obligatory hewing to the line of progressive narrative interest has forced me to select and to omit.

As a result, unavoidably deferred is the full detailed reply to your first obvious question, 'Beyond what you have given, do the Sonnets of the poet's pupil pen confirm the feigned characters, the *personae* identified in the portraits? That is, does the young Shakespeare feign himself throughout in these poems as Mercury, and his friend the stripling Will Hatcliffe as Apollo?'

To this, the considered answer (to be given with chapter and verse when occasion offers) is Yes, he does. Indeed, once equipped with that essential Mercury-and-Apollo clue, together with hints already given, certainly some readers will not wait until they are published to recognize items of the evidence. To cite but one particular out of the number, readers will remember that Shakespeare, unlike any other Elizabethan poet, presents himself in his Sonnets now as an old man *chopt with tand antiquitie* (62.10), now as a youth (138.3, *Mr. W. H.* 72), now as a babe (143.10). And who does not know that there is no poet familiarly seen in each of these three shapes or manifestations except the divine poet Mercury?

And also remaining to be brought out is a study stimulated by Keats's unique perception—that Shakespeare consciously lived a life figurative, of allegory. Evidence that his figure throughout was 'Mercury' as his own age thought of that god, it will appear, has stared us in the face almost in vain, both in ascertained facts of his life and in features of what Chambers called the Shakespeare-mythos.

Only recently have I come upon a notable exception to this common oversight, one which surely should be better known. It is Dr. Richard Garnett's delightful little verse-play of 1905 —*William Shakespeare, Pedagogue and Poacher*. Here, without naming the name, the poet figures from first to last as Mercury. Yet having perceived so much, and with his foot poised to step into the Sonnets' penetralia, Dr. Garnett stopped.

But your other natural questions, 'What is the history of the two examples of the Shakespeare miniature? And where is the *Howard* now?' must have immediate answers.

First, the Victoria and Albert Museum example. All I have learned is that it was included in the collections of Sir Hans Sloane (1660–1753), which were 'purchased by the nation and placed in Montague House 1754 (afterwards the British Museum)'. From there it was transferred in modern times as 'Sloane No. 272' to the Victoria and Albert Museum, and entered as 'No. P.21—1942'.

With the *Howard* we are more fortunate, being able to trace it back into the 17th century. In George Vertue's *Note Books* II, 13 (pr. Walpole Soc., XX, 1931–32) we read:

> May 1726 Mr Halsted's sale of pictures . . . [he livd on Ludgate Hill. he dyd about 2 Jan 1695] there likewise several hds of Hilliard with writing about, gold letters. One of Leonard Dorus Æta. 37. An°. 1591. . . . the Earl of Essex. 1588.

There is no known Hilliard portrait of Essex dated 1588; but still today the *Howard* Shakespeare by Hilliard dated 1588 carries on its frame the 17th-century misnomer 'Earl of Essex'. In 1882 it was already at Castle Howard, where it was later described as the property of the Earl of Carlisle.

It was twenty years ago that I took up my copy of Carl Winter's attractive *Elizabethan Miniatures* (King Penguin), and returned with closer attention to the thirteen outstanding works of Nicholas Hilliard reproduced for him there in excellently faithful colour. Like every deeply interested observer, I found myself most drawn to the two masterly and famous 'unknowns' with their baffling inscriptions—*Dat pœnas laudata fides* and *Attici amoris ergo*. And of these two certainly the more fascinating was the second. For it presented a double challenge. No critic had been able to fathom either the sense of those three words or the meaning of those joined hands.

At that time no suspicion of any 'Shakespeare' possibility in this puzzle had crossed my mind. But Winter's note, *A similar miniature, wrongly described as a portrait of the Earl of Essex and attributed to Isaac Oliver, was formerly at Castle Howard*, roused my curiosity. Did this 'similar' one still exist? And if so, where? Since the one he reproduced from the Victoria and Albert Museum was damaged on the sitter's left cheek, and also badly faded on his left shoulder and breast, might not this other conceivably add some clue?

Yet it was not until early in 1958 that I made any progress towards seeing that 'similar' one. At King's College Cambridge my friend the late Dr. A. N. L. Munby encouraged me to consult that ever-helpful Kingsman the late Mr. Colin Agnew of the famous Old Bond Street firm. And Mr. Agnew informed me that this 'similar' one was the property of the then Viscount Morpeth (now 12th Earl of Carlisle) of Ganthorpe Hall near Castle Howard, Yorkshire. In reply to my appeal by letter, Lord Morpeth kindly offered to give me the sight of his miniatures at the Castle.

And when he laid the *Howard* before my eyes in full daylight, its startling effect on me is something I cannot hope to describe. To me this was far more than a masterpiece of portraiture in miraculously preserved fresh colour and delicate drawing. For here I felt a power of expression, an intensity of thought beyond that presented by the familiar one in the Museum. A pregnant message seemed to spring not only from the eyes but from the whole face and the very poise of the head: stirring in me a rare unreasoning conviction of opportunity at the flood, an urgent presentiment of unseen treasure at hand, asking to be brought to light.

Only in the days of reflection following however did the thought of a 'Shakespeare' possibility first occur to me. On looking back I find it strange that no one so far as I know had ever proposed it, though both art-critics and Shakespear-eans have published their wish that we had a 'Shakespeare by Hilliard'. Strange, because the sitter's fair curling hair and beard, his hazel eyes—if a bit faded in the *Howard*, the irises are well preserved in the *V & A*—and his straight nose are all present in Janssen's bust of the poet at Stratford. The features are clumsily cut; but in customary manner they were 'coloured to the life' to the order of the subject's family.* Also because of the young manhood of the sitter in 1588, when young Shakespeare was 24; and not least because the sitter answers John Aubrey's report, from those who had known the living poet, that 'He was a handsome well shap't man.'

So I began to think that certainly here, all unsuspected, was a possible 'Young Shakespeare' painted in the Armada Year at the time of his Sonnets. But if either *Attici amoris ergo* or the hand-holding gesture contained any sign pointing to the poet, I could not imagine what it might be.

Absorbed though I was in study for *Mr. W. H.*, that *Howard* portrait would not out of my mind; and its 'Shakespeare' thought grew ever stronger. To me the *Howard* was doing what Dr. Johnson said Shakespeare excels in—'exciting restless and unquenchable curiosity'—, urging me to secure it for scrutiny; but I had no inkling that it might come on the market. And by bad luck I was at home in America in the spring of 1959, missing Sotheby's auction of 14 May at which Lord Morpeth's Hilliard miniatures went for handsome prices.

My one comfort was the news that the *Howard* had not gone to a museum but to a private collector. Might he be persuaded to sell? Mr. Agnew inquired through Leggatt Bros., the owner's agents, and found that he was not inclined to part with it. And though at my request Mr. Agnew continued to press his inquiries, more than two years had to pass after that auction before the owner at length changed his mind.

Now Raymond Mortimer's perception of the *Howard*—which (as I suppose) he had seen only in a half-tone engraving

---

* For the authenticity of the present colour, see M. H. Spielmann's authoritative monograph *Shakespeare's Portraiture* 1924, 'unchallenged, except by uninformed opinion.'—C. J. Sisson, *Shakespeare Survey* 3, 1950, 5.

—'His wide-eyed man grasping a hand could be Shakespeare himself' came out in the *Sunday Times* of 28 May 1961. Whether or not this influenced the owner one can only guess. But less than two weeks later Leggatts communicated to Mr. Agnew the owner's offer to sell—at a figure steeply advanced—and I closed with the offer.

When Mr. Agnew had put the precious possession into my hands, there remained the matter of applying for an export licence. Since however the Victoria and Albert Museum held an example of this miniature, that licence was readily granted; and the *Howard*, after passing the Customs in New York, promptly found itself in a safe-deposit box.

What urged me in those days to acquire a painting I could ill afford was evidently nothing more than a hunch, obscure but powerful. Nevertheless, as you have seen, my years of search for the meaning of its unique features in the light of their own time have been rewarded. Here is new light on Shakespeare, his life, and his Sonnets: corroborated independently, both by Hilliard's portrait of Hatcliffe as 'Apollo W H' and by 'Mercury'–Shakespeare's Sonnets to his 'Apollo'. In 1964 *Mr. W. H.* was the vital approach-shot which put us on the green. And here at length, as it seems to me, the luck has held and we have sunk the winning putt.

Index